# Ghost Dancing on the Cracker Circuit

# GHOST DANCING ON THE CRACKER CIRCUIT

## The Culture of Festivals in the American South

Rodger Lyle Brown

University Press of Mississippi/Jackson

All photographs were taken by Rodger Lyle Brown.

Copyright © 1997 by the University Press of Mississippi
Manufactured in the United States of America
00 99 98 97    4 3  2  1
The paper in this book meets the guidelines for permanence and
durability of the Committee on Production Guidelines for Book
Longevity of the Council on Library Resources.

Library of Congress Cataloging-in-Publication Data

Brown, Rodger Lyle.
    Ghost dancing on the cracker circuit : the culture of festivals in the American
South / Rodger Lyle Brown.
        p.   cm.
    Includes bibliographical references and index.
    ISBN 0-87805-905-9 (cloth : alk. paper).—ISBN 0-87805-906-7 (paper : alk.
paper)
        1. Festivals—Southern States.   2. Southern States—Description and travel.
3. Southern States—Social conditions.   I. Title
    GT4806.B76   1997
    394.2'6975—dc20                                                    96-17962
                                                                          CIP

British Library Cataloging-in-Publication data available

# CONTENTS

# ACKNOWLEDGMENTS

I have many people to thank for helping me complete this book, but first I must acknowledge my friend and colleague John D. Thomas. He read drafts, offered advice and bought the gas when we went to a rattlesnake roundup for the first time years ago, and I got the idea for this project. Among the others to whom I owe thanks are Allen Tullos, my advisor at Emory University, who offered bracing critique and encouragement, and Robert Morris, who read drafts and promised I would be rich. Thanks to my mom just for being my mom, to my family for nodding appreciatively when I explained why the book was taking so long and to my many other friends who are kind enough to hang out with me every once in a while. Special thanks, of course, go to my wife, Leslie, for tolerating the mess, and to my sons, Luke and Max, for making me get up early so I could get to work.

# INTRODUCTION

When R. H. "Pathfinder" Johnston published the first automobile guidebook for the South in 1910, he suggested that any driver heading into the region was best advised to pack extra tires, heavy link chains, mud hooks, an ax, an electric flashlight, a shovel, a crowbar, a hundred feet of manila rope, a sack of cement, soapstone, valve parts, extra brake linings and tire tubes and rubber patches and brake shoes, raincoats and galoshes and oilskin canvas, a compass, five gallons of oil, a bucket of grease, and a gun.

And you still probably wouldn't make it.

Pathfinder had made the first car trek from Philadelphia to Savannah two years earlier, busting struts and springs through territory so uncharted that, while lurching along the dirt trails from Nashville to Chattanooga, he had to ask two hundred people for directions. No paved roads yet linked the recently reconciled sections, so naturally there were no highway maps. Pathfinder used old Civil War documents to find his way from town to town, figuring his course by maps originally sketched for wheeling armies and supply trains.

After conquest came the tourists.

Soon, the highways were paved. Farmers lobbied for farm-to-market roads, middle-class bicycle clubs pushed for macadam surfaces, and, once the bikers had traded their two-wheelers for the latest contraption—the car—the begoggled hordes wanted blacktop everywhere to accommodate their need for speed and their desire for Appalachian vistas, Dixie heat and the waters of the gulf. A couple of years after Pathfinder's pioneering mud bog, the Dixie Highway was built, the first set of interlinked paved roads webbing its way like a rope ladder from Michigan to Miami Beach and intended to carry tourists down into what a writer for *Motor Travel* magazine called in 1920 "the land of perpetual sunshine" (Preston 1991).

Between 1915 and 1920, hundreds of highway associations were formed to raise money, build roads and hype the allure of beaches, sun and mountain air. Soon the Robert E. Lee Highway ran through seven southern states, linking the Northeast to San Francisco, the Jefferson Davis Highway ran from Washington, D. C., to the Pacific, and the Dixie Overland Highway ran from Savannah to Los Angeles. In 1921, Gulf Oil opened the first filling stations in the South. By 1924, highways laced the countryside, and the roads had become so numerous and confusing that the U. S. Department of Agriculture appointed a board to designate and map the roads that were federal highways. The highways served important economic functions, allowing swift transport of goods from here to there, but elaborated and embellished beyond that is the restless and spectacular culture of the American Road, one part of the cacophonous mix of myths and symbols composing America's public life.

About eighty years after Pathfinder's trek, I went out from my home in Atlanta and drove around the South to see what I could see along the roadsides in the land of perpetual sunshine. But the picturesque scenes I was looking for weren't the standard ones—scenic overlooks, waterfalls, rolling pastures, colorful and eccentric local characters. I wanted a higher order of picturesque. I was looking not for kitsch but for the resonance of historic struggles. I wanted to find moments and weekends and places shot through with cultural traces. Like Pathfinder Johnston, I wanted to write a guidebook, but not one that consisted of a list of bed-and-breakfasts or curious interstate exits. I wanted to reveal some of the shadow geographies and cultural politics at work in certain public rituals in the South, at places and events created for the anchoring of collective memory. I wanted to mark history in high relief, rub chalk on the contours of the moments through which we move.

Wanting to troll for significance in unlikely places, I started driving to weekend community festivals, such as Peanut Day or Old South Days, the Chitlin Strut or Kudzu Festival. I wanted to see how crops and history are celebrated in Dixie's town squares and what kind of public stories people are telling about themselves as they try to draw lines around something called "community" during the last years of the twentieth century. I had thought it would be fun, but, as it turned out, the more places I visited, the more I began to detect a disturbing pattern. Even though the weekend festivals were times of reunions and laughter, flea markets and parades, everywhere I went I sensed the imminent presence of cultural death.

I found that most of the public rituals in small southern towns are productions of the white communities, and I saw a subtext of mourning haunting the celebrations as towns and families and lives were being wrenched by change. Throughout the countryside I found resonating through the events a sense of loss and a fear about the future, because the main streets were abandoned, the kids all wanted to move off, and history kept getting lost in the blur of new media. Far from being simply annual weekends staged to raise money for the local Jaycees or Kiwanis, the community festivals seemed to me to be responses to the economic restructuring and the transforming conceptions of time and space that characterize the late twentieth century. It seemed that a certain segment of the southern population was creating and perpetuating these festivals as part of a nativistic revitalization movement.

Writing in 1943, anthropologist Ralph Linton defined a nativistic movement as "[a]ny conscious, organized attempt on the part of a society's members to revive or perpetuate selected aspects of its culture. . . . [C]ertain current or remembered elements of culture are selected for emphasis and given symbolic value." That was certainly what I was seeing at these annual festivals commemorating the mule, the hog and assorted agricultural commodities. Such movements, Linton wrote, were "almost without exception" a response by a society's members to certain frustrations. "The elements revived become symbols of a period when the society was free or, in retrospect, happy or great. Their usage is not magical, but psychological. By keeping the past in mind, such elements help to reestablish and maintain the self respect of the group's members in the face of adverse conditions" (231–33).

The best-known examples are the ghost dance movements among Native Americans, although such activities have occurred throughout history. In the seventeenth century, revivalist movements took place among the Pueblo in the Southwest and the Inca in Peru and, in the late eighteenth century, among the Delaware, Shawnee, Winnebago and Seneca. In the early nineteenth century, the movement spread to the Creek and the Cherokee, with prophets declaring that the Indians should stop eating beef, bacon and chicken and return to a diet of venison and turkeys and should break their looms and go back to buckskin. In 1870, a ghost dance movement spread through Nevada, California and Oregon, and, in the 1880s and early 1890s, another went out of Nevada into the Great Plains. James Mooney, an ethnologist who reported to the Bureau of Ethnography on the Ghost Dance movement among the Plains Indians in 1890, wrote: "As with men, so with nations. The lost paradise is the world's dreamland of youth. What tribe or people has not had its golden age, before Pandora's box was loosed? . . . The doctrines of the Hindu avatar, the Hebrew messiah, the Christian millennium, and the Hesunanin of the Indian Ghost Dance are essentially the same, and have their origin in a hope and longing common to all humanity . . ."(1965:1).

The Native American movements were responses to social and cultural deprivations, population loss and the disappearance of familiar ways of life. Occurring when tribal identities were threatened and group boundaries were in danger of collapsing, they were deliberate efforts to restore populations and ways of life by conjuring up a time when all the dead would return, the game would return, and the Americans would be swept from the earth. Different tribes did the dances in different ways: some danced indoors, some outside; some danced nude, some danced clothed; some waved handkerchiefs, others shook claprattles. Different tribes also called the movement different names. The Comanche called it The Dance With Joined Hands; the Paiute called it Dance in a Circle; the Shoshoni called it Everybody Dragging; the Kiowa called it Dance Craziness; the Caddo called it The Prayer of All to the Father; the Sioux and Arapaho called it the Ghost Dance, because it related to the return of the dead. The practitioners cast off their European clothes and belongings and danced for a day of salvation, singing songs such as:

*The spirit host is advancing, they say*
*The spirit host is advancing, they say*
*They are coming with the buffalo, they say*
*They are coming with the buffalo, they say*
*They are coming with the new earth, they say*
*They are coming with the new earth, they say*
*(Thornton 1986)*

The movement faded out after the death of ghost dance leader Sitting Bull and the 1891 massacre at Wounded Knee, South Dakota, but, in an oblique way, it had been successful. Although the dead did not live again, tribal identities were strengthened and the distinctions between Indians and Europeans clarified.

I saw a similar impulse at work in the southern countryside, but it was manifested in a dissipated, confused way—a performed, postmodern way—and submerged beneath a civic rhetoric of fund-raising and community development. The more closely I looked at the stories behind the contemporary southern festivals and at the moods and sensibilities underlying them, the more convinced I became; I concluded that, frustrated and unstable in the face of late capitalism's accelerating cycles of creative destruction and the ensuing social stresses, *the crackers are ghost dancing*.

This book is the result of my roaming through the circuit of community festivals in the South. The book has shifting shapes because to accomplish what I want, it has to be different things. The first purpose of the book is to reveal some of the meanings and histories behind a set of community festivals of a type that has flourished throughout the contemporary South. Another, equally important, is to provide a different sort of guidebook. Just as Pathfinder Johnston recommended that the auto traveler in the South pack rope, grease and a gun, I wanted to offer some concepts and ways of seeing that people can take with them as they read the landscape of public culture.

Guidebooks and travelogues serve important roles in society because, before visiting a site, tourists and travelers can examine the material and dream their excursions. From Homer and Fodor's to Walt Whitman and Jack Kerouac, the literature of the road—epics, novels, booklets, brochures, guidebooks—activate themes, set tones and establish motifs for a visit to a place. Travel writing can play a key role in directing the tourist gaze and helping to situate a visitor within specific landscapes. Just as language, in a sense, obligates us to have a version of the world, so too do travel writing and tourist guidebooks obligate us to have certain versions of a place—certain Americas, certain Souths—by offering frames for experience, catalogues of desires, aids for dreaming, and maps by which we can script our weekends, orient our wonder and schedule our wandering.

To accomplish this end, I have structured the book as a collection of episodes that compose a narrative of progressive revelation and understanding, sort of a vision quest via rental car. Such a guidebook would contribute to the elaboration of a progressive poetics of tourism, be

a kind of workbook in critical cultural alchemy through which someone could make sense of the world in a different way and recognize
his or her own historicity. It would be an incitement to deconstruct
and reimagine a historicized landscape and provide a set of exercises
to help in seeing the hidden meanings enciphered in cultural tropes.
My intention is to help resuscitate a sense of historical awareness and
appreciation not simply by presenting the finished products of cultural
analysis and scholarship, but to transmit a thrill by telling the stories of
my own explorations while practicing cultural analysis.

Raymond Williams has characterized the work of cultural studies
as being part of a "long revolution" (1961). This involves more than
just the opposing of certain ideologies, which are usually imposed
upon people from without. Cultural studies more specifically works
as a counterhegemonic practice. Unlike ideology, which is generally
explicit and codified, hegemony is a complex interlocking of political,
social and cultural forces that make artificial relationships of power
seem natural, inevitable and unchangeable. Because hegemony is so
embedded and inarticulate, Williams says, counterhegemonic processes
require the integration of radical critique with emotional and affective
strategies based on structures of feeling. As a contribution to the long
revolution of cultural studies, I decided to use my road story in an effort
to evoke a sensibility, an awareness of the constant presence of historical
and cultural meaning in the objects and gestures around us, and to
provide a context for interpretation as an antidote for the unmoored,
passionless ephemera of postmodernism.

The resulting book is playful, but it is also serious. It is impressionistic
but also objective. It is about white people but about red, brown
and black people as well, just as a book about water is a book about
earth. It is a book about the South and about America. The narrative,
though linear, makes use of techniques such as the cut, pastiche and
juxtaposition, the better, I believe, to evoke an excited meaningfulness.
Considering the subject matter—festivals—my approach can't be static
and objective; it must contain an element of the carnivalesque, must be
spontaneous and chaotic within a controlled format.

My approach is informed by the interdisciplinary field of cultural
studies. A vague term, cultural studies could probably best be described
as a field in which cultural matters are examined in relation to politics and
power. The concern with politics and culture goes beyond issues such

as who receives funding from the National Endowment for the Arts, or who gets lambasted by moralist critics. Cultural studies topics would be, for example, how different social classes are represented in newspapers, on television or at the movies, how different sorts of technology reflect and reinforce different patterns of authority, and how social relations are expressed in the construction of the built environment and the composition of the landscape. A student in this field looks at the regular stuff of everyday life, asking how it got that way and what its links are with political ideologies. Such a student tries to unweave and unweb the root system of what we call common sense, using whatever theoretical tools are available.

What I have always liked about cultural studies is how people working in the field can find complex politics in the most unlikely places: Saturday morning cartoons, pulp detective novels, Barbie's wardrobe, *Star Trek* fan clubs, the history of the front lawn. Using a little symbolic anthropology, some history, and a lot of literary criticism, one can determine how Barbie's parabolic plastic figure turns out to be, upon analysis, both an oppressive icon for bulimic cheerleaders and a contortionist dominatrix instructing genderbending transvestites in oppositional recontextualization of the conventions of feminine beauty. Or one discovers that the American lawn is not just a good place for kids to wrestle but an expression of middle-class emulation of landed gentry, an artifact in the suburban vocabulary of status made possible only by the support of massive agricultural and chemical industries. After a cultural studies-style read, the once seemingly meaningless acts of watching cartoons or cutting the grass on Saturday morning lose their innocence.

An interdisciplinary approach to exploring southern community festivals was appropriate because of the polyvalent character of the events. They have different meanings to different people, and their various elements have accrued from many different times and places. Although I have concluded that, broadly speaking, the festivals constitute a type of nativistic movement, I do not mean to suggest that they are all alike, nor that they are *only* a response to changing economic and social structures. At the heart of this *postmodern* ghost dance movement are issues of the politics of memory, which involves diverse personal and collective experiences. Whereas "history" is a representation of the past, memory and remembering are the actual phenomena at work in the everyday world, and they are combinations of individual and social circumstances. History enters our lives in the form of memory, and there it becomes magical, taking up residence in the real world of objects, gestures, spaces, words, performances and images. Hence, again, the necessity of telling these stories as part of my own personal experience of exploration and discovery, because the *process* of remembering is as significant as the product.

This book took shape in a specific historical moment and milieu. In 1990, I quit my job as a reporter and went back to school for my doctorate. By this time, the postmodernist turn in the humanities had already occurred, and everything I read was all about how the "classic norms" of objectivity were being displaced by a more self-conscious approach to writing about other people and cultures (Rosaldo 1989). Anthropology, for example—the academic field which explicitly explores human cultures—was one of the first intellectual traditions to be restructured by a postcolonial critique of the West's hegemonic academic practices. Many of my fellow students were traumatized by the crisis. According to the coffee-klatsch caricature, it used to be that you could visit some primitive society, learn the language, finger the food, then return to your university with suitcases full of fieldnotes and stories, jewelry and art. You would go over your notes, figure out who was cousin to whom and how many words there were for, say, "corn," write up your results, publish, get tenure, and then sit around enjoying your life as a smart person with a job, telling everybody at parties how you know twelve different recipes for termite larvae. But it wasn't so easy anymore. (And, of course, we know it never was so simple, but this caricature is indicative of the beating the field had taken.) That khaki-pant-and-sweaty-pith-helmet version of anthropology—anthropology as a Hope-and-Crosby road movie—was vanquished.

Although anthropology had always claimed to be a science that made use of rigorous, objective methods of research, it had depended greatly on the creative intuition of its practitioners to contrive ways objectively to represent aspects of the complex subjectivities of human life and behavior. Try as they might to invoke the rituals of science, it is at the point at which anthropologists or ethnographers (or anybody else) transform their thoughts and ideas into representations that the work becomes vulnerable to criticism.

Any cultural account, any text, any representation, it was said, is a construct, a fiction; it is not necessarily false, but it is made up, partial and invented. Writing about somebody else, according to this critique, becomes a political act, not merely an artistic or scientific one, and, especially within a professional discourse like anthropology, implies cultural authority. Those wanting to avoid being smeared with the imperialist tarbrush would have to deconstruct their own power relations to the people they were writing about, and then, naturally, take a principled stand against the exploitation of such people.

As in society at large, the postcolonial revision included the rejection of simple dichotomies: good, bad; progressive, backward; civilized, uncivilized; modern, primitive; right, wrong. Monumentalist truth claims were condemned as oppressive. All aspects of human culture became subjects of political negotiation, and all through the Western humanities a great wailing went up from the land, and there was a gnashing of teeth and a rending of texts.

The old ways of analyzing and representing others were distancing, normalizing and objectivist. The new postcolonial, postmodern methods moved away from formal vocabularies of moral neutrality and toward a more dynamic and dialectic view of human participation in culture. The old classic modernist mode was afflicted with an illusion of timelessness, an infatuation with a scientism that resulted in cultural norms being reified, clamped upon people like obligatory shackles. Such a scientific, modernist approach failed to show how social forms can be and are used spontaneously and creatively, so the task of social analysis moved away from static structural descriptions and toward topics of social inequality and processes of social transformation. After the postcolonial rupture, people writing about culture—anthropologists, literary critics, historians—became more sensitive to the dialectic between human conduct and the structure of cultural systems, the process of doing academic work and the inevitable contingencies of human actuality.

Understanding how that dialectical relationship works, however, is not simply a matter of employing a professional methodology, grinding some data, and seeing what comes out. Personal engagement is required, and so is a *consciousness* of personal engagement, i.e., an awareness of the fact that one's motivation, situation and background profoundly affect whatever representation one creates. Representations contribute to the formation of social identities, and the goal of any critical approach is to ask what possibilities are being opened up, what forms of expression, activity and understanding are either being promoted or mitigated against. Cultural studies both celebrates and criticizes the roles that intuition and interpretation play in any representation of human beings, their way of life, their artifacts. Workers in the realm of cultural studies try to bring scholarship and attention to detail to the study of the everyday world, while at the same time accepting the chaotic, disjunctive nature of life; the field is a version of academics that does not so much resemble a rigidly defined professional ideology as it does an art form, an alchemy, which works to create resonance between objects in the world and the disposition of power.

Given this, after I started back to school, I sat down one day under a tree and watched undergraduates flip Frisbees and smoke cigarettes, and I tried to think of a subject on which I could rehearse my lessons.

I had been reading about community festivals. "Although sometimes appearing 'corny' in the eyes of an urban sophisticate . . . [t]o an astute anthropologist, the [North American] town celebration is as rich in meaning as a Naven performance in New Guinea or a mock rebellion against the Swazi king" (Manning 1983). I was interested in the rituals of small-town America, the celebrations of identity. Working as a reporter I had often attended such festivals. They were everywhere: Kudzu Festival, World's Biggest Fish Fry, Old South Days, Ramp Festival, Armadillo Roundup, Black-Eyed Pea Day, Gnat Days. Most small towns, on one weekend a year, set aside a stretch of freshly mowed pasture or courthouse lawn, get some cloggers, fry some fish, and kindle for the afternoon various rituals of mythic American community. However, these events may not be as simple as they seem.

These festivals are frequently dismissed as yokel hokum, compotes of redundant kitschtrash, where always being peddled are the same yarn-haired dolls, woodshop-built bins scratched "Taters N Onions," landscapes painted in acrylics on sawblades, jigsawed ducks on tinkertoy wheels. Newspapers usually cover just the face painting and the fund-raising angle of these weekend festivals. But I sensed something more.

Etymologically, "festival" derives from the Latin *festum*, but originally Latin had two terms for festive events: *festum* for public joy, merriment and revelry, and *feria*, meaning abstinence from work in honor of the gods. In classical Latin the two terms tended to become synonymous and led eventually to the French *fête*, the Spanish *fiesta*, and the English "festival" and "fair." According to Alessandro Falassi, a festival is "[a] periodically recurrent, social occasion in which, through a multiplicity of forms and a series of coordinated events, participate directly or indirectly and to various degrees, all members of a whole community, united by ethnic, linguistic, religious, historical bonds, and sharing a worldview" (1987: 2).

When they are good, the festivals are cultural flares: they occur and burn, go off like fireworks, and illuminate for a day or two some landscapes of a place. They are marketplaces, sites of discourse and display, occasions of public memory and recall. As annual institutions performed over the course of changing times, the festivals work as boundary stones, marking territory, staking claims and declaring meanings, and as historical events, cobbled from traces of the past.

I decided that these festivals would be fruitful performances on which to practice my gaze.

My story begins with the Rattlesnake Roundup in Whigham, Georgia, with which I was familiar from my days as a reporter. I then go to three events related to crops and commodities: the North Carolina Tobacco Festival of Clarkton, Inc., in Clarkton, North Carolina, Swine Time, in Climax, Georgia, and the International Banana Festival in the twin towns of South Fulton, Tennessee, and Fulton, Kentucky. It was at these three places that I noticed in clearest form aspects of the life cycle of a festival, as well as how public celebrations are shaped by extracontextual forces. At each event I found rich cultural information—the history of the farm bureau, the significance of the TV show *Green Acres*, the history of the pig as a carnivalesque symbol. And at the heart of each event I found the same underlying impulse: an attempt to perpetuate communities under economic and cultural stress by the manufacturing of annual rituals. The sense of ghost dancing is most especially present in the Banana Festival, an event that was created in the 1960s to promote a town's function as a railroad distribution point for shipments of bananas. With the fruit now shipped by other means and through other towns, the festival is an explicit celebration of, as the festival's official T-shirt declares, "The Void of Bananas."

Next I explore the dimensions of Hillbilly Days in Pikeville, Kentucky, discussing how economic forces shape public representations and how these can be used as devices to facilitate exploitation while at the same time allowing those represented to recontextualize such images as part of a tactic of resistance. This chapter describes a trip to the grave of Devil Anse Hatfield, the patriarch who led one side of the notorious Hatfield and McCoy feud; the visit gives me an opportunity to discuss another issue of representation in popular culture and foreshadow the significance of *The Andy Griffith Show* on my ultimate thesis.

The De Soto Celebration in Bradenton, Florida, while not a community festival, provides an example of public celebration as a site of political conflict and struggle. The organizers of the celebration were besieged by critics who felt it insensitive for the town to be commemorating a man— Hernando de Soto—who spearheaded the movement of conquest in the Southeast in the 1500s. This chapter, like the others, demonstrates that certain ways of viewing history and society are being revised within the realm of public, if not private, performance.

The next chapter, on the Scopes Trial Play and Festival in Dayton, Tennessee, tells the story of how an annual festival event was created by parties with an interest in shaping and affecting the public memory of a historical event (the Scopes Trial) while at the same time keeping discussion of a controversial subject—evolution vs. creationism—as part of a public dialogue.

It was at Mule Day, in Calvary, Georgia, described in the penultimate chapter, where I had my epiphany. Here I saw not only the nostalgic commemoration of the mule and of rural life in general but also evidence that the ghost dance movement I had detected on the cracker circuit is postmodern in nature, that its manifestations are staged through the performance of simulacra and simulation and the manipulation of emblems derived from popular culture.

My visit to Mayberry Days in Mount Airy, North Carolina, concludes my trek on the cracker circuit. It was there that I witnessed what amounted to the purest episode of postmodern ghost dancing. While all the previous events—from Rattlesnake Roundup to Mule Day— contained moments of authentic memory, Mayberry Days was purely a celebration of simulation in the service of remembering life in the small-town South. In this chapter I review the shifts in the sense of time and space that have been aspects of industrialization and post-Fordist economic changes.

A final aspect of the crisis surrounding the representation of others that needs to be discussed is a concern for authority. In other words, who has the right to speak? Traditionally, one could have experiential authority, a kind of accumulated savvy and a sense of place, or interpretive authority, resulting from training and research, which would enable one to read cultural texts. In the classrooms of the 1990s, both types took a back seat to the idea of racial- and gender-based authority. The prevailing sentiment—whether acknowledged openly or not—was that, for example, only women could write about women, and only African-Americans could write about African-Americans. Again, this is a reduction, but such was the intellectual atmosphere when I returned to school. Claims to authority were less automatically accepted as legitimate, and one needed personal credentials as well as professional ones. So when I sought a subject for my research, my choices seemed to be either risk condemnation as patriarchal and imperialist, or encounter another culture and document in excruciating detail my failure to understand it, and thereby be hailed a hero of the refigured field. Instead, I decided to drive out on weekends among southern Americans, an activity with which I was experientially and intuitively familiar, but from which I was also suitably alienated by my egghead persona.

This brings me to the concept of the "cracker circuit." Various people to whom I first mentioned the title of this book questioned whether the use of the word "cracker" might not be offensive to some. The word, which came to the colonies along with the Scotch-Irish, is one of America's oldest pejoratives, expressive of class and ethnic conflict. "Cracker" had been a Scottish colloquialism for "boaster," and Samuel Johnson defined a cracker as a "noisy boasting fellow." By 1755, it was a common ethnic word for white backcountry folk, and, in 1766, crackers were defined as "a lawless set of rascalls" on the frontiers of Virginia, the Carolinas, and Georgia. An Anglican missionary tried to preach to some Presbyterians once but couldn't because they kept howling at him. He responded by characterizing them as "crackers who will bluster and make a Noise about a Turd" (Otto 1987).

When the crackers moved into the frontier beyond the Appalachians, they were called plain folk, hoosiers and hillbillies. Crackers who went south into Georgia and Florida kept the name. Poor farmers living in log houses and cracking corn for food were called "corn crackers." If they were middle-class cattle raisers who ran their stock on the open lands used in common, they were called "whip crackers." After the Civil War, Georgia and Florida sold off public lands to timber interests, and the age of free range was gone. Cattle herding was dropped in favor of cotton growing. As white plain folk were sucked into the cash nexus and thus into debt, pauperized and driven off the land, they moved into the mills. By 1900, cracker was a common word for white southern millworkers or sharecroppers. In Florida "cracker" kept its narrower reference to a poor, hyperrural backcountry folk, but in most southern states, "cracker" lost its specificity and became a common word used by black people for white southerners, or by white southerners themselves to invoke a sectional ethnicity and humble origins. Before Atlanta's baseball team was the Braves, it was called the Crackers.

I couldn't think of a better word to evoke a generalized, rural southern white cultural ethnicity. As it turned out, nearly everybody who participated significantly in the festivals I went to was white. There were always some black folk but never in proportion to area populations. The festivals were usually run by local chambers of commerce, or the Kiwanis, the Lions, the Rotary, the community clubs. These were the folks who wanted to ghost dance for the old Main Street, for imagined places and remembered times when values and hierarchies that favored their interests were still in place; before the federal government busted up local power structures; before the gigantic sucking sound wasn't factories going to Mexico, but was business moving from Main Street to the mall and Wal-Marts out on the highway; before manufacturing took over the countryside as the major employer; before national wage and labor laws in the 1930s and 1940s put the nail in the head of the South's distinctive labor-intensive, low-wage economy; before civil rights legislation ended Jim Crow; before the croppers and tenants and small family farmers were finally run off the land, the last hope of a viable agrarian alternative was snuffed by the farm lobbies, and the Jeffersonian vision of America was hung in high capitalism's Hall of Memories; before the kids all moved off; before, as one festival participant put it, we had all this Tee-Vee and Nintendo.

There is plenty of cracker in me, and I finally decided to tag the collection of festivals I was attending "the cracker circuit" after a man at a festival called it that himself. The man drove around to festivals and malls with a fog machine, a bush hat, and a bowie knife, showing people his enormous alligator named Allie. We were talking, and he was telling me what it was like trying to make a living by showing off a gigantic sixty-year-old alligator. He was retired from the army, had been a sniper, a noncom; Ross Perot was his hero. He complained about how it was hard to get the big stores like Kmart or Penney's to let him set up his display. He said to me, sounding almost hurt, "You tell 'em you want to bring an alligator into their store and they look at you like you're Joe Shit the Ragman."

Then, when we were talking about how he got started in the "amusement business," he said, "This friend of mine has got this big steer, Max, and he takes him around to these things, and I had just got out of the army, and I was looking for something to do, and my friend, he said, 'Get yourself an animal and take it 'round the cracker circuit.'"

# Ghost Dancing on the Cracker Circuit

# CHAPTER ONE

# STUFFING SIN IN A LARD BUCKET

## Rattlesnake Roundup at Whigham, Georgia

It's late on a cold Friday afternoon in January, and an itinerant snakehandling cowboy named Buckley stands on a rise overlooking U. S. Highway 84, which runs between Thomasville, the county seat of Thomas County, and Cairo (pronounced Kay-row), the county seat of Grady County. This is the deepest part of south Georgia's sandy coastal plain. A few miles farther south is the Florida state line, and only fifty miles beyond that is the Gulf of Mexico. To the west is Lake Seminole, where the Flint River meets the Chattahoochee and forms the Apalachicola; to the southeast is Lake Micosukee, and fifty miles beyond that flows the slow black water of the famous Suwannee.

Near the edge of the red clay bluff above the road, Buckley, who enjoys the congenial good looks of a hefty *Smokey and the Bandit*-era Burt Reynolds, has propped up three flat and wide boxes to serve as temporary billboards declaring his trade. On one box, his promotional pitch has been hastily spray-painted in red, each parabolic "S" fanged with the bold slashed promise of reward, a simple, sensational gambit for attention sure to make anyone (including me) pull over and stop: "*$NAKE$! $NAKE$! $$Rattle$nakes Wanted. We pay Cash$$.*"

Buckley has set up his weight scale and snake boxes on the side of this south Georgia highway because tomorrow, the last Saturday in January, is the Whigham, Georgia, Rattlesnake Roundup, and, as Buckley tells me, he needs to buy himself some snakes. Buckley's a snake buyer for the Mustang Trading Company out of Texas. His business is snakeskins. You can tell just by looking at him. He's a walking advertisement for the hide trade. His straw cowboy hat is banded with a choice strip of python. His burly torso is wrapped in a rattlesnake vest. His pants are likewise belted, his feet are likewise shod, and his wallet, which he pulls out of his back pocket with the well-practiced ease of a quick draw, is made of the same.

A family affair

He says it was a "spurn of the minute" thing that brought him to Georgia for the roundup. He had a free weekend and his company needed skins, so he recruited a friend to ride along, and they drove all night from Texas. But now it looks like it was all a waste of time. Buckley explains that earlier this Friday morning he tried to set up his snake box billboards in Cairo. He had expected to do a heavy trade there because it's the closest town to Whigham that has any motels for the snake hunters who are coming to the roundup with their tin boxes and canvas sacks and plastic ice chests and percale pillowcases full of rattlesnakes. Buckley figured for sure he'd score some snakes because he offers good money, top dollar. Four bucks a pound. Dead or alive.

"I need me fifty, a hundred pounds of snakes to make the trip worth my while," he says, squinting beneath his straw hat and rhythmically squeezing the handle of his aluminum snake hook. "I figured for sure I could get me that much. Twenty, twenty-five good snakes and I'd have me that much. I figured for sure, 'cause I pay good money, top dollar."

He bobs his head with convincing sincerity. "*Good* money. *Top* dollar."

But things aren't working out like he planned. Buckley says he fell victim of a conspiracy to keep him from buying any rattlesnakes. He had just gotten his snake box billboard set up in the corner of a grocery store parking lot back in Cairo when the law pulled up and told him to get the hell on out of town. They said they don't need his type coming into Grady County and trying to buy up all the rattlesnakes and spoiling Whigham's community spectacle.

Buckley isn't having much luck buying rattlesnakes along the side of the quiet road. He has only three so far, bought from a couple of kids who caught the snakes in some woods behind a welder's shop and didn't want to wait any longer to redeem the reptiles for cash. The others, though, especially the ones who hunt for volume, are saving their sacks of snakes to sell to the herpetologists from Silver Springs, a reptile garden in Clearwater, Florida, who have a deal with the Whigham Community Club to stage the center-ring snake-wrangling show and buy all the snakes collected at the roundup.

With the sun going down behind him, Buckley stands atop a red dirt bluff, idly clacking his snake hook, wistfully gazing back across the Grady County line, which he has been warned about crossing, and, in a low but emphatic squint-eyed voice, explains his unwelcome at Whigham's annual rattlesnake roundup. "They kicked us out of Cairo," he says, lifting his snake hook and clacking the jaws toward the darkening east, "because we were the only ones telling folks what their snakes was really worth!"

Buckley leers, winks, taps his snake hook against a reptile box, bites a match between his teeth, and wags it with his tongue as if it were a baton directing a conspiratorial orchestra in his head. "Somebody's getting kickbacks. They say they're only using the snakes in shows, say they use them for education and research. But they been doing this for twenty-five years. And that's three hundred snakes a year. At *least*."

He pauses for effect, to let me do the math in my head. When I nod, a deep awed nod signifying respect for the numbers, Buckley leans toward me. "You tell me they just put all them snakes on exhibit."

Buckley explains the economics of rattlesnakes: "You buy a rattlesnake for fifteen dollars—and you can sell a belt for seventy-five dollars, the rattle for ten dollars and the head for fifteen dollars—make them into a paperweight or something like that, you know, like put the head on a necktie—and you can even sell the meat if you got enough of it; they make it into dog food. Now all that's gonna make you a tidy profit. Now you tell me they just want those snakes for show? Use them just for education purposes? *Shee*-it."

I nod again, jotting some notes, and tell Buckley I sure would do what I could to check out the scam. I tell him he just might be on to something, and he says, "You do that, boy. You check it out. Somebody's getting kickbacks. There's more money in them snakes than you'd think to figure. Something's dirty."

Buckley says he is straight up and honest in his snake dealing. No forked-tongue double-talk about do-gooder research for him; he's flat-out willing to pay twice what the snake hunters will get at tomorrow's roundup, and he's not afraid to admit that the snakes he buys will end up as boots, wallets, belts and snakeskin hat bands. And no two-bit smokescreen about public education, neither. He'll say it right up front—he'll flat-out tell me—he wants to nail them snakes to a board and hack off their heads and peel their hides and dip the heads in Lucite and feed the meat to the dogs.

And there's a lot of meat and hide on an eastern diamondback rattlesnake. *Crotalus adamanteus* is the heaviest venomous snake in the world. The snakes can weigh up to thirty-four pounds, grow to more than seven feet long, and live up to eighteen years. The rattlesnake prefers to leave people alone, but when one is threatened its body swells, its head flattens and the rattle at the end of its tail sings out with a mightily persuasive rhetoric. When they strike, the rattlesnakes hurl themselves like explosive springs, lashing forward two-thirds of their body lengths. When the naturalist William Bartram tramped through the Southeast in 1773, he saw rattlesnakes which, when coiled, made a heap as high as his knees. Bartram wrote of how he had heard that when Georgia was first settled, there were rattlesnakes ten feet long and as thick as a man's thigh, but by the time he came through, there weren't any that big left.

Bartram wrote this about rattlesnakes in the South:

> They are supposed to have the power of fascination in an eminent degree, so as to inthral their prey. It is generally believed that they charm birds, rabbits, squirrels and other animals, and by steadfastly looking at them posses them with infatuation: be the cause what it may, the miserable creatures undoubtedly strive by every possible means to escape, but alas! their endeavours are in vain, they at last lose the power of resistance, and flutter or move slowly, but reluctantly, towards the yawning jaws of their devourers, and creep into their mouths, or lie down and suffer themselves to be taken and swallowed. ([1791]1988: 222)

I hadn't seen a snake yet since driving into the country earlier that day, so I ask Buckley to show me one in his box. As he lifts the lid, he pauses and turns, narrows his eyes, cracks a smile around the match in his teeth and says, obviously enjoying himself, "Gotta watch out. The big one went crazy earlier."

Inside the box, a thick gray-and-black eastern diamondback coils in a hypnotic mandala. Buckley dumps it from the box onto the dry winter grass and pokes it with his hook, making it strike out into the emptiness.

6

Slowly the rattlesnake lays its head like an apostrophe upon its looped body. We all stand around and stare until the sun blinks red and sits down in the distant pines.

I had come into the county on assignment from a newspaper in Atlanta, sent along with a fellow reporter, John D. Thomas, to see what the story was behind this roundup of reptiles. My first assumption was a common one, although wrong. I had thought the roundup might be related to the peculiarly southern snakehandling Pentecostals, the few and fringe and far-between who test their fundamentalist faith by drinking deadly concoctions and taking up serpents in ecstatic frenzy. But I was quickly set straight during several phone calls, including one with a laughing clerk at the county library who said that the roundup was nowhere nothing near a religion, just a regular once-a-year thing, a time when everybody gets together to visit and have a good time. You know, like a fair: a parade, arts and crafts, funnel cakes, rattlesnakes.

Early Saturday morning I take my notebook and camera and go to the Whigham Elementary School for the 6:30 a.m. "hunters' breakfast." The cafeteria is filled with folks, mostly men and their boys, but also men with their wives and men with their families, and a few with their girls. The room projects that odd yet somehow pleasant violation of scale that occurs whenever heavy knots of men in thick camouflage coats and caps come together in spaces usually occupied by children. The walls are taped with mimeographed lunch menus and cut-out construction paper letters that encourage reading, and, at the moment, near the framed color snapshots of homeroom classes are the sign-up sheets for people who want to go out on a snake hunt.

Everybody files through the serving area for the prehunt meal of eggs, toast, sausage, coffee and grits. As they've always done in years past, the oldest men from the Whigham Community Club serve the breakfast. Standing stooped behind the steamer trays, shoulder to shoulder, these men in their seventies and eighties wear aprons tied up around their necks, and pass the trays along one to another as one old man forks the sausage onto your plate and another lays on with palsied hands the toast, and another spoons on the pure white looseness of grits, and another the eggs, and another the packets of jelly.

I sit and talk to a man who has come to the roundup to peddle junk at the flea market, spending twenty minutes trying to figure out if we know anybody in common. (Since I'm from Savannah and he's from Thomasville—two hundred miles apart—we reckon there's got to be somebody, and sure enough, we soon find out he went to high school with the older brother of a guy I used to work with at a photocopy store. That's the kind of discussion that goes on a lot at events in the South.) When I finish eating, I go to sign up for the hunt. Standing in line, I speak with a man named Carnes.

"I'm going out with Cox," Carnes says. Carnes is thin and whiskered, his jaw moving slowly and constantly like he's still chewing on the memory of his link sausage. He is wearing a plaid flannel shirt and quilted nylon jacket and a baseball cap patched with the logo of an herbicide; if he were ever to be portrayed in a television movie, Harry Dean Stanton would have to play his role. "Cox has always got a snake in the past. He's always been good. He'll get you a snake. My kids like to watch the snakes, and Cox he'll always catch you one if you want to go watch. The hunt's the best part. We seen him before. We come ever year. Cox, he's good. He'll catch you a snake."

Carnes pencils "Carnes and family" on the sheet of lined notebook paper. I step up after him and sign, filling in the last spot on the Cox list, and poking holes through the paper, which is taped to the lunchroom's cinderblock wall.

We meet up with Cox and a group of about fifteen on the edge of town at the abandoned high school. Cox is a pharmacist in Cairo, but was raised in Whigham. Clean-cut and well pressed, he looks like Clark Kent in a safari hat with a snakeskin hatband. Cox explains to us that the day before, community club members had gone out and found some gopher tortoise holes loaded with snakes. They had blocked the burrows so that on this Saturday morning they could take out groups and show them how the hunt is done. While waiting for a Boy Scout troop to show up, Cox asks if anybody has any questions.

Someone asks how the Rattlesnake Roundup works. Explaining that hunters have been out for a couple of months collecting snakes, Cox says, "If the festival depended only on the snakes caught on one day in this county, it wouldn't be much of a festival."

Snake hunters, he says, start coming after the diamondbacks once the temperature drops to forty degrees. The hunters walk the woods, looking for stump holes, rubbish piles and gopher holes. Especially gopher holes, which are the burrows of the gopher tortoise—*Gopherus polyphemus*—one of only three true tortoises found in the United States.

8

They have been around for 60 million years and are as big as helmets. They used to be found all through the Southeast, but their habitat has shrunk so that now they are found in significant numbers only in southern Georgia and northcentral Florida. The gopher tortoises—everybody just calls them gophers—burrow into the sandy soil of the coastal plain, sometimes going ten feet deep and thirty-five feet in length. The gopher burrows provide habitat for dozens (some say hundreds) of species of animals, spiders and bugs, like the Florida pine snake, the gopher frog, the endangered indigo snake, and the bountiful eastern diamondback.

A boy asks Cox a question. "Anybody ever get bit?"

"Oh, no. We know what we're doing." Cox had his hand in the pockets of a green Rattlesnake Roundup windbreaker. He wore a felt fedora and new two-tone bush pants.

"How do you get 'em to come out of the hole?"

"Put a little gas down there and they come right out."

"These snakes run better on high-test or unleaded?" someone asks, and we laugh.

"We're using reg'ler," Cox says, and we laugh some more. I would come to find out that this was not the first time the joke had been told at a rattlesnake roundup.

The Boy Scouts finally show up. Cox gives them the shovel, posthole digger, black plastic tube and lard bucket to carry. We get in cars and drive a couple of miles out of town to a cornfield that is crunchy with the brown stubble of cut stalks. We park in the field and walk into the woods. Cox leads us to a spot where rotten logs are stacked over a gopher hole.

"You sure there's a snake in there?"

"Checked it yesterday."

Cox says that when he listened the day before, he heard the rattlesnake puff up and rattle. "And it sounded like a big one."

Cox tells everybody to stand back as he uncovers the hole.

"When it come out, you be moving," a father says to his son.

"You look out, girl!" A brother pushes his sister toward the hole. She slips and scrambles in the leaves, squealing and skittering backward and saying, "*Stah*-op!"

Cox kneels, shines a flashlight into the hole. He sticks the black plastic pipe into the burrow, rotating and twisting it to find and follow the contours. Seven feet, at least. Cox stops pushing. He puts the tube to his ear.

"Sure enough. He's in there."

Everybody stiffens.

Cox says, "Anyone want to listen?"

Folks take turns holding up to their ears the black plastic auditory link to death. Girls, boys, men, women recoil from the hissing tube. The noise sounds close, like you shouldn't let it touch your head. It sounds like a murderer outside your bedroom window.

Cox calls for the gasoline. A kid named Rusty pulls a screw-top Coke bottle from an old cotton glove he has stashed in his pocket. Cox pours a bit of the gas into the tube. The group is silent and still as we stand around, finding footing in the cluttered underbrush, double-checking a secure escape route in case we have to run.

Cox wraps his mouth around the end of the black plastic pipe, swells his cheeks, and blows, filling the gopher hole with the vapors of gasoline. Then he holds up his hand and speaks. "Quiet, now. Quiet."

After five minutes of total silence, Cox touches index finger to thumb, flashing the "Hey, we got 'em, a-okay" sign. We watch with thin-lipped grins as the wedge-shaped head of a massive rattlesnake slides slowly up and out of the hole.

All five feet of the snake is out of the hole. It moves toward the people crowded around, and a small arc of the circle bursts as a cluster of Boy Scouts panics, yelping and tripping over themselves to get away from the length of certain painful death that curls groggy and thick in the brown pinestraw and black leaves. Cox lifts it with his hook. The rattlesnake hangs limply, curling only slightly, raising its head to figure its predicament and taste the air with its tongue before Cox drops it into the white plastic lard bucket.

The crowd relaxes. Then Cox says, "Wait. There might be another."

Cox listens at the tube. "Sure enough. A bonus!" He blows more gasoline into the hole and, after a few minutes, a second, smaller, snake crawls out. "A bonus, sure enough." Then he again sticks the black plastic tube up to his head, like a suspicious doctor working the stethoscope. "I'll be. There's a third."

More gasoline.

More waiting.

No response.

Cox rams the tube into the hole, hoping to stir up the snake, but nothing emerges. It has been about ten minutes since the last snake came out of the gopher burrow. Cox concludes that the snake isn't coming out of the hole. Maybe he used too much gas and the snake was poisoned.

"Rusty," Cox says, "start digging."

(I can't remember if his name was really Rusty or not. If it wasn't then, it is now.)

Rusty and a couple of men talk among themselves, pace off a length of dirt, and estimate where the back end of the burrow would be. Figuring as best they can, they plunge their shovels and hole diggers into the ground.

"He's got us buffaloed, boys."

Cox takes off his commemorative Roundup windbreaker and dirties his brand-new two-tone wilderness britches as he digs hard into the hole. Finally, he reaches his hand deep into the chopped and mutilated earth and whips out his prize by the tail. Satisfied, the huntmaster grins and flings the gas-groggy half-dead snake into the lard bucket, there to writhe with the others.

In winter, rattlesnakes don't move with the speed that makes them such terrors in the rocks and dust of the classic westerns. These snakes in the Georgia woods are slow from the cold and poisoned from the gas vapors, and, as they crawl from the holes, the hunters simply pluck them up with a snake hook, a rake, or a stick. Some snakehunters pick them up by their tails and use a golf club to guide them into buckets. Another good place to hunt is around the edges of farmers' fields. Where corn is left in the field, there will probably be rats, and where there are rats, there will probably be rattlesnakes.

There's not a lot of remorse involved in hunting rattlesnakes. In addition to the routine lack of regret felt by hunters of any type, there's a supercharge of cultural snakefear and snakehate that makes this harvest of diamondbacks something more than regular bloodsport. A lot of people hate snakes so ferociously that they want to kill everything, venomous or not, that has been biblically condemned to crawl upon its belly: "And the Lord God said unto the serpent . . . thou art cursed above all cattle, and above every beast of the field; upon thy belly shalt thou go, and dust shalt thou eat all the days of thy life. And I will put enmity between thee and the woman, and between thy seed and her seed; it shall bruise thy head, and thou shalt bruise his heel."

Most people don't bother to consider the ecological role of snakes. It's the rattlesnake's misfortune to have its habitat overlap with that of a Judeo-Christian culture that loves westerns. The rattlesnake—its flat viper head loaded with symbolism—is to many a thing of danger and horror. A rattlesnake roundup is a chance for humans to gas Satan, grab evil by the throat, stuff sin in a lard bucket.

With the hunt over, Cox lets the crowd members pose for photographs. Children and old people hold the listless snakes in the air on the ends of long sticks, feeling their heft. Dads pop snapshots.

I watch, getting a kick from the closeness of the snakes as people flip them with sticks and toss them in the air. The snakes slide off the hooks, flash their pale undersides, land with thuds. I am on my knees taking pictures, when, two feet away, a four-and-a-half-foot rattler falls and tries to coil but is pinned with a stick by a man with a jack-o'-lantern face, half grimace, half sick grin. The stick forces the mouth open, and there is nervous laughter at the snake's helplessness. I look at the white-pink jaws and the fangs. I know that if this day weren't a special festive occasion, and if the snake buyers didn't prefer live snakes, a shovel blade would follow the stick, and the viper's head would be separated from its diamondback with a quick and socially sanctified stroke.

Kill a snake: no blame.

With the snakes limp in the lard bucket, we drive back into town to catch the brief parade, which features horse clubs, politicians in vintage Mustangs, mule-drawn carts, antique cars with magic-markered posterboard taped to their doors, and festival queens from surrounding counties (Miss Pine Seedling, the Swine Time Princess from the nearby town of Climax).

Then something happens: bringing up the rear of the parade are four high-stepping walking horses ridden by black men in porkpie hats and red T-shirts printed with the name of their club, Midnite Riders. As they ride past and the crowd begins to move toward the playground at the elementary school—drawn along down the road after the end of the parade like people caught in a current—a rough, stocky woman hollers out to one of the horsemen. "Hey, boy," she laughs raucously. "Gimmee a ride!" He smiles and nods and then ignores her.

This is the first time that I notice it: other than the few men driving the mule wagons, the Midnite Riders are the only blacks in the parade. The crowd on Whigham's sidewalks is almost all white, too.

I think about this not-insignificant fact as I walk toward the snake pit.

In the American language, rattlesnakes have been known as sizzle tail, buzz tail, buzz worm, chatter viper, snattle rake, sand eel and rattled snake (Klauber 1956). The Indians of the Southeast—Cherokee, Creeks, Choctaw, Chickasaw, Hitchiti and Yuchi—called the rattlesnake thunder's necklace, and he was the chief of all snakes. Once when all the animals of the world were gathered together to make up diseases and maladies as a way of fighting back against the humans who kept killing them, the rattlesnakes suggested a way to make people die. The rattlesnakes said they could make humans dream about eating rotten fish and being hugged by snakes. The dreams would make the dreamers lose their appetites, sicken and die. In the Indian cosmology, rattlesnakes were related to lightning and rain, and were allied with deer and ginseng.

The southeastern Indians carefully avoided rattlesnakes, only killing them when they especially needed one for medicine. Even then, they performed appropriate rituals before hunting the snakes.

The Indians played a type of stickball that was something like lacrosse, and players in the ballgame sometimes tied rattles on their heads to make themselves scary or ate rattlesnake meat to increase their ferocity, because it was said that rattlesnake meat makes a person hot-tempered. The oil from rattlesnake flesh was considered good for sore joints and rheumatism, a malady especially feared by the southeastern Indians and thought to be caused by someone killing a deer improperly. The Cherokee believed that seeing a snake at the beginning of a journey was an omen of death, and that moccasins that had absorbed smoke would make snakes get out of your way. The Chickasaws and Choctaws considered the snake to be treacherous, and characterized deceitful people as speaking with a snake's forked tongue (Hudson 1976: 165–68).

When a person got sick, to keep witches away the Cherokee priests would sometimes dance gigantic spiritual rattlesnakes around the house, only leaving a space between the head and tail where family members could pass through. The priests used rattlesnake fangs to scratch a person before sucking out any magic objects that had invaded the body.

People were sometimes transformed into snakes as punishment for eating foods that weren't prepared properly. If they did not show the proper care and respect when killing a snake, they would be surrounded by dozens of serpents, which would torment them until they went insane. Since snakes were thought to coil from right to left, the priest would warm his hands over a special fire and rub a snakebite victim's body in a circular motion from left to right, unwinding the snake out of the body. Anyone who dreamed about being bitten by a snake was treated by the priests in the same way as if he or she really had been.

American settlers treated snakebite by mashing the head and pasting it on the wound, or swallowing a fresh snake's heart, or rubbing rattler fat on the bite, or splitting a chicken and applying it to the bite and removing it when the chicken turned green. Although some snake lore was adapted from native beliefs, settlers also came up with their own. Some believed that an African-American with red gums could safely suck out venom, but one with blue gums would die. Others believed that anyone bitten too soon after drinking milk would surely die, and that it was only safe to suck venom if a silk handkerchief were put over the wound.

Indian ceremonies called the Town House Dance and the Eagle Dance were said to make the rattlesnakes angry and jealous, so the dances were only performed in the fall after the cold weather came, when the snakes were in hiding. Twentieth-century Americans in the Southeast believe differently. These days, it is after the cold weather has come and the snakes are in hiding that rattlesnake hunting begins.

By Saturday afternoon, the air has warmed a little. Small breezes are streaked with the smoke and smells coming from funnel cakes and fish being cooked in hot oil. The playground behind the elementary school is covered with booths and tables where people sell their arts and crafts and collectible junk—old license plates, ax handles, ninja throwing stars. People wander around with bags of boiled peanuts or pork rinds, eating as they walk. They will buy snap 'n' pops and little bullwhips for the kids; maybe Dad and the boys will get their pocketknives sharpened for a dollar, maybe Mom will buy something that she thinks is cute, and maybe (but probably not, since it's all so expensive) somebody will even buy an item made from a rattlesnake—rattle earrings, a snakehead paperweight, a snakeskin belt, a pair of snakeskin boots or a skeleton in Lucite.

The defining spectacle of Whigham's Rattlesnake Roundup is the snake ring, which is marked off by sections of rusty fence pipe encircling the infield of the baseball diamond on the playground behind the Whigham school. In the center is a flatbed truck where a snake show is held—snake-milking demonstrations, lectures on safety.

Outside the snake ring a crowd of people stands ten thick. Inside, men cluster around boxes and lard buckets. One by one they pull out the snakes, weigh and measure them, then drop them into one of several large boxes with clear Plexiglas walls. When a snake is dropped inside, those already there roil and vibrate their tails. As the snakes get more excited, so does the crowd, and people exchange big-eyed glances and quick, quiet, open-mouthed grins. If someone walks by a box of snakes, usually a snake will strike toward the person and hit the Plexiglas wall.

That's what people come for: to see the snakes, to experience fear and then a release from fear. Some stand fascinated for more than an hour staring into the snake ring, almost hypnotized by the spectacle of hundreds of rattlesnakes writhing in heaps. Watching the snakes' undulations, the unfeeling eyes, the vicious arrow-shaped viper heads, the keenly graceful and feared fangs, people in the crowd slowly and politely jostle and reposition to get a clearer view. The boxes are about ten feet in front of the first line of people around the ring, but a few still recoil with a jolt when a snake rises and slips the length of its white underbelly along the clear walls of the snake box, seeking escape.

I go inside the snake ring and stand close as the Plexiglas boxes fill to one layer with the snakes. Some coil slowly in the chilly shadows. Others, in the sun, are fully active, moving restlessly like waves on the plywood floors. Whenever I walk near a box, the sound of rattling rises up; it is almost universally compared to the sound of bacon frying. I watch as people point video cameras down into the boxes, recording the turmoil as lively snakes roll over listless ones and braid themselves together.

A few of the snakes seem maddened and angry. These few are not still. As people walk past or press camera lenses close to the Plexiglas, one or two of the most active snakes rise and hammer the clear box wall, striking with a widespread jaw. It is a compelling sight. I watch one as it hits repeatedly, and the walls soon become smeared with blood running from the rattlesnake's self-inflicted damage, the blood pink-streaked with leaked venom from its broken fangs. Soon its jaws are hammered unlocked, and will no longer close. Its desperate drumming against the box walls slows to an arrhythmic and infrequent rate like the last loose-armed roundhouses from a beaten boxer, the snake still vicious in the eyes but crippled in the vital mouth, which is seemingly frozen in a silent, broken anger that inspires a momentary wincing, reluctant pity. As new snakes are tossed into the boxes, one or two of the angriest will take up the fight and begin again the threatening, demanding, pitiable mad pounding—startling the crowd with their strikes, breaking their fangs against the box walls, and ruining the retail value of their heads.

15

(I never did discover a rattlesnake conspiracy, although I did find out that Ross Allen, who founded the reptile garden at Silver Springs, Florida, sold fifteen thousand cans of rattlesnake meat as novelty items in 1946 for $1.50 a can. The community club, I learned, was just protecting its interest when Buckley was run out of the county. Who wants to go to a rattlesnake roundup if there aren't any rattlesnakes?)

By late afternoon, we have enough material for the story. I have been on a hunt, eaten fried snake meat, watched the heaps of snakes writhe in their boxes. We find the car and drive back to Atlanta.

The newspaper article came out, and I moved on to other things. I didn't think too much about Rattlesnake Roundup until two years later, 1991, when I quit my newspaper job and entered a program at a local university to get my doctorate. It was here, when I was thinking about what I could do to practice cultural studies, that I recalled the crowds lingering around the snake pit.

When January came around again, I went back to Whigham to see what I could see.

American settlers came into south Georgia in the early nineteenth century, just after Andrew Jackson had crushed the Muskogees, the Seminoles, the Spanish and the British, and, with some geopolitical maneuvering and a few unrestrained bloodlettings, opened up south Georgia, Alabama, Mississippi and Louisiana. Most settlers passing through south Georgia went on through the pine forests and left the wiregrass country alone, believing that nothing of worth ever grew near pines. In due time, of course, the value of pine trees became apparent. The lumber was cut, the sap was distilled to make turpentine, and the wiregrass country was finally settled, first by cow herders—nicknamed "whip crackers"—and then by farmers, who now had new hard, sharp plows that could cut through the iron-tough, centuries-thick wiregrass mat of roots and thatch.

In 1867, the Atlantic and Gulf Railroad located a station midway between Thomasville and the Chattahoochee River and named it Cairo, after an old post office in the area, which itself had been named Cairo because it was located in the fertile valley of the Ochlocknee River, a valley that had been compared by a frontier classicist, in what must have been a moment of fanciful excitement, to that of the Nile. The next year, lots were surveyed for another town on the railroad, and, in 1888, the town of Whigham was incorporated. These are still the only two incorporated towns in Grady County (Grose 1974; Brunton 1976).

16

When Grady County was created in 1904, the folks in Whigham felt that their town should have been named the county seat, but Cairo had been campaigning for it since 1903, and a local sawmill owner from Cairo was an influential member of the Georgia legislature. The competition between Cairo and Whigham, despite the fact that one is more than ten times the size of the other, continues to this day.

Whigham is a quiet, small town, and the railroad that first gave it shape and substance no longer matters much. Passenger service ended years ago; the depot has been decommissioned and now houses the Master-Mix Cash and Carry Feed, Inc. Once in a while a train will sidetrack to pick up some corn and peanuts. In 1930, Whigham's population was 442; in 1990, it was 600 (205 black and 395 white).

On my return visit to Whigham, I got there on a Friday, the day before the roundup. That evening I bought a chicken gizzard dinner from the Pac-a-Sac and sat on the curb watching sheriff's deputies and the men and boys from the volunteer fire department direct traffic into the festival grounds. Nearby, old men in overalls picked up branches under the pecan trees. Vendors pulled in with their trucks and trailers and Winnebagos and station wagons and singular homemade vehicles of sheetmetal and two-by-fours. All of them had faded bumper stickers from the Chitlin Strut or Peanut Festival or Mule Day. Across a sidestreet in an asphalt-shingled house on the edge of the pecan grove, I watched a woman wipe dry her evening dishes. Behind her I could see magnets shaped like butterflies flocking on her refrigerator. All the other windows besides the one above the sink were nailed over with sheets of translucent gray plastic for insulation during the brief winter. She had been washing dishes and watching the cars and trucks and trailers pulling into the schoolgrounds, but dusk had reversed the surveillance; the fading light made her the better lit. Darkness stilled the trees, and I watched the woman's window as if it were television.

I sat and tried to think what Rattlesnake Roundup meant. It was my first exercise in deploying some of the concepts that are part of the toolkit of cultural studies.

When I was a boy, I once ordered a pair of X-ray Specs from the inside cover of a comic book. The ad showed a man wearing a pair of the glasses, holding his hand up in front of his face, and magically seeing the bones in the back of his hand. In the background was a small drawing of a woman, her skirt knee high and swinging loosely. Her presence suggested that the X-ray Specs would allow you the ultimate insight, as the glasses rendered clothes transparent. I sent away for a pair.

*Scientific wonder! It can't be true but look for yourself! Greatest illusion of the century! Apparently sees bones thru skin. . . . Girls will never trust you with these, but let them look for themselves and apparently see legs right thru your pants. Amaze and embarrass everyone!*

I got ripped off. It turned out that when you put them on, no matter where you looked, you saw the bones in the back of your hand. You didn't see through anything into the next layer of reality; you saw the bones from the back of your hand. Look at a woman's skirt: *the bones from the back of your hand.* Look at the door of your neighbor's house: *the bones in the back of your hand.* Look at your foot: *hand bones.*

Something similar to that experience happened when I went back to school and first started reading theory. One of the fundaments of cultural studies is the concept of hegemony. The coinage of the word as it is used today is credited to an Italian communist named Antonio Gramsci who was put in prison in the 1920s by Mussolini's fascists. Gramsci tried to understand why, considering their increasing misery, the working classes didn't rise up and overthrow the ruling class. He decided that it was because the working classes had come to accept the order of things as natural and inevitable. Gramsci, as Friedrich Nietzsche had before and Michel Foucault would after, understood that power was not simply a question of physical force, was not manifested only in the form of billy clubs and balled fists. It is that, surely—power does indeed grow from the barrel of a gun—but it is also something else: a flux of energies harnessed in patterns of behavior, habits of thought, systems of knowledge, structures of discourse. In this sense, "hegemony" is a sort of naturalized ideology, which saturates, according to Raymond Williams, the whole process of living, the whole substance of lived identities and relationships, to such a degree that the pressures and limits of what can ultimately be seen as a specific economic, political and cultural system seem to most of us the pressures and limits of simple experience and common sense. Hegemony is the sense of reality, a lived system of meanings and values, which is determined by the dominance and subordination of particular classes.

As with the X-Ray Specs, after I began to read contemporary cultural theory, everywhere I looked I saw the bones in the back of Gramsci's hand: hegemony. It was there in the most unlikely places—children's alphabet books, women's underwear, *Gilligan's Island* reruns—some pattern that reflected the uses of oppression in modern society. In the television program *Gilligan's Island*, for instance, where once I saw merely loopy hijinks, I now saw the naked ligaments of power. There's the Professor who represents the domination of the techno-elite, embodying an asexual rationality that keeps alive futile hopes of liberation, preventing the castaways from fully integrating with their new tropical environment. The Skipper is the dominating but dim-witted authority figure who rules through sheer force of beer-belly mass, but whose control also is dependent on the implicit sanction of the techno-queer professor and the classic capitalist robber baron leeches, the Howells, Lovey and Thurston the third, who command respect and obedience even though their wealth is useless and intangible on the desert island. This establishment of a few at the top of a fictitious yet naturalized hierarchy is such a strong cultural habit that merely by writing a check on tree bark the Howells can have Gilligan, Ginger, Mary Ann and the Skipper groveling in the sand, serving coconut cocktails and waving palm frond fans. Only the Professor remains aloof, free from the taint of mammon, and suitably so for the 1960s, when the myth of politics-free science still held sway. Gilligan himself represents the working class as infantile knucklehead.

I considered Rattlesnake Roundup in this context, looking for the blunt force head wound of hegemony. As I sat on the curb watching vendors unpack bootleg Simpsons T-shirts, Metallica posters, ax handles and butterfly knives, I wondered: could the roundup represent rampant phallocentric celebration, a reiteration of masculine domination?

Or perhaps it was a symbolic McCarthyite action, a sort of purge of insidious domestic dangers, with the annual ritual of rattlesnake roundup presenting a version of the social order that is supposed to be believed by the rest of the people, a declaration that the white men in the Whigham Community Club—and they are all white—are the ones who really wield the clubs and sticks and bent golf clubs and old shovel handles of authority in that town, and that it is only through their intervention and control that the fatal forces of nature and chaos are kept at bay.

Then I thought that maybe the roundup was less hamfisted and Freudian, where snake=penis=power, and more a textual affair, inspired by the movies. Although seasonal, community-wide rattlesnake eradication campaigns date back to colonial days (when they were sometimes called "rattlesnake bees"), westerns were big when the first (formalized) roundup was held in Texas in 1958, with Whigham's starting two years later, in 1960. In westerns the rattlesnake is always coiled, always a danger, always deadly, never a part of a balanced ecology. The rattlesnake was always a chance for a gunslinger to practice his quick draw, perform a woman-saving courtship ritual and slay the phallic rape-race-threat. This hypothesis would fit with the environmentalist critique of roundups; and, just as Native Americans have been transformed in the national imagination (no longer seen as demonized killers), so, too, are animals like the rattlesnake—once thought to be satanic and deserving of death—now considered a positive force in the ecology.

Then I thought: Why don't I just ask? When I did, I got a totally unexpected answer.

"We used to host community fish fries," James Cox tells me later on when I call him at his house. He is a retired postmaster and a founding member of the community club. Everyone calls him Mr. James. "But then before you know it, all the groups in the county, the Rotary, the Kiwanis, they're having fish fries too! So there wasn't any profit in it. We needed us a new attraction, so we came up with the roundup. But even now we still have the fish fry. Every year at the roundup we have the fish fry. Everybody knows we put out the best plate at the roundup. If you like mullet. It's a mullet plate.

"This used to be quail country, and we had a number of bird dogs getting bit by rattlesnakes. Then someone suggested we have a snake hunt. There'd been one in Crestview, Florida, I believe, and one in Texas. But at the time, it was quite a novel thing. We had heard about an old gentleman around Adele and Sylvester who hunted snakes, so we sought him out and he showed us the snake hunting method.

"We didn't realize what we were getting into. For the first one we told the hunters to bring their snakes to a filling station on the edge of town that we had as headquarters for the roundup. And that first time, traffic backed up a mile on 84. The second year we had it on a vacant lot and put the snakes in a cotton wagon. Then the crowds started getting bigger. We had a growing giant and didn't know it.

"Nobody can really remember who first proposed the snake hunt. Some say it was Clarence Mobley or Julius Newberry. They'll say, 'Oh, I remember Julius,' and such."

Seeking the source, I call Julius Newberry and ask if the roundup was his idea; he modestly demurred, saying that it was Clarence Mobley.

"Clarence was president of the club at that time, and he really had more to do with it than I did."

I ask Mr. Newberry why the display of rattlesnakes is such an attraction.

"There's no nut like a snake nut, I'll tell you that. People get around the snake ring and stay for all day, ooohing and ahhhing. A couple years ago we had a handler get bit. That was quite a show. People have been coming for years to see something like that."

On Saturday I go back to the snake ring, where the club members are hooking snakes out of boxes and tubs with bent poles. They drop a snake in the dirt, press the hook hard behind the snake's head and pick it up by the tail, holding it at arm's length. The snakes are too weak to curl up or lash sideways, so they hang in curves like tired ribbons as a club member carries them to a pine plank magic-markered with feet and inches. If the big rattlers just naturally curl like fat stiff wire uncoiled, desiring to resume an easeful arc, the men use the hooked poles to press the head against the post and get a full measure of their length.

They are weighed in a can, measured against a plank, then dropped into the Plexiglas boxes.

Outside the snake ring, Tracy Cobb stands next to his GMC Sportster SE Sierra pickup truck. The truck bed is stacked with snake boxes, like a pile of building blocks, and the boxes nearest the lowered tailgate have built-in Plexiglas windows. Inside the boxes are rattlesnakes. On top of the stack of boxes sits a friend, a man in his early twenties. His mouth hangs open, and when he talks a rim of dip snuff swells along his lower teeth, marking a dark line and making his lip protrude, as if he is beginning the slow stretch so that he can be fitted with a Kayapo lip plate. He offers appreciative guffaws as Tracy tells me about snake hunting, and how his little brother doesn't work and just hunts snakes, but that's not so bad, really, when Tracy himself isn't working (fixing the machines at a textile mill in Tifton), he's hunting snakes, too. That's what they do. Hunt snakes.

"I was just raised into it," he says, when I ask him how he got into rattlesnake hunting. "Mama and Daddy did it, so we did, too. Until I was big enough to hunt the snakes I drove the truck."

He has the shy soft-spoken demeanor of someone used to aggressive public attention only once a year when he, his wife, his parents and anybody else who wants to come along go to Whigham to deliver their load of snakes. In recent years, the Cobbs have become a snake-hunting dynasty. They first won the hunt in 1979, and from 1989 through 1993 dominated the categories for the most and the largest. They hunt Colquitt and Worth counties in south Georgia. They've seen the habitat decline, but tell me that the number of snakes remains high. In 1990, the roundup's total haul was 398 snakes; in 1991 it was 457, breaking the 1969 record of 418. The all-time high, 583, was set in 1992.The Cobbs brought in 125 and had the two largest, 10 and 10.2 pounds.

Tracy's mother has a slightly weathered cuteness about her. She has curly dark hair and wears a purple sweatshirt decorated with a design of a winged white horse flying among stars, like something from the cover of a fantasy romance novel. She tells me that a man named Randy Campbell buys the dead snakes. She smiles toward a man wearing spaghetti-western chic—a long dirt-length duster, horseman's boots and a cowboy hat. The ladies seem to like his look. Campbell runs an outfit called Southeast Skins. In the snake ring he stands around joking while the boxes of snakes are emptied and the live ones measured, duly noted, and dropped into the Plexiglas boxes. At one point, when the club members open a flat box, the snake doesn't seem to be there. They look in. They turn the box over and a dead snake falls in the dust. Campbell hustles over. He thumps its head, nudges it with his hook, pins its head and still, for safety's sake, grips its throat. Carrying it looped in his hand like a length of rope under the flaps of his duster, he walks out the gate, through the crowd, past the Cobbs's pickup to his own truck. His brow is furrowed. He is a man going about a serious business, although his expression also projects a sense of sheepish indignity—he's cool, wears a duster, a cowboy hat, slick boots, he's a rattlesnake man and has a cool truck, but still he's someone who has to pick up the dead.

Coming back from his truck, he stops and grabs Mrs. Cobb and hugs her to his side, saying how he's cold and how he needs to get him one of these-type heaters.

Tracy Cobb says, "We're always after the biggest. Always looking for that next one to be the biggest yet."

Nobody's ever been bit, Tracy tells me. "It ain't dangerous, we don't think about that, we wear snake boots and chaps and all." What motivates him is what motivates most sportfolk: the competition.

Mr. Cobb, Tracy's father, is a bit excitable. He is quick to defend the sport even when it's not being criticized. When he hears us talking about snake hunting, he jumps right in. "We got to thin 'em out somehow.

I seen the habitat decline, but the numbers remain high. You take one female, hatch out ten or fifteen babies, and five of them survive." He laughs with the thought of the incredible numbers. "There's plenty of snakes out there. Last year the total set a record. This year the numbers were a little lower 'cause of the warm weather and the rain. They'd be laying out around their holes and they'd miss 'em." The Cobbs say that since the use of gasoline has been prohibited, they have to dig the snakes out. To do this, they work together, one listening through the hose while another digs in burrows that are sometimes thirty feet long.

Mr. Cobb says he and his wife got started hunting snakes when he got out of the service in the late 1960s; he needed a hobby, a challenge, and Mrs. Cobb likes to get outdoors. They agreed that the sport gets in your blood and becomes addictive. Since snakes come back to the same holes every year, the Cobbs hunt in the same places. Critics say that rattlesnakes are very loyal to their territory, and that hunting them is actually like picking cabbages.

The Cobbs say they eat a right smart amount of snake meat. "Meal it and it tastes like fish. Flour it and it tastes like chicken. They's lots a bones in it. Like eatin' a bream." Mr. Cobb says he's hoping now that snake hunting can make a little money for him—not a lot, but some. "See, with deer hunting you don't make any money back. But snake huntin' is like cash huntin'." Mrs. Cobb adds, "You get four dollars a foot for the dead ones and seven dollars a foot for four foot and over, for the live ones. The price is going up because of the competition for the snakes."

The Cobbs have a snake house, complete with pens, heaters, water, and carpet, where they put snakes caught during the cold weather. Mr. Cobb says the snakes don't eat too much in the winter because it's their hibernating time, and the big ones, he adds, never eat. "That's the biggest tragedy of it. You can't get the big ones to eat."

A woman standing nearby asks Randy Campbell what he does with the dead snakes. A shadow falls over his eyes as he assesses the questioner. Then he becomes ebullient and almost boisterous. His boots scuff the dirt and he kicks up the flaps of his duster.

"Why, young lady, I got kids to feed!" he bursts out, totally finessing her question. "We in hard times, you didn't know that? These er the nineties! I got kids waitin' for me at home! I told the kids they could stop sitting on the fence like buzzards, I'm bringin' meat home tonight!" He puts his arm around this stranger, hugs her, lets her go, walks on.

Tracy's wife and two-year-old daughter walk over. They all joke about how snake hunting is a family tradition. Tracy nods toward his daughter and says, "We're starting on the third generation."

His wife wears a baby-blue high school cheerleader's jacket with a hood that zips up the middle, but which is now unzipped and spread like little fly wings off her back shoulders. She seems exasperated. "She is *not* going to hunt *snakes!*" Everybody laughs at her vehemence.

I ask Mrs. Cobb what the neighbors think of their snake hunting habit, their snake pens, their snakes. Mrs. Cobb leans forward in confidence. The others keep talking, their heads uplifted and their laughter projected in arcs. She leans forward toward me like she's bending beneath low-hanging branches of trees.

She whispers, "They think we kind of like the Addams family."

I had come to Whigham to check out the roundup and reckon its significance, and I believed I was closing in on it. Falassi has written about festivals in general: "Both the social function and the symbolic meaning of the festival are closely related to a series of overt values that the community recognizes as essential to its ideology and worldview, to its social identity, its historical continuity, and to its physical survival, which is ultimately what festival celebrates" (1982:2). So it is with Rattlesnake Roundup; having begun thirty years earlier as a fund-raiser, it has evolved, and now it celebrates and perpetuates the community. The community represented, however, is the white one.

Whigham's roundup is a white thing, a cracker thing, not overtly or explicitly; it just is. Racial segregation is the sine qua non of southern history, and it is an indisputable subtext of the roundup, perpetuated by the inarticulate momentum of social mores. There are black folk who come, and they are welcomed, but they're like visitors, and they remain distant, their numbers very small. The community club, the roundup's sponsor, is all white. The parade was practically all white. When I asked a man in the snake ring wearing camouflage pants and a knife on his belt why there weren't more black people at the roundup, he looked puzzled, glanced around like he hadn't noticed it before, shrugged, and said, "They don't like snakes." The Whigham city clerk, a white-haired woman getting ready to retire, had said, in answer to the question, "The blacks, they have their churches."

Later on, I called the NAACP in Cairo and asked the local chapter president why there weren't more black people at the roundup. He said, "People just have different interests," and in the spaces between his words I heard the tired silences fostered by traditions of exclusion. Then he said, "Let them catch their snakes. They're a dying little conservative town, anyway. The times have passed them by."

Small towns across the South are dying, but Whigham's not going without a fight. Lining the two blocks of downtown Whigham are fifty-two streetlamps made to resemble turn-of-the-century gaslights and referred to as Whigham's Amber Way. When I talked to townspeople about Whigham, they kept telling me that when the streetlamps are all lit up at night, it makes quite a sight (they are right).

Whigham's Amber Way lines the stretch of U. S. Highway 84 that at one time was the town's main street, with parking meters and stores. But that's pretty much gone now. There's still a streetlight in Whigham, and some businesses, but the highway has been four-laned, and Whigham's downtown street has been widened and black-topped. Most of the parking is gone, and so is the retail shopping; the street reminds me of Baron Hausmann's demolitions in nineteenth-century Paris, though of course on a much smaller scale. At night when all the lamps are turned on along the empty road and sidewalks, the desolate main street looks like a runway for the space shuttle.

The streetlamps were put up as part of the state's Community of Pride program. The Community of Pride program was started to help small Georgia towns keep their chins up as they were racked by structural changes. Whigham's streetlamps, however, are little compensation for the loss of the town's high-school-aged kids.

Whigham lost their teenagers when the state of Georgia forced the consolidation of the town's seventy-five-year-old high school with the high school in the county seat of Cairo, killing Whigham's "Indians" and turning them into Cairo's Syrupmakers. "That was a setback," the city clerk told me. "We miss our kids.

"We were hard put when we lost our high school. You know, that keeps the spirit up and everything centers around the school. You've got so much parent involvement, you've got the baseball, basketball and that sort of thing. And we just lost that. I never ever as long as I live will get over losing our high school."

Without the high school, town loyalties and town energies begin to dissipate. Retail shopping goes to Cairo, or Bainbridge, or Tallahassee, and with fewer farmers, the role of a small agricultural town has limited options. Through the lobbying efforts of the community club, two textile mills have located in the countryside around Whigham, and they employ a few hundred people, but they live out and scattered around along the highways and in the woods. The town no longer has a natural coherence; the economic forces of the last half of the twentieth century have torn it apart and scattered its kids. Nowadays it takes extra effort to keep the sense of community alive, extra symbols and extra rituals. As the trains stopped coming and legal segregation was dismantled and the high school closed and the kids were sent away and the businesses locked their doors and the young people moved on, the annual Rattlesnake Roundup took on more of a crucial ritualistic role in keeping the white community together.

What worries some people in Whigham is how long they will be able to keep holding the annual snake hunt, and how long they will be able to keep their community alive. Without some sort of commemorative vigilance, they know they will be swept away.

There's a legend about rattlesnakes that seems appropriate to the situation in Whigham. According to the southeastern Indians, there used to be a monster snake, the Uktena, living in the southern Appalachians. James Adair, a trader who operated in the Southeast in the eighteenth century, believed that the Uktena really existed. In his book on American Indians, he wrote:

> Between two high mountains, nearly covered with old mossy rocks, lofty cedars, and pines, in the valleys of which the beams of the sun reflect a powerful heat, there are, as the natives affirm, some bright old inhabitants, or rattle snakes, of a more enormous size than is mentioned in history. They are so large and unwieldy, that they take a circle, almost as wide as their length, to crawl round in their shortest orbit; but bountiful nature compensates the heavy motion of their bodies, for as they say, no living creature moves within the reach of their sight, but they can draw it to them. . . .
>
> Those who know say that the Uktena is a great snake, as large around as a tree trunk, with horns on its head, and a bright, blazing crest like a diamond upon its forehead, and scales glittering like sparks of fire. It has rings or spots of color along its whole length, and can not be wounded except by shooting in the seventh spot from the head, because under this spot are its heart and its life. ([1775] 1930: 249–50)

If anybody ever killed the Uktena, all the other snakes on earth would rise up, and everybody would get bitten. The diamond in the Uktena's forehead was a magic crystal. Hunting for it would lead to almost certain death, because the light caused the hunter to run toward the snake, instead of away. "Even to see the Uktena asleep is death," Adair wrote, "not to the hunter himself, but to his family" (251).

The belief system of the southeastern Indians was greatly concerned with categorization. Animals were divided into three classes: the four-footed animals were associated with this world, the birds with the upper world, where things were pure and ideal, and snakes, frogs and lizards with the underworld, the place of madness and disorder. The Uktena, which was also part bird and part deer, represented the ultimate transgression of boundaries, the disruptive, the carnivalesque. It represented chaos, loss of control, the violation of codes, and the blurring of categories. The Uktena was fearfully powerful because it represented the extinction of patterns, the anxiety of paradigm shifts, and the death of cultures. It represented the ultimate human terror: change.

In the 1990s, the symbolism of the monster serpent Uktena is relevant to the fate of rattlesnake roundups. When the roundups began in the late 1950s and early 1960s, the animals were considered expendable dangers. In popular western TV shows and movies, rattlesnakes and Indians alike were portrayed as having no inviolable link to the land. Currently, however, just as public consciousness has shifted regarding Indians, who are now perceived as having a sometimes overly mystical connection with the land, the rattlesnake is seen to have a valuable ecological role as a predator of rodents. Hunting rattlesnakes by dripping gas into gopher tortoise burrows has drawn criticism from environmentalists, and the use of gasoline has been officially prohibited. The only other option is digging out the snake, which totally destroys the burrow.

The nature of spectacle in the roundup has also decreased. At one time, Silver Springs sent safari-clad handlers to put on a snake show—milk the snakes, give lectures. But Silver Springs got out of the venomous snake business—despite the money to be made in the selling of snake meat as a novelty—after an employee was bitten and died and the family sued, and after exit surveys showed that visitors to the attraction had a decreased interest in venomous snakes. At the snake ring now, there's no show where the herpetologist drinks the venom or makes the rattlesnakes strike at red balloons. And the club no longer takes groups out on demonstration hunts, because they can't assume the liability.

One charter member of the community club I talked to admitted that maybe the environmentalists have a point. "Well, I think they are probably right. I wouldn't say this at the community club, 'cause I'd get drummed out. We kill some other animals in those holes we get snakes out of. Turtles, possums, skunks, and the main thing I hate, we have a big beautiful snake here [the eastern indigo] that gets in that hole, and he's about extinct. I imagine he probably is by now.

"I think I'm the only fella who thinks we may have to shut down one day. But I wouldn't say that out loud 'cause I'd have to move.

"We've talked more than one time over the years about changing to some other theme, because a lot of these rattlesnakes don't come from Grady County. I don't think there's as many rattlesnakes as there used to be, or, let's put it this way, they're in thicker places I feel like than usual. And with the environmentalists and the different ones, it's something we've thought about changing, but we don't know what to change to.

"And it seems people will always come to see the rattlesnakes."

# CHAPTER TWO

# HISTORY'S ALL WE HAVE LEFT

The Tobacco Festival (Clarkton, North Carolina),
Swine Time (Climax, Georgia), and the
Banana Festival (South Fulton, Tennessee)

The New South, as C. Vann Woodward has written, was built on rail-roads. The Civil War had left the region's rail systems in shambles, with few bridges, much torn-up track, and little money for making improvements. But once Reconstruction ended, New South leaders set about rectifying this situation. In 1870, the southern states east of the Mississippi had 10,690 miles of railroad; by 1890, that total had more than doubled to 27,655 (Woodward 1951 :120). The Democratic Party that came to control the South for a hundred years was so thoroughly identified with railroad interests that in Virginia, for example, nearly every chairman of the state party during the 1870s, 1880s and 1890s was ei-ther a railroad president or director. "The constant theme of New South editors and orators was cheap resources, business opportunities, railroad developments and commercial enterprise," Woodward writes (6).

Since modes of transportation and communication play a large part in determining the dispersal of people across the landscape, towns began to grow up along the rail lines. Communities lobbied hard to have railroads run through their towns, and railroad companies themselves worked hard to colonize undeveloped land and support agricultural improvements. People and crops meant passengers and freight. But then cheap cars, good roads, big trucks and agribusiness wrought their changes. The train depots closed as passenger traffic declined and the distribution systems for agricultural products were redesigned. The founding of the railroad stations had literally put many towns on the map, and the closings of the train depots were profoundly traumatic experiences that challenged the communities' perceptions of themselves.

After Rattlesnake Roundup, the next three festivals I visited—the North Carolina Tobacco Festival, Swine Time, and the International Banana Festival—all involved communities responding to shifting trends in agriculture and transportation. Each of the festivals clearly shows how the events are attempts to revive or perpetuate communities by giving symbolic value to certain current or remembered elements of culture. At the same time, each festival offers rich sources for cultural history and moments of interpretive grace; I learned, for example, about the historical evolution of the semiotics of the pig, the troubling cultural politics resonating in the sitcom *Green Acres,* and the railroad company responsible for America's embracing of the banana as a popular food. This and more are present at such festivals as the celebrants conjure with their artifacts and memories so that they might live again.

### Hank Kimball — Enemy of the People

Many of the storefronts along the two or three blocks of Main Street that used to be downtown Clarkton, North Carolina, are abandoned. Their windows are sheened over sheet-metal gray with two decades of grime. The window sills are trays for the display of horseflies and mouse dung and the intricate fil-igree of desiccated moth wings. Most of the downtown trade has been drawn off by the discount stores along the highway and the malls around Lumberton. The un-walked concrete sidewalks sprout spikes of grass along the cracks. But this Saturday is different from most Saturdays during the year. The curbs along both sides of Main Street are lined with people.

Armored National Guard as-sault vehicles are rolling down the middle of the street in front of me, their diesel engines in low gear,

A Banana Queen

30

once in a while revving and roaring out gray-black exhaust. Suddenly one of the machines explodes with bursts of heavy-caliber automatic weapons fire. Nearby sit two elderly people in lawn chairs; when the machine gun fires, they snap their heads back and down, their shoulders rising with a jolt toward their ears. Adults standing along the side of the road wince toward each other, smiling grimaces about the gunfire, while their kids, some jumping and some just staring, exhibit the unequaled equipoise of truly fascinated children as they follow with a slow turning of their heads the grinding rotation of the armored assault vehicle's tread. The kids tug at their parents' hands, wanting to break free so they can grab the brass shell casings spit from the weapon. Picking up the shells, they flip the brass in the air, shaking their hands in surprise at the heat. Everyone claps for the gunner to do it again, but the vehicle moves on, lurching more than any jumpy horse in harness, revving and grinding up the asphalt and careening on down the road. The gunner fires another burst in front of the First Baptist Church, where volunteers are serving coffee and cold drinks to the church members sitting in chairs on the lawn. The machine gun obliterates all other sound for the few seconds surrounding each side of the banging *whop whop whop*, and the Baptists hold cups of Coke out to their sides so as not to spill them during the rapid exploding smacks of air. The assault vehicle was not designed to be a demure and domesticated feature of festival parades. It punches along, rocking on its tread behind a shrill and unkempt high school marching band.

After the assault vehicle comes a flatbed of cloggers. Behind that, the Evergreen Princess sits up on a red convertible, followed by the Junior Miss Evergreen Princess, the North Carolina Strawberry Festival Princess, the Blue Devil Band, the Tar Heel Band, Miss Williams Township, Junior Miss Williams Township, the Jaycees Baby of the Year, the Bladen County Little Miss Christmas, the Fair Bluff Watermelon Princess, the Junior Miss Watermelon Princess, and the Tobacco Queen and her Court, riding on flatbeds decked with green crepe paper and hauled by a tractor on loan from a local tobacco warehouse.

Located about ten miles south of the Cape Fear River and about fifty miles from the coast, Clarkton is a tobacco town in the Bright Belt, a swath of the Carolinas and Virginia where farmers produce a light-leafed, flue-cured tobacco. The first European settlers in the area were the Scotch-Irish, who came and built a courthouse at a landing on the nearby Cape Fear River. The town was called Brown Marsh when the railroad first came through in 1861, but in 1874 it was renamed Clarkton after the man who built the first cotton gin in the county and who was the first Democrat elected there after the state was redeemed from Reconstruction.

After the Civil War, Union soldiers spread a taste for southern tobacco across the country. The invention of efficient cigarette rolling machines and the wildfire spread of cigarette smoking as a cultural habit created such a demand for the light, flue-cured cigarette tobacco that companies sent men out into the field to teach farmers how to grow what was called the "thirteen-month crop," so named because next year's seedlings had to be sprouted before last year's plants were harvested. When cotton prices dropped, farmers began to plant the noxious golden weed and rake in the money. The first crop grown in Bladen County, where Clarkton is located, was planted in 1886, and the first tobacco auction market was set up in Clarkton in 1898 (Tilley 1985:144). As late as the 1920s, the Bladen County newspaper was printing the basic instructions for tobacco cultivation on the front page. Farmers have been growing tobacco in this part of the country for most of the twentieth century, and Clarkton has been honoring tobacco with a festival since the end of World War II.

Folklorist Roger Abrahams has written about one type of agricultural festival: "They are resounding times and elaborated places for excited exchange, for bringing out, passing around, for giving and receiving the most vital emblems of culture in an unashamed display of produce . . . precisely so that the community may boast. The emblems explode with meanings, for they are invested with the accumulated energies and experiences of past practice. They epitomize not only the seasonal passage but the history of the culture, a history spelled out in terms native to the group and appropriate to the place and the season" (1982: 161).

That's what I expected when I decided to go to the forty-fifth annual Tobacco Festival at Clarkton in the fall of 1991. I thought I'd drive into the Bright Belt and see the crop enlarged, prolonged, magnified, amplified, miniaturized, and made into toys, the fertility of the earth and the abundance of the community's most significant cash crop celebrated by reproduction of its iconic emblem. Tobacco is important stuff: it built the earliest American fortunes, and the culture and economics of tobacco cultivation in colonial times helped shape the ideology of our founding revolutionaries. Being such a key emblem of America, the plant, I thought, should be anthropomorphized and worshipped like a pagan god. I had once seen a picture of two young women dressed in bikinis made from tobacco leaves at a tobacco festival in Moultrie, Georgia, during the 1950s. That's what I was looking for.

At one point during the parade, after the assault vehicle and the cloggers and the queens, I got excited when I saw a float approaching up the road. On top of the float was a person decked out in the costume of some dark vegetation. Surely this was what I had been hoping for. I shouldered between people and maneuvered with my camera to the edge of the road. Maybe it would be the mayor wearing the town's tobacco suit. The flatbed rolled closer.

But it wasn't a tobacco leaf; it was a sweet potato. A woman was wearing a brown sheath and green gloves sewn with corkscrewing tendrils. Her banner announced Tater Day in nearby Tabor City.

I never was to see any reference to the tobacco crop other than a leaf drawn in grease pencil on the cheek of a festival organizer and the dry dust in the air at Jimmy Green's Bright Leaf warehouse during the beauty pageant. In the 1990s, tobacco, it turns out, is not a very popular or successful festival theme. As with Whigham's staging of the Rattlesnake Roundup, Clarkton's persistence in holding the tobacco festival is an effort to postpone civic dissolution. It is a stubborn celebration of an agricultural heritage that no longer matters for most people except in their remembered sense of place and community. Although I never saw women in tobacco bathing suits, my visit to Clarkton provided me with an example of a southern community festival that not only contributed to my eventual understanding of ghost dancing on the cracker circuit but also led to a smaller revelation. My examination of Clarkton's Tobacco Festival demonstrated how rich and complex such phenomena are and how, by contemplating chains of association, historical insights can come from unlikely sources. It was because of my desire to see tobacco bathing suits that I learned that Hank Kimball, the addle-brained county agent played by Alvy York on *Green Acres*, was *an enemy of the people.*

I had driven in to Elizabethtown on Thursday and spent most of Friday reading microfilm at the Bladen County Library, where I found the first mention of what was to become the tobacco festival on the front page next to a list of Bladen countians charged with traffic violations and drunkenness. "Representatives of the Extension Department and the Bladen County Farm Bureau met on Wednesday night, September 10, for the purpose of making plans for farmers and Extension Achievement day, which will be held on Friday, October 24, in Elizabethtown," the *Bladen Journal* reported (September 25, 1947). The 1947 event was to be the climax of the Farm Bureau membership drive. Among those named to the publicity committee for the Farmers and Extension Achievement Day was the publisher of the *Bladen Journal*, herself a frequent author of editorials supporting the Farm Bureau and select crop control programs. "Farmers and Extension Achievement Day will be the climax of a drive to increase membership in the Farm Bureau which has been responsible for many benefits in this and other counties of the state" (October 16, 1947). Two weeks before the first Farmers and Extension Achievement Day in 1947, the name was changed, for some reason nobody could remember, to Farmers' and Farm Women's Day.

Whatever its name, it was a tobacco festival, because farming in Bladen County and the entire Bright Belt meant tobacco. An editorial that summer in the *Bladen Journal* testified to the region's dependence on the leaf:

> With the opening of the Border Belt Tobacco Markets next Thursday . . . "the golden weed" becomes king in Eastern North Carolina and the larger part of our population will feel the effect of the king's presence. . . . For the next few months King Tobacco will hold sway in our section and his golden influence will swell the coffers of many, leaving good cheer in his wake.
>
> Debts will be liquidated in many cases, homes will be brightened with new equipment and new furniture, young students will start to college because of King Tobacco, new machinery will make the farm burden easier, new cars will shine in the family garage and thousands of other avenues will be opened by King Tobacco as he reigns among us. We welcome this king into our midst. (July 31, 1947)

At the Farmers' and Farm Women's Day in 1947 the mayor of Elizabethtown (the county seat) and the manager of Sears, Roebuck presided over the 4-H club's pig chain competition between Hampshire pigs and spotted Poland China pigs. Flapping and feather-shedding chickens were thrown down from buildings. Greased pigs ran through the street. The 82d Airborne parachuted in. There was a baby contest and a parade of babies. The British had just banned American tobacco imports as a way of conserving cash for rebuilding after World War II, so when the former governor spoke at the Farmers' and Farm Women's Day, he promised that if everybody joined the Farm Bureau, they would try to get tobacco included under the Marshall Plan, which would guarantee the sale of lots of cigarettes.

Farmers' and Farm Women's Day was such a success that three Bladen County towns—Elizabethtown, Clarkton and Bladenboro—decided to shorten its name to Farmer's Day and make it an annual event, rotating the host duties. At Farmer's Day in 1948, a man named Mr. Pierce gave a sharpshooting exhibition that was highly praised by the visiting soldiers from Ft. Bragg, but the shooting had to be stopped when school children kept running into the line of fire. In 1952, when the famous cowboy star Al "Fuzzy" St. John rode in the parade, his horse went crazy and nearly trampled some kids; the newspaper reported that "only the cowboy's excellent horsemanship prevented injury."

Clarkton at this time was still a flourishing tobacco auction market, and every fall the *Bladen Journal* would fill with ads: "Sell Your Tobacco in Clarkton Tobacco Market—Bring Your Dry Cleaning to McNeill's Cleaners." "Welcome to Clarkton Mr. Farmer! While You Are in Town Stop by and Let Us Service Your Car or Truck."

Living in Bladen County meant supporting tobacco, so, when scientists began criticizing the plant as a public health hazard, the *Bladen Journal* rallied in support of the local cash crop. In 1955, the newspaper eagerly reported the findings of some research on lung cancer. "British Tobacco Experiments Unable To Induce Cancers" the headline declared on July 28, 1955. "The report of the British Empire Cancer Campaign that 16 month experiments fail to show any connection between cancer and smoking is further evidence that lung cancer is not a simple problem with a simple solution," said Timothy Hartnett, chairman of the Tobacco Industry Research Committee. Nonetheless, despite the promising research reports, there was an uneasiness creeping into the land, along with foreboding signs. For two years Farmer's Day wasn't held. In 1957, the little town of Bladenboro revived it as Old Fashioned Bargain Days and Farmer's Festival, and the newspaper, on October 3, 1957, described the event as "trade days designed to be a stimulant to business and a mark of community determination to grow and prosper. Regardless of the name of the Friday celebration, it is good for townspeople in the various communities to set aside a special day to have their rural neighbors in for a day of entertainment." Also that year the wireworms and the black shank struck the crop, and too much rain washed the fertilizer out of the sandy soils and drowned the tobacco in the bottoms. Bladen County also suffered a rash of witchweed. In the column "This N That," it was reported that "[l]ots of people think M. G. 'Sprunt' Hair had the right thought when he came up with the claim that witchweed may be caused by certain fertilizers . . . hope the experiment people get hot on the clue and trace it down. We've also heard that the fertilizer could have been purposely tampered with as a means of aiding the Communists. . . ." And in 1959, the first Tobacco Queen, Sarah Love, of Clarkton, was crowned, after which she went on to an unsuccessful bid for the title at the National Tobacco Queen Pageant.

By 1961, it had all fallen to Clarkton. Bladenboro and Elizabethtown had stopped holding the event because it was too much trouble to haul in tents, and Clarkton already had enormous tobacco warehouses. The big news that year was that Miss North Carolina was going to attend. Everybody fondly remembered her from the pageant, where she had performed Lady MacBeth's sleepwalking scene. On October 4, 1961, the *Bladen Journal* reported that the International Tobacco Queen, Emmalee Gaddy, "ambassadress of tobacco to the world," had come through town. "She is the working partner of all those who earn their livelihood within the confines of this Industry. Miss Emmalee Gaddy is a student at Columbia College, Columbia, S. C. From Tampa, Florida, to New York to Istanbul, Turkey, this enchantingly lovely and intelligent young woman is telling the story of Tobacco to all who are interested enough to listen."

By 1964, there were ominous developments regarding the tobacco industry. The surgeon general issued his report on smoking. County agents urged diversifying to hogs, livestock, poultry, soybeans, sweet potatoes or strawberries. By 1966, bulk curers were coming in, and this technological innovation meant more than just a small change in the way things were done. Combined with crop control programs and acreage allotments, it was the death of the tobacco culture. "Back before the arrival of the 'computer age' it was difficult to tell which the farmer took more pride in, the strength of his team of mules or his own ability to cure tobacco," pondered an editorial in the *Bladen Journal* in August 1964. "Tractors have replaced the mules and now something called 'programmed curing' may replace the farmer at the controls of the curing barn. Curing tobacco, once an art gained through years of experience, has become a science. The change may bring a shift of personal values for the farmer, but it also promises to eliminate the errors often made in curing tobacco."

The increasing use of science in agriculture not only brought a shift of farmers' personal values but helped eliminate the farmers themselves. By the time of the 1991 North Carolina Tobacco Festival of Clarkton, neither farmers nor tobacco were being honored. The head of the festival organizing committe was a woman who worked as a personnel manager at a local knitwear factory, and when I asked her what connection she had with growing tobacco, she recalled a few times visiting an uncle— now dead—who grew some tobacco back in the 1960s. "The only time I put in tobacco was when I was five years old, and this man gave me a dime to leave him alone, so I didn't sucker tobacco or that type thing." Then she added, "And I used to smoke. But I've quit. Smoked for fifteen years. I done my part for tobacco."

After the parade had passed, the streets emptied. The people were drawn along toward the playgrounds behind a vo-tech school where the festival was being held. With everyone gone, the desolation of the town was stark. I cupped my hands to shade my eyes and peered in the windows of a store with chained and padlocked doors. The shelves, sagging along with the floor, had fallen away from the wall, spilling empty shoeboxes. On the counter stood old displays of bow ties, crewcut men smiling from the peeling sunbleached cardboard, suggesting the happiness that a clip-on could bring.

The ties were gone. There were cans of insecticide and packs of underwear on the floor. I went around to the back of the block to see if I could find a way in. The lot next to the store was empty, and I crossed the broken and uneven tile and concrete of a long-demolished building, the linoleum of the empty lot left in ragged sections among gravel and dirt, like hints of an ancient fresco. Inside the abandoned store, the broken drawers of a broken chiffarobe peeled leaves of veneer. There were wire racks, sodden clothes, and leaf litter from the trees and weeds growing up toward the concave roof; the sun came in through pumpkin-sized holes in the ceiling. I stepped lightly, afraid of breaking through and impaling my feet on rusty nails.

On the other side of the building, under what had to be a decade's worth of pine needles, were stacks of old soda bottles that had once held pop. These were *real* pop bottles. It was as though the cases had been stacked on the side of the building to await pickup and refilling, but the bottling service never showed back up—as though, suddenly one Saturday afternoon while Kennedy was president, the Rapture and the Wrath came, the streets emptied, the pop bottles were left stacked in their crates. The seasons passed; pine needles drifted down, burying the crates. Rains came and the pine needles rotted, filling the squares around the bottles, and the water leached through the wooden crates, which were now themselves black and rotted. When I dug into them, the crates crumbled, but finally I found one that was still whole, and I filled it with a selection of the bottles—Wink, RC, Patio—bottles Opie himself could have drunk from, bottles cast in old rocket ship shapes from back in the era of Sputnik and the Mercury program, from the days when the downtown was still used, when folks still drank soda pop from bottles, when the Tobacco Festival was called Farmer's Day, when there had still been lots of farmers and lots of people smoked.

I put the pop bottles in my car. Back out on the main street of Clarkton, I found my way to the festival grounds by following the sound of machine-gun fire.

Just as there was no tobacco in the parade, there was no tobacco at the festival, except for the outline of a leaf drawn in grease pencil on the cheek of a woman who was sitting at a table selling hot dogs out of a Crock-Pot. "No," she said, when I asked if there were any crop displayed at the festival, "I don't think you'll find any here." She looked over the playground.

There was not a lot of anything there. The National Guard had set up an M-60 belt-fed machine gun which some Boy Scouts spent all afternoon taking turns firing. The state penitentiary had a display of homemade shivs confiscated from the cons (the Boy Scouts liked those, too). There was a wood-planked flatbed for cloggers, and some vendors were selling craft items made with lots of lace and dowels. There were not many people. Everybody I talked to said they had come today "just to see what they got this year": "Yes, it's not but just a little ol' festival. We try to just keep it going. Just a little something for us, you know, not too big. I know there's not much here. We were supposed to have this lady back this year who made ducks out of tobacco leaves, and made these prettiest little roses, but I don't know what happened to her, why she couldn't come. Yes, there's not much here, but it's nice just to get out, see people."

The people of Clarkton used to get help for their festival from the tobacco companies, but, during the 1980s, the companies began to drop out and cut off their support. For almost four decades the National Tobacco Festival had been held in Richmond, Virginia, until in 1986 the tobacco companies killed it by withholding their money. The event died, and when local people tried to start the festival back up, the tobacco companies said the only way they would contribute was if the word "tobacco" was nowhere to be seen. The companies pulled their support from Clarkton's festival as well, but in a small town it's easier to keep something going: a Crock-Pot of hot dogs, a display of confiscated homemade weapons, cloggers, and you have a ritual.

Philip Morris used to send "Little Johnny," the world's only living trademark. The national tobacco council would send the International Tobacco Queen. Senators, governors and movie stars would come. But it's all over. I asked the lady with the tobacco leaf drawn on her cheek why the tobacco companies don't contribute to the festival anymore. She paused a second before she answered. "I don't really know. We wrote to them asking for money but they never sent us any. All they sent us were some plastic banners," she says, forking a hot dog into a Sunbeam bun, "and some hats."

As I was hanging around just talking to people, once again I noticed that the crowd and contestants were all white. I asked somebody about race relations and got this reply: "I don't think we've really had any racial problems here. Everybody's just grown up together. If you had a farm, you grew up with each other. I do remember whenever they were marching and that type of thing, that they came in and tried to get the blacks here to march and they would not. Now that's just hearsay, but I don't really remember them doing anything, because everybody, like this black lady that used to baby-sit for us, she's just like a mama to us. We've just grown up together. We've visited each other's homes. We got black people we call aunt and uncle, and that's just how they are."

I remembered seeing an article earlier that morning at the library. It was a report from August of 1980 about three hundred youths, blacks and whites, brawling in the nearby town of Bradenboro. They fought for two nights. A curfew was imposed. The police chief said, "The problem was liquor, plain old drinking and dope. They got to hanging around and drinking a little bit and that started the whole thing."

When I mentioned it, the woman I was speaking with said, "You've always got some bad examples, but that occasion was a rarity."

"Oh," I say. "Okay."

The subtext of mourning was much more obvious at Clarkton's festival than at Whigham's Rattlesnake Roundup. Both events were hosted by communities that were dispersed geographically, but were still symbolically, if not economically, centered around their main streets. The parades in both towns still traced routes along what had been the most significant streets, and the organizing committees were made up of members of the older, white families, even if they lived in other counties or towns. However, Clarkton's long-time dependence on tobacco led to the town's rapid decline, as crop controls, third-world growers and the industrialization of the growing and processing of tobacco forced the farmers out of business and off the land. And, of course, the changing social attitudes toward tobacco have also severely affected Clarkton's celebration. On the other hand, Whigham's more diversified agricultural base—cattle, soybeans, peanuts—has allowed it to support more of a rural-farm population even though the financial activity has been dispersed from its small-town center.

It was the very decrepitude of Clarkton's festival that led me to a deeper understanding of a certain aspect of the South's history, and thus to a fuller comprehension of Hank Kimball, a character on the television show *Green Acres*, who had previously existed for me merely as walk-on comic relief. After my visit to Clarkton, the dossier on Mr. Kimball was presented to me. All history is, in a sense, hidden yet ever-present, and taking one artifact or aspect of the world around you and pursuing it to its origins can lead to some interesting connections. I had gone to Clarkton looking for a festival of plant worship and women in tobacco bikinis, but what I found was that Hank Kimball, Hooterville's county agent, was actually an enemy of the people.

Here's how I reasoned that.

I had discovered in my reading that the big names appearing at the very first Farmers' and Farm Women's Day were a former governor who was "an ardent supporter of the farm program," and R. Flake Shaw, the executive vice president of the North Carolina Farm Bureau and a member of the board of directors of the American Farm Bureau. Mr. Shaw was to be introduced by the local county agent. County agents, I found with a little further research, had evolved from efforts by governments, farm organizations and business people around the turn of the century to fight the boll weevil. Their demonstration techniques proved effective, so more men were sent into the fields to demonstrate new crops and methods which would help improve living conditions in a countryside racked by populist upheaval throughout the 1880s and 1890s.

In 1914, Woodrow Wilson signed into law the Smith-Lever Act, creating the extension service. Sponsored by Georgia Senator Hoke Smith and South Carolina Congressman A. F. Lever, the bill was supported by chambers of commerce and the country's largest banks. A competing bill supporting increased vocational education had been supported by the Grange, Farmers Union and the American Federation of Labor. International Harvester and John Deere favored the use of "extension" agents because they could serve as transmitters of improved technology and as middlemen for suppliers. The union groups favored vocational education because it would help the folk adapt to changing times (Scott 1970).

By 1917 there were 860 county agents in the South, compared with 540 in both the North and the West, plus an additional 66 black agents for the South. During World War I, the county agents expanded their roles and served on draft boards, organized wholesale purchasing and controlled distribution of rationed materials.

At first, local groups called farm bureaus were formed to help raise appropriations for funding these demonstration agents. Eventually the assorted bureaus coalesced, and in 1921 the American Farm Bureau Federation was formed. This benefited the wealthy farmers, as the federation worked against poorer folk by opposing federal programs like the Farm Security Administration, which would help tenants and sharecroppers buy their own farms (Baldwin 1968). The local branches were heartily supported by businessmen, and since their funding was connected to the American Farm Bureau Federation, county agents sometimes became agents instead for fertilizer and farm equipment companies and recruiters for the Farm Bureau. Although the government tried to control the connection between the Farm Bureau and the county agents, the two were never really separate. Ads in the September 25, 1947, *Bladen Journal* for the farm bureau membership drive that appeared on the eve of the first Farmers' and Farm Women's Day instructed potential members to send their three dollars to "Farm Bureau membership Chairman, care of AAA Office, Elizabethtown, N. C."

Farm activists have called the Farm Bureau "the right wing in overalls" (Berger 1971 ). A 1946 newspaper editorial complained that the farm bureau only represented the "time merchants, warehousemen and large farmers." Rexford Tugwell, a former New Deal official, in 1949 called the Farm Bureau the most sinister influence in America. Populist former Texas agriculture commissioner Jim Hightower wrote in his

41

book *Hard Tomatoes, Hard Times* (1973) that the Farm Bureau, land-grant colleges and universities, agricultural experiment stations, and agriculture schools had neglected the family farmer to benefit corporate agribusiness, which increased mechanization and concentration of ownership and devoted time to developing products like a hard, tasteless tomato that wouldn't bruise when picked by robotic claws. Along with the National Association of Manufacturers, the American Farm Bureau Federation opposed early child-labor laws.

The county agents did do a lot of good by helping people learn how to preserve foods, practice better sanitation, and use more productive seed. And the 4-H, which takes up most of the time of today's agents, is a force for good. But the county agents were also part of the modernizing trend toward capital-intensive agriculture that destroyed once and for all any alternative arrangement of independent family farms or large-scale cooperatives.

County agents weren't easily accepted by conservative farmers who did not like college boys coming around telling them that everything they had been doing was wrong. The ambivalent sentiments of the country folk toward the agents as state functionaries is evident in the portrayal on *Green Acres* of Hank Kimball, by far the best known, if not the only, county agent on television. Mr. Kimball, as played by Alvy York, is eternally trapped within his own useless, fruitless half-thoughts, delusions ironically appropriate for the functionary of a system designed to destroy the countryside in order to save it.

In 1939, the population of Clarkton was 458. Today it is 654. In 1945, on the eve of the beginning of Farmer's Day (which would evolve into today's Tobacco Festival), there were 3,480 farms in Bladen County, with 2,900 of them counting as tobacco farms. The average farm size was 68.6 acres. In 1980, there were only 719 farms, the average size being 182 acres; 340 of them were tobacco farms. In the short period between 1959 and 1964, the number of farms with fewer than 50 acres shrank by 30 percent. The number of farms with 500 acres or more increased by 17 percent. From 1949 to 1964, the number of all flue-cured tobacco farms fell 53 percent (U. S. Census of Agriculture).

It was into one of the abandoned, ramshackle yeoman farmer houses that big-city lawyer Oliver Douglas moved with his lovely wife, Lisa, in the small, southern town of Hooterville on *Green Acres*. This 1960s sitcom was the flipside to *The Beverly Hillbillies*; instead of showing bumpkins in the city, the program featured sophisticates transplanted to a rural community. Whenever Oliver Douglas, the penthouse jurist turned dirt farmer with utopian agrarian impulses, starts extolling the virtues of the Jeffersonian vision of America as a republic of independent farmers, patriotic fife music begins to play. The Hooterville natives—the merchant Sam Drucker, the farmer Mr. Ziffel, the peddler Mr. Haney—listen patiently for a moment, screwing up their faces at the fife music, to which Douglas is oblivious. Finally one of them will make a wisecrack, deflating Oliver's populist bubble, and irreverently ask where the hell that fife music was coming from.

They don't mean to be rude; it's just that they know something that the idealistic Oliver doesn't: that the vision of America as an agrarian democracy is no longer a feasible one. And, unbeknownst to them, and with ultimate irony, the demise of that vision is represented within the cast by the man who enters the scene and deranges any stable, comprehensible community identity—the bumbling, but always lovable, apparatchik, Hank Kimball—enemy of the people.

Before I left Clarkton, I spoke with Madeleine Clark, who was described to me as the area's unofficial historian. She told me about the settlement of the town and the old days of the festival, about how things used to be when the downtown was a viable, lively place. Now that the downtown is a historic district, she's working to have it put on the National Register of Historic Places so they can get money to fix it up. But nobody cares enough to help her.

"Nobody cares until they get really old," she says. "But when you're old, then all the stuff is gone. And my own committee! We had a little meeting not too long ago and I was a-wantin' to apply for some money for the historic district, and I won't say which one, but he's a funny one. Anyway, he says, 'Why, who wants to do anything to see something like that?' And he named off some stores and how they looked so bad and all, and I said, 'Well, sometimes, you know, they do things to the stores and really go ahead and fix 'em up.' But, see, we don't want 'em to fix 'em up except to fix 'em to how they looked a long time ago. Right now, the downtown is on a study list, with the state, and they're waiting for me to get information on every one of those stores, and they think that most of them will go on the National Register. I told this fella that, but he just wasn't interested in doing anything with what we got. But, you know, I'll keep going anyway, because history's all we have left here."

**Thinking with Pigs**

Linda Faircloth steps down from the cinderblock special events platform into a small crowd of excited admirers. Camcorders nudge their snouts over the shoulders of her fans. Instamatics pop pointless, unneccessary flashes. Fortyish, blond and weathered, Ms. Faircloth cradles in her arms the reason for all the attention: Scarecrow Pig, her winning entry in the best-dressed pig contest at Swine Time in Climax, Georgia.

Ms. Faircloth hands the two-month-old pig to a boy whose arms are smeared with blurry blue-black india ink tatoos. She needs her hands free to accept the trophy and shake hands with the judges and talk to her fans and show them her pigs. She's smiling. She's proud of herself. And for good reason. To win the contest she beat out a record-breaking lineup of sixteen entries, including Clogging Hog, St. Nick Pig, Pig Robin Hood, Pig Aerobics Instructor, and The Hog That's Ready To Go Shopping.

Not only did Ms. Faircloth win, she won for the second straight year.

Same costume.

Different pig.

"We raise hogs for the Sunnyland slaughterhouse," she tells me. "Each year I just go and pick me one out, put a shirt on it, and stuff it with straw. I can't believe I won best-dressed pig two years in a row."

The best-dressed pig contest is followed by the hog calling contest, the baby crawling contest, the chitlin eating contest, the greasy pig chase, and the kiss the pig.

It's fall, the first Saturday after Thanksgiving, and I have come to Climax because I'd seen the Swine Time float at Whigham's Rattlesnake Roundup—not a float, really, just a car, an old fifties Chevy, carrying the Swine Time princess—and the name had nagged at me for months. Climax is only eight miles west of Whigham down Highway 84. Each year the Climax Community Club sends a float to Whigham at roundup time, and each year the Whigham Community Club sends a float to Climax at Swine Time. On the festival circuit, each town within a reasonable hour or so of driving time from another will send a float or a queen or a little miss princess to ride in the parades and stand composed within the tableaux of icons, emblems, gestures and fragmented historical recollections with which these white southern communities decorate their sense of place, inventing and reinventing their public selves in the face of a transforming late-capitalist agricultural-industrial economy. Examining the spectacle of captured rattlesnakes had proven a fruitful exercise; I wondered what I might find at a festival of hogs.

Climax is so named because it is the climax of the contour across south Georgia, the highest point on the railroad between Savannah and the Chattahoochee River, which is the border between Georgia and Alabama, about thirty miles to the west. The town was founded in 1883 and incorporated in 1905. It never grew larger than a few hundred souls. As rail traffic declined, Climax did, too. Then it rose again, only this time not centered around real relations of production but around the invented, pieced-together annual festival. Still no larger than a few hundred souls, the town can now boast about something in addition to its geological prominence: "Home of Swine Time" is painted on the fenders of the Climax police cars.

Cliff Wells is a retired rural mail carrier and a member of the Climax Community Club, and he used to coach a little basketball. I talk to him before the parade on Saturday morning and he tells me Swine Time began around 1973, when a group of people came back to Decatur County to celebrate the county's sesquicentennial. "We had a lot of people from Climax that participated in the seskwi, and they had a big time, and they said we don't need to let this thing stop. Let's just start us a club of some kind."

The collective civic identity of Climax had been in flux, but the "seskwi" provided the germ of an idea, and that's how the community club got started. A lot of the men in Climax work down south of there at the kaolin mine in Attapulgus, and many others work in industry over at Bainbridge, where the Chattahoochee and the Flint come together and go on to the gulf as the Apalachicola. Since people were scattered over the the area, they had to make a formal, concerted effort to meet and assert the identity of Climax. Once formed, the club needed to have activities and raise money. They saw the success Whigham was having with Rattlesnake Roundup, so they decided they would start a festival, too.

"There's a good bit of hog farmers in this area," Mr. Wells tells me when I ask him how they chose the pig theme. "And so when the community club started thinking about a project, we looked around at names and we figured Swine Time might be best, you know, cause there's so many things you can do with it. You know, there's the chitlin eatin', and hog callin' and greasy pig chase. And this year we added the new one, the kiss the pig. We have jars out around town, and see, we have a woman mayor and a woman postmaster, and the town clerk's a woman, and a co-chairman of Swine Time is a woman, and so we got five women and five men running, and who gets the most money in their jars has got to kiss the pig. So people vote for who they want to kiss the pig, and the money goes for a firetruck for the volunteer fire department. Our mayor, she's a school teacher, she makes us a good mayor, I'm having a lot of fun with her. I'm saying 'I'm gonna make sure you win,' and she said, 'That works both ways!' 'Cause I'm runnin' too.

"My wife came up with that one. She saw an article in the paper and she saw that somebody they had a kiss the pig contest and some lady had to kiss a pig at half time of a basketball game. So she cut that out and saved it and she said, 'Well, this is the year for the kiss the pig contest.' "

Pigs have had a place in rural southern life since Hernando de Soto drove a herd with him when he made his march from Florida to the Mississippi about 450 years ago. In 1860, a Columbus, Georgia, doctor who didn't look favorably on pork consumption wrote in *Godey's Lady Book* that the South was at the center of a "great Hog-eating Confederacy" and the "Republic of Porkdom." He wrote that "fat bacon and pork" was all anybody in the South ever ate, "continually morning, noon and night, for all classes, sexes, ages, and conditions." Hog's lard was "the very oil that moves the machinery of life" and in it southerners fried everything from vegetables to fritters and pancakes, "and indeed fried everything that is fryable, or that will stick together long enough to undergo the delightful process" (Hilliard 1972: 42). In 1877 the Georgia commissioner of agriculture praised hogs for being efficient sources of protein and the perfect food for workers, as pork was "especially suited to supply the waste of the frame incident to manual labor; and is not only the most convenient and economical food for the negro laborer, but is preferred by him to any other kind of meat. Many planters, who have not bestowed personal attention upon their hogs, have been painfully reminded of this partiality by the mysterious disappearance of their porkers." The commissioner also praised the pig for being edible from snout to tail. "Besides the pieces proper, the trimmings are made into the most delicious sausages, which none but a Jew, or a Mohammedan, could refuse"(Janes 1877: 17). Hog-killing time in the fall was a major seasonal event, and hog raising was a life-sustaining practice among the poor and not-so-poor in the devastated countryside after the Civil War.

Most people are familiar with the hog's role in southern culture, but in Western civilization the animal has an even longer, richer history, so various and ancient that it's not surprising to find the hog picked as the theme for a number of swine time-chitlin fest events on the cracker circuit. I wonder whether the Swine Time organizers know that, in Attic comedy, female genitalia was linked to the pig; that prostitutes were called pig merchants; that "porcus" was a Latin nursery word used by women to refer to the pudenda of little girls ( Stallybrass and White 1986: 44–59); that "to pork" and "makin' bacon" remain today slang terms for intercourse; that the pork industry's campaign to promote hogflesh as "the other white meat" sounds nasty; or that the kiss the pig contest resonates with layers of pornographic meaning and a legacy of the medieval carnivalesque. I wanted to ask, but I didn't.

Instead, I ask Mr. Wells if the the festival is popular, and he says, "Oh yeah, people have a good time. *Pigs are a lot of fun.*"

The Swine Time parade is led by the Bainbridge Cub Pack 159. After the Cub Scouts comes the Climax Grand Ole Opry, with two folks dressed up like Minnie Pearl and Grandpa Jones lip-synching on a flatbed pulled by a tractor. Following are the Swine Time Queen's Court, the Miss Swine Time Little Sisters, Little Miss Decatur County, Miss Dogwood, from nearby Attapulgus, and Little Miss Pine Seedling—I couldn't see where she was from—Miss Gum Spirits, and Miss Blue Crab. A van with darkened windows advertises Letha's Unlimited Hair Care, and then come the Dance Electric Cloggers.

And, finally, walking down the street are some women in frilly black saloon-gal dresses, yellow balloons tied to their wrists with ribbon. Fake pig snouts are rubber-banded to their faces. Their mouths curl open in laughter, their lips coming up and cupping around their teeth. When kids step near to catch tossed candy, they all exchange porcine mimicry, quick chugging snorts, and a high wailing squeal like a rusty hinge.

The women pass, sashaying to the music of Ray Stevens, and the parade ends. Everybody walks toward the Swine Time grounds. All my life I have been attending festivals and ritual holiday weekends, and I have always been aware of the profound *personal* significance of such celebrations, but only after reimagining them from a cultural studies perspective did I begin to see their *public* features and to sense the rich threads of historical allusions and cultural politics found in such events as Swine Time. The gestures, floats and crafts booths appeared to be hypertext links—click on the icon and whole skeins of cultural history spill at your feet.

I sit down on the grassy bank of a roadside ditch next to a Baptist church group selling fried fish in styrofoam boxes, and, with the image of women wearing rubber snouts in my mind, I think about the shifting semiotic functions of the pig.

Being able to eat and digest its own shit, as well as the shit of others; having sensitive skin susceptible to sunburn, and tending—like other tender mammals who have to manufacture their own sunscreen—to roll in mud and dung and a wallow made from its own urine stirred into the dirt; being endowed with a squeal like a baby in pain; being able to eat and digest human food as well as their own; being at least as intelligent as a dog; and being a beast that is allowed to live only in order that it might die, good for little but its meat and the animal most often depicted on restaurant signs wearing overalls and willingly offering itself up for slaughter, the pig has been useful to think with.

The pig has humped its way out of the wallow of pre-history toting quite a semantic burden. When Jesus cast out demons, he sent them into a herd of swine "and the herd ran violently down a steep place into the sea (they were about two thousand) and were choked in the sea." In medieval sermons, the greedy, the lecherous, and the vomitous drunk were called hogs "vyle and ungoodly of body and usage." The pig sty was a place most foul. To German reformists, the pope was a sow and Jesuits were swine born from the union of a sow and a dog, who were, according to the reformist slander, taught their love of luxury by a professor of Epicurean philosophy named Pig. Herded and slaughtered swine became symbols of demonized Others—a role still contained somewhere deep within the activity of chasing greased pigs. In some belief systems the flesh of the pig was proscribed; in others the celebration of food was embodied in the rich swelling oozing fat of the sausage. The pig carried along with it over time the loaded and conflicted charge of the carnivalesque: it was the emblem of the the lower bodily strata—that ribald and earthy realm of filth and excrement, the world of charivari and inversion, where shit is slung, the world turned upside down, kings and the Church mocked, and butchers get butchered by the pigs. Pigs are stars in the medieval Boschean landscapes where the nuttiest gag is to blow a bellows up a feller's arse to make him fart. An inflated pig's bladder evolved into today's party balloon (Stallybrass and White 1986: 50–85).

In the city, the meaning of the pig shifted. On urban streets the pig's manure lost its usefulness as fertilizer and became simply odious and disgusting, and the human love-hate ambivalence toward the pig began to tilt more toward hate. Pigs wandered the cities, sometimes biting and killing small children. But the pig still provided a useful image: members of the urban underworld in the early nineteenth century began calling police "pigs" and "grunters." To the new bourgeoisie in the eighteenth century, the carnivalesque pig became the symbol of the bumpkins and boors, the ignorant and slovenly, the peasants from off the farm. The name eventually sprang back onto the bourgoisie, who, after the economy stripped and starved urban labor, themselves became the undisciplined gluttons. The resemblance of piglets to children has been noted—both exist in realms of indiscriminate and unrestrained eating, shitting and squealing. Today the banishment of the pig from city streets, its confinement to farms far from the sight of most people, has tenderized the meaningfulness of the pig, and rendered it into a comical cartoon character. But traces of the pig's symbolism remain in everyday language like cracklings in corn bread: what a ham; don't be a pig; that porker's wearing pigtails; hogshead; hog wash; a pig in a poke; pig sticker; pigskin; go hog wild; get hog tied.

I'll warn you now: think twice before you jump on a greasy pig.

Everybody stood in a circle while three men lifted a big hog by its back legs and rubbed it with what looked like motor oil and vaseline. The hog thrashed; when let go, it stood and paced around. A man said, "Anybody want to give it a try?" So I, in my participant observer mode, decided to see what it's like to wrestle a greasy hog. I set down my satchel with my camera and notebooks. I was wearing only my T-shirt and jeans. I cautiously walked up to the hog, considering what hold would be most likely to clamp and trap the shining animal.

Deciding that a headlock would do, I reached down and lurched to lock my arms around the hog, but it kicked forward with a grunting squeal like the scraping of heavy furniture across a wooden floor, and was gone from my arms in a sudden, muscular bolt, its back feet clipping my elbow with a hard knock, tagging my funny bone and paralyzing my arm to the shoulder. The hog didn't run far, stopping a few feet away, free from my grasp, and even free from my conniving, because at that point, shaking the vibrations from my arm, I concluded, okay, I wrestled a greasy hog and lost. I can accept that. I smiled and held up my hand to the grinning folks standing around, shook my head, wiped the smear onto my T-shirt and left the hog to be wrestled by someone else. I walked back across the Swine Time grounds to the special events platform.

A man in a plaid shirt and straw hat won the hog calling. His hands were bigger than the trophy. While they laid out carpet on the cement stage for the baby crawling contest, mothers knelt with their kids, put their noses together and said "C'mon now, C'mon now," in that ferris wheel singsong of baby talk, and then moved to the other end of the carpet. When they said "Go," the babies looked around; two began to touch, one began to cry, and another, panting forward toward the coaxing of his mother, won.

I had easily spotted the stylized ritual of capturing the Signified Other that was embodied in the greasy pig chase. The ancient sexuality component was obvious in the kiss the pig contest, as was the piglet/baby connection in the best-dressed pig event. All of that was the residue of the carnivalesque, traces of ancient European folk culture. Now I wanted more recent history. The semiotics of the pig is interesting, but I was looking for the resonance of historic struggles expressed in public spectacles. The baby crawling contest brought me almost up to date. Just as my experience at the Tobacco Festival surprised me with a revelation regarding *Green Acres* and county agent Hank Kimball, so, too, would Swine Time surprise me with further deep-cultural curiosities. As the mothers consoled their kids, lifting them high in the air to shake off their crying, I walked away following a train of thought that would lead me to link the baby crawling contest to a legacy of master-race eugenics.

Beyond the element of spectacle itself, there is some larger pattern at work tying these festivals together, a common, underlying impulse, some deeper connection which I had not yet comprehended, but which I was beginning to sense. These sorts of festivals—Rattlesnake Roundup, the Tobacco Festival, Swine Time—do their cultural work by creating sites for the symbolic display of community. They become places where the pieces of the celebratory repertoire of emblems and icons and gestures are refashioned, re-presented to create some version of the world. But in addition to the local laughter and boosterism, I sensed an undeniable uneasiness and anxiety as well; the festivals seemed like fluorescent lichen growing on fallen trees, celebrations of unstable illusions in the face of economic and cultural transformations.

In 1940, about 40 percent of southerners farmed. In 1980, only 3 or 4 percent did. The communities in the countryside fragmented as more than 14 million southerners, blacks and whites, left the farms during the fifty years after the end of World War II. Originating during those years of dispersal, these community festivals are ways of bringing people home to imagine community and recollect shared versions of the present and the past. As public celebrations, they express a kind of postmodernism-in-the-country: the festivals draw their gestures and events piecemeal from a historical repertoire, and their sources seem ironic now. Although the events have a genealogy that can be traced back through political barbeques and church picnics, their most immediate ancester is the agricultural fair, which was part of the delivery system of modernity that shattered the countryside.

Agricultural fairs have the image of being rustic, but civics and economics were always at their core. Elkanah Watson, the father of agricultural fairs, started his competitive sheep shearings in the late 1700s to provide wool for the mills he owned and to foster anti-British sentiment. The move toward scientific agriculture hit full steam after the Civil War, and, by the turn of the century, local agricultural fairs were a major source of new information for farmers. One southern state, North Carolina, had thirty fairs in 1914; four years later it had 251. Besides spreading the word about new animal breeds, seed varieties, chemical fertilizers and efficient machines, the fairs were also a major conduit through which the state impressed modern, scientifically sanctioned behavior on rural people. In parts of the South, traditional collective recreations like log rolling and corn shucking were supplanted as agriculture was mechanized and rural people were drawn into public and federalized systems. And once the traditional links with the land were severed, the national system of agriculture extension retooled harvest festivals into token, ritual competitions; county agents taught women and girls how to keep a clean house and can tomatoes and men and boys how to use better seed and run new machines. They offered prizes if you learned your lessons well.

Here's where I detected the trace of eugenics at the Swine Time's baby crawling contest. Agricultural fairs offered prizes not only for hogs, cattle, quilts, and jam, but for babies, too. Scientific rationality in the industrial age colonized any aspect of life it could, and the baby contests were contrived to demonstrate hygiene and scientific principles of nutrition to an ignorant, remote population. A better babies contest in Louisiana in 1916 was described as "a popular yet scientific movement to insure better babies and a better race. It consists of entering, examining and awarding prizes to children of five years or less on exactly the same basic principles that are applied to live stock shows. . . . The Better Babies Contest insures a better race of Americans . . ." (Ownby 1990: 185–86).

By 1935, American agricultural fairs had worked so well that a book sanctioned by the U. S. Department of Agriculture declared them "out-moded and in process of decay." Having served their productive purposes, the fairs were converted to spectacles of social ideology. The author of this book, Wayne Neely (1935), spotted the central contradiction at work within the institution of the agricultural fair: originally intended to improve farm production, they did so with such success that farming rapidly became mechanized and capitalized, the result being overproduction and collapsed prices.

So the great success of agricultural science turned out to be a Pyrrhic victory: farming lost its farmers. Local fairs were once again retooled, this time to instruct rural people in consumption, not production.

Neely, clearly understanding that the action at the fair is never merely play but ritualistic performance that articulates cultural and political meanings, surveyed the scene and wrote: "Recently . . . the tendency has been to make these exhibits reflect or idealize the relationship which exists between the farmer and his industry and the larger society. In other words, the fairs in recent years have endeavored to emphasize the matter of an attractive, significant and satisfying rural social life" (217).

Neely said that the one thing country people didn't have to worry about anymore was stimulating agricultural production. "We witness the perplexing paradox of farmers' inability to sell their live stock and crops for sufficient money to pay their taxes and interest, at the same time that hungry and ill-clothed men walk city streets. Neither the agricultural fair nor those agencies most closely associated with it can solve this fundamental problem. But within certain limits the fair can and does function in marking the relationship of the farmer not only to rural society but to the whole social structure" (217).

Agricultural fairs were transformed once again. They became trade shows—places to display new products—or were supplanted by a new type of event: school fair, grange fair, township fair, farmers' fair, fall festival, community fair, community festival. These were no longer educational, but they still served a political purpose: "[I]t is a socially initiated attempt to shape the experiences of the individual or to transmit to him accepted ideals for purposes of social control or of preparation for social participation; it is a purposeful process of making him a participant in the institutional life of society" (155).

By 1960, about 9 million southerners had migrated out of the region; millions more had moved to southern cities and towns. The countryside was enclosed and depopulated. Sharecroppers and mules became rare. The harvests were mechanized. These days, the countryside wants industrial development. Manufacturing already is the most significant employer in rural areas, drawing labor from scattered rural settlements. With the people dispersed and working for the factories and mills, communities are no longer consolidated around the functional market on Main Street.

The mobility of the American people, along with the pattern of creative destruction intrinsic to capitalist development, leads to a degrading of spontaneous, local memory. Material production no longer creates community, so communities are created through symbolic productions. To compensate, contemporary culture creates sites for remembering and re-presenting communities through memories surviving in reconstituted objects, with manufactured heritage erected as signs of distinction.

Memory has a magical purpose—it creates selves and places. Community festivals like Rattlesnake Roundup, the North Carolina Tobacco Festival, and Swine Time are intended to repair what the modernization of agriculture accomplished. The festivals doing this work rely on today's common currency of simulations and fragmented imagery, stitched together according to the logic of collage and laminated with a veneer that signifies historicity.

It's important to note that one other thing modernization accomplished in the South was the destruction of codified segregation. Many black southerners were more than happy to see the coming of the Wal-Marts and new strip malls because it meant they no longer had to step 'n' fetchit at Mr. Man's Main Street store. It's only the crackers who publicly parade their anxiety over the economic, political and demographic shifts.

All across the field of the Swine Time grounds is the low funk of frying chitlins. I walk through the smoke that blows through the awnings, tents, and canopies pitched over tables, racks, stacks, heaps and clotheslines full of stuff for sale. It is a marketplace where you can buy and barter, get items cheap, find things you can't find anywhere else (around south Georgia anyway) like fart spray and ninja death darts. It's a south Georgia rendition of a market fair, a moveable souk. Like the stylized lynching of the greasy pig chase, and the residual eugenics embodied in the baby crawling contest, the arts and crafts marketplace across the Swine Time grounds is also a hyperlinked icon, a replica of a historical formation restaged to serve a meaningful contemporary cultural purpose. It harkens to a lost world of the handmade. It is a stylized gesture of communality, an improvised performance. It's a nostalgic re-creation of that ancient ritual of community: trade.

Sturbridge Fair, in Cambridge, for example, the model for John Bunyan's Vanity Fair, was the most famous of the English market fairs, a place where Genoese merchants sold silks and velvets, Flemish weavers sold linen, Norwegians sold tar and pitch, Spaniards sold iron. Isaac Newton bought his first book on astronomy there. Such medieval fairs worked to bring country people into the web of larger markets, but, unlike the situation at those events, the trade at Swine Time is in nonessentials, and the inventory is out of control. I walk around and make a list: Hong Kong prints of Indian maidens in snow and unicorns in space, gun racks made of deer hooves, skinned coyote heads and rabbit hides, ax handles, butterfly knives, Bocephus hats with peacock feathers, snap 'n' pops, Jesus jigsaw puzzles, chowchow, pepper jelly, switch combs, ninja spikes, stalks of okra sprayed with shellac, pork rinds, bootleg tapes of Ton Loc and Randy Travis, hats reading "Rebel," "Party Naked," "Grateful Dead," "Roll Tide," "Skid Row," and a popular series of hat bands reading "Vicious Power Happy Bitch," "Bitch and Proud of It," "49 Percent Bitch, 51 Percent Sweetheart," "I Go from Zero to Bitch in Six Seconds," and "I'm Suffering from PMS— Putting Up With Men's Shit." There are New Testaments opened to a passage about love, framed in lace and nailed to plywood hearts painted pink.

At this point in my studies and my travels, I review what I've dis- covered thus far in my investigation of the cracker circuit. First: towns, villages, settlements, and communities rise, fade, and fall like crops in a field as the seasons pass and times change. Second: the movement of capital operates as a magnetic force, sucking people after it as it circulates. Third: as this movement of capital crosses up with the chaos of human actuality, it works on the cultural landscape just as wind and gravity and water work on the dirt and leaf of the geological one. Fourth: there is a habit among humans to dance meaningful movements through streets and parks and public squares as ways of celebrating the tribe or nation or clan, a habit of dancing dances that draw meaningfulness from deep silences, and set up resonances within a surreal vernacular grammar of icons. And lastly, I've learned this: *the Uktena rules.*

I drive north away from Swine Time and toward home. On the road, I eat from a barbeque plate, soaking my car seat with vinegary sauce, and think about where I will go next.

### The Void of Bananas

I went to the International Banana Festival on the eve of its destruction. Heading westward across the prone slash of Tennessee, unrelenting country music on the radio, I drove past tobacco barns, smoke leaking from between old weathered and split boards as farmers cured their leaf; past pale tobacco spilled on the roadsides; past a man who looked like the actor Brian Dennehy standing by a mailbox; past Paris, Tennessee, home of the World's Biggest Fish Fry; past billboards that said "Mud Volleyball Tournament for Epilepsy" and "Make Time for Footcare. Dr. Schussler, DPM"; past fluorescent plastic-letter signboards reading, for example, "Taking Applications—Two Piece Snak." I drove beneath TVA power lines, and, through tidal waves of static on the radio, I could decipher the faint signal of Atlanta Braves baseball. Small frogs made scallop designs hopping across the highway in my headlights.

South Fulton is in western Tennessee. One block north is the Kentucky state line, and, across it, the town of Fulton. The Mississippi River is about twenty-five miles farther west. About thirty-five miles north-northwest is the confluence of the Ohio and the Mississippi, where Illinois, Kentucky and Missouri wave to each other across barge traffic. New Madrid, Missouri, the center of the great 1811 earthquake that shook the entire country, is just across the Mississippi. This part of Kentucky and Tennessee was part of the Jackson Purchase, bought by Andrew Jackson from the Chickasaw in 1811. The Chickasaw were removed and the area filled with so many settlers from the worn-out lands of the East Coast that it is known as "The South Carolina of Kentucky." The town was named after Robert Fulton, the engineer who experimented with underwater explosives and built the first steam warship, *The Fulton*, in 1815. This area was Confederate during the war, but most casualties around here were caused by measles.

I arrive in South Fulton the night before the Banana Festival. On a little park in the middle of downtown people are setting up their crafts booths. I talk to a woman who has blurry Polaroids of herself and Donna "Elly May Clampett" Douglas framed and displayed on her table, which is set up under an awning hung from the edge of her Winnebago. Tomorrow, Saturday, she's going to try to sell gold-plated chain by the foot, unwinding it off plastic spools and snapping it with shears. Her eyes are ringed with black makeup. She tells me that Donna Douglas is great and as sweet as can be. "That's me and her there," she says, tipping the framed Polaroids toward me.

I've always had a thing for Elly May, so I tell her about the time I met Donna Douglas when she came to a big suburban pentecostal church in Cobb County, just outside Atlanta, where I was doing a story on pentecostalism in the suburbs. All the tables at this singles ministry potluck dinner were decorated with candles in bell jars and folded pink construction paper place cards reading "Elverna Bradshaw's Table," "Ol' Duke's Table," or "The Cement Pond." I sat at "The Billy-Yard Room." You had to wait until your table was called before you could get in line for food. When Donna Douglas came out, she was dressed like Elly May, in a frothy white dress, and she told stories about Jed and Jethro and Granny—only she called them Buddy and Max and Irene— and about how she had been just a li'l ol' gal from Louisiana who got carried away by worldliness, until she found the Lord after she could no longer get any work in Hollywood.

The woman says that sounds sweet, and then she tells me of a market-festival promised land in Arkansas where Donna Douglas holds an arts and crafts event, and tens of thousands can come and sell their stuff. She says that sometimes Donna Douglas will show up dressed like Elly May and come around and talk to people. That's how she got the Polaroids. "She's just as sweet as can be. She'll let anyone take their picture with her."

A little ways on, I talk to a man named Jasper Cook, from Texas. He's missing four front bottom teeth. He's wearing a floppy red-and-white striped hat and a black plastic Batman cape tied around his neck. The cape, much too small, flares out like the cellophane flourish on a commemorative bottle of nine-dollar champagne.

"I had a big woodworking shop with saws that cost eight hundred dollars," he says, telling me how he came to be here at the International Banana Festival. "I sold that, sold my house, sold my furniture, sold everything and bought me a thirty-foot—we used to had a twenty-six-foot—bought me a thirty-foot travel trailer and a bigger truck to pull it with, and where we hang our hat is our home. We got two cemetery plots in Texas, a post office box and two dollars in the bank, so I guess actually really that's still home. I's born there.

"Our wife and I aren't old enough for social security yet, but she will be this week. We do this flea marketing . . . well, not flea marketing, just these special occasions, like last weekend in Paducah at the Tater Day and this one is a banana festival, this kind of thing."

While he talks I look through the stuff on his table—glassware, rings, hair clips. When I pick up a Chinese air pistol and heft it in my grip, Mr. Cook barely interrupts his storytelling to flick his sales pitch at me; he says in a voice low and straightforward, just for me, "I'll give you that pellet gun for twenty-five dollars, and throw in two hundred pellets."

Letting that settle in, he continues with a somewhat stentorian recitation: "I used to be an editor of a little ol' tabloid in Montgomery, Alabama, back in forty-nine, fifty. Along in there. Fifty-one. They had the Alabama Rural Electric News. I was in their statewide office. Seventy-two-page tabloid. Once a month. I wrote editorials. I hepped put it all together. I been in radio, TV, and I'm a comedian."

Mr. Cook reties the black plastic Batman cape around his neck. "I'm also a preacher," he says, finishing the knot and lifting up his voice once again. "I fill in preaching sometimes when somebody's sick, on vacation, what not. In fact one night not long ago it was 9:30 Saturday night, and the district superintendent (this is a Methodist church), he lives fifty miles away, he calls me and says, 'Jasper, I need you in Coleman tomorrow morning.' And I say, 'What? You know Coleman is seventy miles from me.' I say, 'You believe in giving a guy notice.' And he said, 'Well, the preacher's wife got real sick all of a sudden, and they took her to Fort Worth and he went with her and ain't nobody there.' Well, you know, I'll fill in. Big churches, little churches. It don't matter to me. I'll still preach. I always will as long as I live. I never read in the Bible where it says when you're sixty-five you quit. It don't ever say quit. So I said, Well, okay.

"Oh, yeah. I been having fun." Mr. Cook's eyes glitter mischievously, and his loose lower lip flutters in the wet toothless space in the front of his grin. He bobs his head toward the left and then toward the right, indicating two other booths where men in shirts and ties are stacking pamphlets and small free Bibles. "This group is Nazarene Church," he says, "and this group is Mormon, and I'm Methodist, so I been having fun with 'em. See, there's a Scripture (and you have to take something out of context though to get this joke), but there's a Scripture, and I been askin' 'em, did they know why Paul really had a shipwreck? They know about Paul, apostle Paul, and his shipwreck, and they said they didn't know why Paul really had a shipwreck. And I ask them for a King James version—it's only in the King James version; the new versions is too trendy—in Acts in the twenty-seventh chapter in the fifteenth verse—I'm not going to quote it all—but it's just a short verse, and the last four words says, 'We let her drive.' "

He laughs, and I laugh too, even though the joke didn't work on me like it did the Nazarenes and the Mormons.

"They caught on to that one," he says, finishing up his laughing, his voice all chuckly. "We had fun with it. See, all that means is, we just let her go, just let the ship ride into the wind, but it says, We let *her* drive, so that's why they wrecked. Like the apostle Paul let a lady drive, you know.

"So, yeah, I'm having a good time. Most preachers know a lot of jokes. I know a ton of 'em."

Mr. Cook grows a little contemplative. "We enjoy life. My wife is from a little ol' place from near Paducah. A little ol' place, a crossroads called West Viola. There's a Viola and a West Viola. There's nothing there anymore, just a crossroads and two, three houses. But her folks are buried there, so my wife and I come up and of course she puts new flowers on the graves and all, and we go to a festival or two along the way to help pay for gas and such.

"I can do pretty good sometimes. My prices are reasonable. That's why I can sell when nobody else is. Reasonable prices. My biggest sellers? It'd be my guns and knives and rings. I got real turquoise and chorodium. You don't have to polish chorodium. Silver you got to polish. Also sold a lot of salt-and-pepper shakers. Lots of Aunt Jemima. They love the Aunt Jemima. And had a run on earrings up in Paducah. I sell 'em three for a dollar. They cost me twenty cents each. I'm making forty cents on every sale. That gets 'em over here. And I had some bullwhips too. Sold all my bullwhips.

"I tell you. There's good events and there's bad ones. I had a fellow here earlier tell me somewhere there's a Ham Festival. He told me where it was, but I forgot. But you know, they also tell me the biggest thing around here is over in Benton, Kentucky. It's a Tater Day. They's quite a few Tater Days, you know, but they say that'n in Benton is *big*. I'll get me some more Chinese pellet guns and Mexican bullwhips, and go make a little retirement money. Maybe do some preaching along the way.

"And they like these what they call butterfly knives. Kids love those. Them and bullwhips."

The sun is going down, and still only seven or eight vendors' booths have been set up. Mr. Cook and I stand there and look out over the Banana Festival grounds at the few people walking around.

"You know, they say there's supposed to be ten thousand people here tomorrow. But it don't look like there's going to be a couple hundred." He sounds a little concerned. "This Banana Festival, it's not quite what some people said it was."

I tell Mr. Cook I better get moving on, and he says, "For you, I'll let you have that pellet gun for $22.50, and the two hundred pellets still come with it free."

Up to this point, my exploration of the South's festival culture had not been guided by systematic logic. My methods of picking which events to visit were chaotic enough to make my selections actually qualify as random. After I came back from Rattlesnake Roundup and decided to rehearse my schoolwork and diagnose the zeitgeist of the cracker circuit, I began reading state tourism booklets, the backs of magazines, and posters on telephone poles, as well as talking to strangers and friends, hearing about public celebrations, listening to people like Jasper Cook tell me of fabled ham festivals where craftsmen reap bountiful harvests selling surplus earrings and Chinese pellet pistols. Once you start looking, of course, you see thousands of them. Whenever I heard about one with a theme that interested me—an agricultural commodity, a historical event or character, or a novelty gag—I would find out where and when it was, make exploratory phone calls, count the gas money in my pocket, figure what assignments might be coming due around the same time, and reckon distances and driving times. About once every four or five months all the factors would come together, and I would ride out to visit a place.

I was finding the festivals to be rich, multifaceted events, the meanings of which were as varied and numerous as the crowds that attended them. Even though I was practicing a crude textualism, I knew that the terms of analysis should not be taken as terms of substance. There are all sorts of complexities, tensions and uncertainties that determine any individual's actions. People go just to get out of the house, or to eat the fried fish plate, or to help their church group direct traffic, or to see their sister's group clogging on the south stage at three, or because they've never been and figured they'd finally check it out, or because they've always gone. But beyond those specific, local meanings, I was picking up signs of an eerie trend. I'd been to Rattlesnake Roundup, Swine Time, the North Carolina Tobacco Festival of Clarkton, Inc., and now the International Banana Festival, and everywhere I went I detected the imminent presence of cultural death. Death and regeneration are constant processes, of course, but over long phases, one is often predominant over the other—as in periods of boom and expansion, or of bust and decline—and collecting enough of a sample leads to the detection of bigger patterns. I couldn't help but sense that there was something going on in the countryside—entropy, dissolution, decay— and that I was seeing it expressed in these annual weekend episodes of public culture.

The sense of community on the cracker circuit, I concluded, is a residual cultural formation, meaning, as Raymond Williams (1961) explained, that it was formed in the past and is still active in the current cultural process, but has been superceded by a new dominant order. When Williams developed his analysis, from the 1950s to the 1970s, he noted that the idea of rural community was still a residual formation, but had been incorporated into industrial capitalism as idealization and fantasy, as exotic leisure. What has happened since Williams is that on the cracker circuit, the reality of rural community has become increasingly scarce, and it has been replaced by the *idealization* of community—that is to say, the countryside has been colonized by an idealization of itself, just as the real structures that determined past communities are being dismantled, shredded and scrapped.

The next morning I'm standing in the lobby of the City National Bank in South Fulton, Tennessee, looking at the pictures in a display called "Thirty Years of Banana Festival Memories," and thinking maybe I should go and buy that pellet gun from Mr. Cook, when two women walk in. One is tall, with short hair and fruit basket earrings. Her name is Virginia. She says she lives a couple of miles outside town. Her friend's name is Kitty, and she's up visiting from Huntsville, Alabama. Kitty says she comes to the Banana Festival every year, and when she comes her kids always say, "Mama, bring me back something from the Banana Festival."

On the bulletin board of Banana Festival memories are a hundred or more old black-and-white photos taken from the event's heyday in the 1960s. Kitty points to one photograph of a woman with pinned-up hair and cat's-eye glasses.

"There's you, Ginny. Up there with your cake."

Ginny's smile is modest. Kitty tells me that Ginny has won seventy-five ribbons for her baking. Ginny continues to look at the photos, nodding slightly, proud and polite.

We stand quietly looking at the Thirty Years of Banana Festival Memories, and then Ginny turns to me and says, "You goin' to be here for the puddin'? That's the main event."

I say, sure. I wouldn't miss it. It's a one-ton banana pudding.

She puts her hand on my arm, wrinkles her nose a little and says to me as though confessing a confidence, "The pudding's not as good as it used to be. We used to use boiled custard. Used to cook it. Now some company gives them the mix, and it's just not nowhere near as good."

I say, that's too bad; I would have liked to have eaten from a one-ton custard.

Ginny continues, "This is probably the last year for the festival. You can't get nobody to do nothing. Them's that's good get worked to death, so they don't want to do it no more."

Her friend Kitty shakes her head, and the two ladies commiserate on the decline of the Banana Festival.

"Oh, it used to be something," Ginny says. "Used to hang bunches of bananas from the parking meters, but then everybody hogged them all up, just drive by and load 'em in their trunks. Used to have a style show, a tour of homes, quilting. It just isn't the same anymore."

Kitty says that her husband sent up a sack of tomatoes from Alabama. "And when I got here, Ginny didn't even have a banana in the house. So I told my husband, he should have sent bananas instead."

The irony of this statement lies in the fact that, thirty years ago, sending bananas to Fulton was like sending coals to Newcastle. The town was the distribution point for all the fruit shipped north out of New Orleans on the Illinois Central, which had taken control of America's banana traffic in the late 1800s when the IC's southern agent, James Tucker, became convinced that he could ship bananas using special refrigerator cars running at express speed. At the time, probably one in ten thousand Americans had ever tasted a banana, although they were quite popular in New Orleans. James Tucker died before the banana shipments started, but his brother, Joseph Tucker, who was the general superintendent of the railroad, finally made the first shipment of twenty-two carloads in 1880. The next year, 331 carloads were carried by the line. The banana trade was so successful that the Illinois Central expanded its fruit house to protect the bananas during the loading. By 1900, eight thousand cars a year were shipped. And in 1947, an all-time record was set when the railroad hauled 52,250 cars of bananas (Stover 1975: 189, 385). Bananas could make it from a New Orleans wharf to a Chicago rail yard in thirty-six to thirty-nine hours.

For most of this time, Fulton, Kentucky, was, as John Stover, a historian of the Illinois Central put it, the "wasplike waist" (189) on the entire IC line, a thousand-mile network between New Orleans, Chicago, Madison and Sioux Falls. In 1898, an ice factory was built in Fulton. In 1919, the ice company expanded and moved into a building which at that time was the largest one-story building in the world. Fulton quickly developed into the spot on the railroad where northbound trains out of New Orleans and other gulf ports iced their cargo. Bananas were shipped up to Fulton, iced, and sent on other lines to the rest of the country. Fulton became the Banana crossroads of the United States. The townsfolk called Fulton the Banana Capital of the World.

"This used to be a railroad town," Ginny says. "Everybody worked for the railroad. Now maybe two trains come through here anymore. The tracks used to run right down the street, but they tore 'em up and paved over them. I used to know everybody in town, but the Goodyear plant opened over in Martin and now I don't hardly know anybody."

After World War II, gas rationing ended, car sales went up, air traffic became more common, and rail passenger traffic declined. In 1945, passenger service made up 15 percent of IC revenues. In 1951, it was down to 8 percent (Stover 385). Trains were being idled. Lines were being shut. Depots were being closed. By the 1950s, the banana traffic was being lost to trucks. In 1962, the Illinois Central carried 164,000 tons.

Swept up in the internationalism of the Kennedy era, and spooked by the increasing din of cargo trucks on interstate highways, the business interests in Fulton started the International Banana Festival in 1962. President Kennedy sent personal greetings. Kitty and Ginny point to a picture of the time when the Marimba la Reina Del Ejercito came to town from Guatemala and, according to the promotional booklet distributed at the festival, "with music the clarion call of friendship, the Latins and Americans hummed a tune of understanding." President Johnson once sent "distinguished diplomat" Averell Harriman.

Harriman hailed the Banana Festival's "key role in the relations between the United States and Latin America." The United States Information Service made a movie of the festival and its centerpiece, the largest banana pudding on the globe. During those years, about twenty-five young people from the banana-exporting countries would come to the Fulton festival.

"They were called 'ameegos,'" Ginny says. "Those young folk that would come visit for the festival. We called them a*mee*gos. Used to have marimbay bands and everything. But not anymore. Too much trouble. Haven't had anything like that in a long, long time. The ameegos had to stay at people's homes, you know, and they just got tired of that, too. We'd have these visitors from South America and people would have to put them up. We called them a*mee*gos, I think that was it, and I think people just got tired of cleaning up their houses. And it wasn't too long after the festival started that the banana trains stopped coming through."

In the late 1940s, the line was running a thousand banana cars a week; by 1966, it had dropped to eleven thousand for the year. In 1971, only 360 cars were carried, less than one a day. The interstates made it easy for trucks to take over from trains. The railroads tore up the tracks. The abandoned ice plant, once the largest building of its type in the world, was torched by an arsonist in the 1980s.

I feel lucky that I came to the Banana Festival when I did because the word on the street is that this is the last year for it. This year they almost didn't have *any* bananas. Dole, the giant fruit company, had said they weren't going to send any. But then the mayor went on TV and made a special plea, and finally, after the news of the Banana Festival Without Bananas went out on the wire service, Dole sent 240 boxes, 95 of which were needed to make the one-ton banana pudding and the rest of which were given away free at local businesses.

At a card table manned by volunteers, I buy an official Banana Festival T-shirt. It depicts the two towns with a parade coming down a street between them. In the middle of the parade is the one-ton banana pudding. The artist's drawing is flanked on each side by scrolls. One scroll is the recipe for a one-ton pudding. The other scroll is inscribed with a testimonial statement that should serve as an epitaph for all the struggling small towns abandoned by the shifting streams of capital: *Banana laden Cars No longer arrive here for distribution, but the Void of Bananas has not dampened the spirits of the residents of the Twin Cities.*

Sadly, though, the Void of Bananas finally has dampened the residents' spirits. Because free bananas are hard to come by, the chamber of commerce is thinking about changing the theme to railroads, because, when you look at it, a lady at the chamber tells me, the festival also celebrates the memory of *trains*. If it weren't for the *trains*, you wouldn't have had the *bananas*. At the Fulton Women's Club building, the local school kids display their art projects illustrating the golden age when the trains still rolled through town, a theme detached from their own memories but commemorated once a year in the town's annual ritual. Written on the pictures are "Chug on to the Banana Festival," "Let's Go Loco at the Banana Festival," "The Singing Banana Trail," "Banana Man in a Cage," "Uncle Sam, Honest Abe, and Betsy Too are Sewin' Bananas Red White and Blue." Almost as though preparing the town for the theme change, the festival booklet announces a big new feature this year: "The Trackless Train," a twenty-seven-passenger train that rides around town. "This should prove to be a very enjoyable feature as we bring back the mystical days of the railroad to our towns."

Ginny and Kitty tell me they hope I have a good time, and they say it's too bad I couldn't have come to Fulton back when the Banana Festival was really something, back when they boiled the custard for the pudding. They nod goodbye and walk into the City National Bank, saying, "Let's see if we can find us a banana in here."

I'm still looking at the pictures, sketching some of them. Another woman comes in. She moves quickly. She is small and wears dangling banana earrings. We talk about the Banana Festival, and she tells me I need to go down to the women's club and check out the arts and crafts show.

I ask her if she has anything in the show.

She says yes. Her response calls attention to the present absence that helps define the cracker circuit.

"I made some little niggers out of crushed pecan shells." She tells me they're not for sale. They took too much work to make.

CHAPTER THREE

# HONORING THE COB

## Hillbilly Days at Pikeville, Kentucky

Back before the age of reptiles, great layers of marble, schist, gneiss, granite, shale, sandstone and coal felt the crushing forces of the earth, and they cracked. These rocks, Precambrian crystalline, Paleozoic sedimentary and carboniferous metamorphic, crumpled and were uplifted. Rains fell, and the rocks were made wet. The water ran, and the rocks eroded, were worn down and cut crosswise by ancient rivers that had been running there first across the lands long before the mountains themselves were heaped up into ragged surges of rock and dirt. At least once since their first birth and that first upthrusting—as best the geologists can tell—after bearing silent witness to the formation of the Atlantic, these great rises of rock and dirt were blown by the winds and washed by the waters and worn by their weight all the way back down to lowland before being folded once again in subsequent upliftings. And then again once more these resurrected heights were dissected by unstoppable waters which spilled across the rocks and, draining the lands, shaped great long valleys from the soft shale and soluble limestone, and left long parallel ridges of sandstone and schist, the hard rocks which would not dissolve, like bone left in the wake of flesh. The valleys were then filled and the mountain tops covered with oak, poplar, hickory, hemlock, cedar, ash, maple, spruce, white pine, white birch, beech, basswood and tulip trees. These forested lands would be hunted by unremembered peoples and then by Shawnee and Cherokee, and it would come to pass that these mountains would be named the Appalachians.

In April 1993 I would go into those mountains, looking for a coal miner who called himself Dirty Ears.

I had lately been reading about the politics of culture—about how modes of social behavior and mediated representations are shaped to serve political and economic ends. This was a development of my learning about, during my examination of the Tobacco Festival, some of the effects of county agents and the extension service. I had discovered how, for example, traditional beliefs about agriculture—planting by the moon, reading nature for hints about the weather—were discouraged and replaced with more scientific methods not only to increase productivity, but also to draw more farmers into the cash economy and make them purchasers of consumer goods. The result of these cultural interventions by agents, as we have seen, was to contribute to the depopulation of the countryside and to the development of agribusiness.

So, looking around for an event that would involve the politics of representation and cultural intervention, I remembered once hearing that every year in eastern Kentucky hundreds of Shriners from across North America come together in Pikeville, the seat of Pike County, in the heart of eastern Kentucky's billion-dollar coal field. When I checked

Teaching children about hillbilly heritage

it out, I heard that they did indeed come, to howl and drink, dressed in hillbilly burlesque—patched overalls, floppy hats, and oversized boots, scuffed and holey; that they drove busted-up trucks decorated with chamber pots, animal hides, headless baby dolls, broken toilet seats, and broken outhouse doors cut with crescent moons; that they were the little-known but wildly popular subset of the better-known Ya'rab Shriners, the Imperial Ancient and Arabic Order of the Mystic Shrine shriners, the ones with the fezes, rubies in their belly buttons, and big cardboard scimitars, the ones who lay synchronized go-cart rubber in parades.

I made some phone calls and confirmed the rumor. The Imperial Clan of Hillbillies, I discovered, was what they call a "sideline" degree to the Ya'rab Shriners—a club within a club—and their two honored symbols are the corncob and the crescent moon. Their emblem is a whiskered doofus in overalls hefting a crockery jug of 'shine. When they speak, they call each other "cuzzin." When they gather, they drink corn likker. When they write in their newsletter, *Hillbilly News*, they feign a grotesque parody of the illiteracy that allowed the original inhabitants of the mountains to be easily exploited by coal and timber companies a hundred years ago: "Howdy Cuzzins . . . We'uns done enlightened a batch of poor flatlanders at our recent eye-nishation an the ret of us ole ridgerunners shore had a great time a runnin them thru the creek . . ."

I imagined that the cultural politics must be thick during Hillbilly Days, with the Shriners parodying the cartoon hillbilly stereotypes like Li'l Abner and Snuffy Smith, which were themselves parodies of the caricatures of mountaineers popularized during the late nineteenth century. A parody of a parody of a caricature, staged in the middle of depressed east Kentucky coal fields—this I had to see.

The first known European to venture into the Appalachians was a twenty-six-year-old German named John Lederer. He was sent by colonial Virginia governor William Berkeley in 1669 to find a route to the Indians, with whom the French had been profitably trading, on the other side. Lederer followed a river to its headwaters in the Blue Ridge, wandered for days in the snow, and finally went back home. Two years later, two more explorers under orders from Governor Berkeley followed the Roanoke River into the mountains, saw a backwash of the New River, thought it was the Pacific, and went back home. Another two years later, a man named James Needham reached the French Broad

River, but was killed by his guide, an Occaneechi Indian, who cut out Needham's heart and waved it in the air to express what he thought about the English. In 1716, Virginia governor Alexander Spotswood led some cavaliers into the mountains, where they hunted buffalo, elk, deer, bear, panther, wolf, fox, and beaver in the meadows, fields, and prairies of the Shenandoah Valley, which the Indians burned regularly to keep clear of forest. Spotswood gave his men each a golden horseshoe inscribed *Sic Juvat Transcendere Montes*—"So pleasant is it to cross the mountains."

In 1726, another German followed the trail blazed by the Knights of the Golden Horseshoe, built a cabin, and sent back word *auf Deutsch* that the mountains were the place to be. So they started coming. The Germans came first, from the Rhenish Palatinate and Würtemberg. They had gone to New York, been scorned, gone to Pennsylvania and filled it up, turned south, and driven down into the great valley, the Shenandoah, into the Blue Ridge. After that came the Scots-Irish.

The deepest and most rugged mountains were hunted by the Indians, but their permanent towns and fields were kept in the lower hills. Settlers would finally squeeze deep into the narrow valleys and hollows, which were choked with rhododendron, and up the steep slopes, which were blocked with fallen trees taller than men.

Families settled in the coves and hollows of the Cumberland Plateau, the Blue Ridge and the Smokies. As the families grew they pushed deeper into the mountains and up the slopes. The backbone of the mountain economy was the family farm, where the crops were corn, oats, wheat, hay, sorghum, rye, potatoes. Most farms had a vegetable garden, a beehive, an apple orchard, and pear, plum, and cherry trees. Cattle, sheep, and hogs, their ears nocked, grazed in the forests along the slopes. Since the land was open, farmers used split rails to fence their crops and protect them from the free-range stock. They covered their beds with hand-woven coverlets and accompanied their meeting house songs with tunes on the dulcimer. They used homespun blankets and homemade baskets, and they colored cloth with vegetable dyes. Their quilting patterns had names like Waves of Ocean, Sunflower, Democratic Banner, and Catch Me if You Can.

The hardwoods in the forests rained down a rich mast of chestnuts, acorns, walnuts, hickory nuts, and beechnuts. The woods were full of mules, beef and milk cattle, steers and sheep. Hogs, having fed on the mast, were then brought in and fed corn so their flesh would firm up. The mountaineers were remote but not totally isolated from the rest of the world. They did a heavy trade with the towns and farms in the flatter lands. Drovers herded the stock raised in the forests down trails and turnpikes through the breaks into Virginia or Kentucky's bluegrass regions, selling the animals—cows, hogs, sheep, chickens and turkeys— on the tobacco and cotton plantations. One year 160,000 hogs passed through Asheville, North Carolina, on their way from Tennessee and Kentucky to South Carolina and Georgia. Flocks of turkeys numbering three hundred to five hundred were also driven down dirt trails to the low country. The mountaineers gathered ginseng, yellow root, witch hazel, sassafras, galax, goldenseal and bloodroot. A pound of ginseng, which was shipped to China, could bring five dollars or a pair of boots. The big roads back then were the Kanawha Turnpike in West Virginia, the Wilderness Road in Virginia and Kentucky, and the Buncombe Turnpike in North Carolina. The big road these days is the Daniel Boone Parkway, and that's the one I took as I headed into the mountains.

The landscape along the way is desolate despite the blooming redbud beside the road. In fact, the trees make it seem more so, as the sparse pinks and reds set off the empty, immature forests of thin, leafless and wispy trees that cover the round hills. For the road to run flat, the mountainsides have had their shoulders cleaved and cut into stepped layers ribbed with drill scars, which makes going into these ancient Kentucky coal fields seem like driving between a set of tamed and unmotivated replicas of Scylla and Charybdis. The mountains seem depopulated, but that is the illusion created by such a limited-access scenic parkway. The national forest is an implied wilderness, but the emptiness is belied by the shot-riddled road signs and pieces of plywood that are nailed to trees and that carry messages of the region's economy: Wanted Clean Fill Dirt; Will Steam Clean Heavy Machinery; Yard Sale— Avon and Whatnots. I am tempted to follow the signs to places like Dwarf and Upper Quicksand Elementary School, but I keep going, on through the great Hazard Coalfield, past the Dairy Cheer—Home of the Smashburger, whose sign reads "Happy Birthday Tiffany. Elect Jesus Savior Lord of Your Life"—and past the Green Door Lounge, where the name of the band playing this weekend is Mistaken Identity.

I have no problem finding Dirty Ears. Walking along the sidewalk in Pikeville I see two men wearing floppy felt hats and red jackets embroidered on the backs with gapped-tooth spiky-whiskered dope-eyed slack-jawed hicks. I ask them if they are hillbillies and they answer me with the nail-driving enunciation of semi-Brit Canadians. I say, Canadian hillbillies? And they say, Yep, Canadian hillbillies. One of them is a retired "flight leftenant." The other is a businessman. They tell me Dirty Ears should be over by the park.

Dirty Ears is standing in the middle of the road wearing a long, torn coat and the floppy felt hat, which is the Hillbillies' carnivalesque inversion of the Shriners' starched, erect fez. A racoon tail hangs from a cord down his back. A patch sewn to the front of his coat reads "Dirty Ears."

"Well, we were on our way down to Portsmouth, Ohio, to a River Day festival, and we was a-talking about why there wasn't nothing here in eastern Kentucky like that, somethin' for *our* people." Dirty Ears, along with his friend Shady Grady Kinney, are the founders of Hillbilly Days. He's telling me about the birth of the event in 1977. "And we were Shriners, see, and at that time there were only about nine Hillbilly Clans nationwide. They were still in the early stages, so they never had all gathered in one place before. So we got a-hold of the Imperial Remand, Jim Harris, who had all the say, and asked him would he like to have a gatherin' here in eastern Kentucky of all the clans. And he said 'Yes, I think it would be a wonderful idea.' Sort of a convention-type thing, see."

Dirty Ears, whose real name is Howard Stratton, is standing in the middle of the street next to a truck hung with animal carcasses. He leans in and twists a knob and cranks a recording of *Jerry Clower Live!* Haw! I'm having a hard time hearing him tell me the story of Hillbilly Days.

"So we talked to a man, Rutherford, here, asked him, and then went to the mayor and asked him for the use of the city, and he agreed to it, and not only did we include the Shriners and the Hillbilly Clans, but we included the local people."

The cofounder of Hillbilly Days, Shady Grady Kinney, walks up. His floppy felt hat is heavy with buttons reading things like "Kiss Me I'm a Hillbilly" and "Hillbillies Like Big Jugs." Dirty Ears introduces us. Shady Grady speaks like he's gargling; his voice is a rattling growl like deep gravel under car tires. He's retired from forty-five years of coal mining. His father was a coal miner. His boy is a coal miner. He likes the union okay; the only problem was that any time he thought he was getting ahead, any time he thought he might be able to buy a car, or get something nice, the union would go out on strike, and he'd use up all his money. When he tells me his name, I say "Kinney?" And he says, *"Kin*ney. I'm not one of those *Ken*nedys. But I'd like to have their money!" And he says it as though he says it all the time, as though at least the early sixties has defined his name as the negation of aristocratic wealth and privilege, just as the name of the region itself—Appalachia— has come to serve as a metonym for poverty and exploitation.

Before the Civil War, there was little demand and no real market for the natural resources in the Appalachians. Some small-scale timbering was done—groups of men would cut trees and float them down to low-land towns on spring flood waters—but there was no extensive mining or lumbering. Southern leaders had deep agrarian biases which prevented them from encouraging large-scale industrial development (and helped them lose the war), but, after the surrender of the Confederacy, the leaders of the New South had different attitudes, and the industries of the North had greater needs, as well as most of the money. Ronald Eller, in his classic *Miners, Millhands and Mountaineers,* has collected statistics and recovered voices that document the industrial exploitation of the mountains in excruciating, undeniable and unrelenting detail.

In 1873, he writes, coal production in Kentucky was three hundred thousand tons. By 1890 it was 2.7 million. Coal mining sucked people into unsettled mountain counties that still by 1890 were not heavily populated. The area boomed, resembling western gold rush towns. In McDowell County, West Virginia, thirty thousand people moved in be-tween 1900 and 1910. Coal camps ran for miles through the hollows and along valley bottoms, the houses strung out beside poisoned creeks like roadside litter. Northern capital flowed in from Boston, Michigan, New York, Ohio. Coal company scouts drove wagons into the mountains, pitched tents, dined in dinner jackets, ate by torchlight and lantern, and bought up mineral rights from largely unschooled mountaineers, whose ignorance and poverty is today mocked by the hillbilly stereotype.

In 1907, a local editor in Beckley, West Virginia, said this about the magic of "king coal":

> Towns and cities springing up where before stood dense forests or waving fields of grain; thousands of coke ovens gleaming along the pathway of the iron horse and clouding the noon-day sun with their endless streams of smoke; armies of men collected together from every quarter of the globe to dig his vast treasures from the mines; heavily loaded freight trains plunging through mountain fastnesses, fording

great rivers and spanning wide canyons to carry to the world its precious supplies of fuel—these are some of the accomplishments of old king coal, who is working out the miracle daily before our eyes. (Eller 1982: 130)

After 1915, as industries geared up for wartime production, the price rose from eighty cents a ton to six or seven dollars. In Pike County, the number of mines went from eight to forty-five between 1916 and 1920. Then came the bust. The reopening of European coal fields, lower demand, and too many holes in the ground led to overproduction. Between 1900 and 1925, twenty-four hundred men and boys were killed in the Appalachian mines. From 1923 to 1927, two hundred thousand miners left the coal fields, not to return to farms, but to move on and labor for wages in factories (Eller 1982: 154–57).

Pikeville, the county seat of Pike County, is located deep in eastern Kentucky's Appalachian Mountains, on a horseshoe bend of the Levisa Fork of the Big Sandy River. The Big Sandy runs as a border between Kentucky and West Virginia. Like most towns, villages or settlements in these parts of the tightly packed mountains, Pikeville is elongated, stretching along the river on the valley floor, and is shaded from the sun. The town is most famous for being the site of the trials resulting from the Hatfield-McCoy feud. An editorialist in the local newspaper writes under the pen name Red Dog—which is a name for toxic slag from the coal mines.

In the 1970s, during the energy crisis, fuel prices skyrocketed, and Pike County became the largest coal-producing county in the nation. There were ninety new coal millionaires in Pike County. Spendable income in the county spiked up 50 percent to $200 million a year. Assets in Pikeville banks doubled to $319 million, making it the second-largest banking center in Kentucky. The most flamboyant of the local coal millionaires, Claude Canada, once mined coal for nineteen cents a ton, but the Arab oil embargo pushed the price to seventy dollars a ton. During the boom Canada made so much money that he gave away Cadillacs to his foremen every year; the Cadillac dealership in Pikeville was the fourth busiest in the nation. Canada owned diamonds, thoroughbreds and twenty-one Rolls Royces. Then the bottom fell out. Claude Canada was shot to death in 1980 while trying to break into his wife's farmhouse in Jessamine County. While I am in Pikeville for Hillbilly Days, the newspaper runs a story about the last slurry pumps, shuttle cars and Pepsi machines from Canada's coal empire being finally sold off at auction.

All the talk is about the decline of coal.

"I worked thirteen and a half years coal mining," Dirty Ears says. "You take my mine, now, the payroll was about a million a month. Four hundred people. And that mine shut down. Now that's hurting. And they was other large mines, too. There were a lot of big mines that shut down, good paying, forty, fifty thousand dollars a year, you know. And people, they're moving out, aren't they, Grady."

Grady nods. Jerry Clower "haws!" Dirty Ears keeps on. "Our young people are moving. When the mines shut down this town be nothing but a ghost town. Won't be nothing, 'cause that's all they got to depend on."

The signboard in front of the Pikeville First Presbyterian Church reads: Welcome Hillbillies. *Come Worship With Us.*

The Indians would say "Okaeepoeze!" ("God is nigh") when they came in sight of the mountains. Those same mountains inspired different reactions in some New South boomers. Here's one from Tennessee: "What we need to make East Tennesse the most prosperous and desirable section of the South is capital. That would be a panacea for our financial ills and would disarm poverty of its terrors. It would put us on the high road to wealth. . . . We need hundreds of blazing furnaces distributed over this region, along the foothills of our mountains, lighting up their gorges and developing and utilizing the iron embedded in their bowels. . . . What a magnificent field for capitalists!" (Eller 1982: 53).

After the Civil War, 75 percent of the Appalachians was woodlands. There were enormous stands of oaks, spruce, hemlock, chestnut and poplar, trees eight feet in diameter and a hundred and fifty feet high. By 1900, only 10 percent was still virgin. The black walnut, yellow poplar and ash had begun disappearing in northern forests, so the lumber barons moved south, and, between 1890 and 1920, they bought out and cut over the mountain forests.

As lumbering became a profitable venture, timbermen used splash dams to help get the logs out of deep mountains. Splash dams were made of earth and backed up streams and creeks. A powerful load of water was stored behind the dams, and logs were stacked in the stream beds downstream. As wooden gates were pulled out of the dams, water would flash flood down the creeks and wash the cut timber out into the deeper streams. Sometimes dams on several tributary creeks were opened at the same time. A mass of rock, water and timber would roar

73

down a mountain hollow, stripping the creek banks. Steam-powered skidders and band saws accelerated the deforestation. Log slides and splash dams destroyed riverbeds. Great woodfires, the result of lightning or sparks from machinery igniting slash piles and sawdust, were an annual phenomenon in the Blue Ridge and would burn for weeks across the ripped landscape.

As suddenly as it started, the lumber boom was over. The big trees were gone. By this time, a generation of mountaineers had been drawn into wage labor. Farms were overgrown; skills and traditional knowledge were lost. Thousands abandoned the mountains for jobs in factories and mines. In 1910, a mountain school superintendant for the Southern Baptist Convention wrote about the effects of the timber boom: "When I first started my work in these mountains, 30 years ago, when the forests were untouched, the mountains were full of sparkling brooks and creeks which required two or three weeks rain to make muddy; today, a few hours' rain will muddy them. . . . many of the mountain streams are dry throughout the summer and fall, while in winter, the waters descend in torrents and do vast damage, rendering worthless the bottom lands which used to be the most desirable for farming purposes" (Eller 1982: 110–11).

Dirty Ears calls over another Hillbilly, a sales representative from Fort Mill, South Carolina. He's a low-country Hillbilly, and the incongruity of his wide-mouthed coastal drawl is striking up here around east Kentucky's sharper twang.

His clan is the closest to turning in $1 million to help the crippled kids. "We're at eight hundred and some thousand dollars right now, and we're almost to a million. We have a coon hunt that annually raises thirty thousand dollars. We have car shows too, anything we can think of."

He says sixteen of his clan came up this year for Hillbilly Days. "We brought our band with us. It's called the Grits Band."

I ask him if he plays bluegrass. He looks around, seeming a little embarrassed.

"Well, actually"—he scopes it out to see if anyone else can hear him—"we got a synthesizer. We *can* play bluegrass, you know, we do that for a fund-raiser too. We used to play it more, that's how we got started, as a bluegrass band. But it got to where"—he leans closer toward me—"maybe up here they like bluegrass music, but other places that kind of died out a little bit, you know, so we just got to where we play all kind of music."

He tells me that being a Hillbilly and coming to Hillbilly Days is fun for a lot of reasons. First, he says, of course, it raises money for the crippled kids. But second is that he's gotten to know all these fellas from all around the country and in his motel where he stays are the same people been staying there every year for probably eight years, people from Virginia, Canada and Detroit, Michigan, and you just look forward to seeing them every year and everybody just has a big ol' time.

He says that during Hillbilly Days they have a Shrine initiation down in the local gymnasium. I ask him what they do during initiation. He says, oh, it ain't really nothing. "As a matter of fact," he continues, "a lot of people think that there's a lot of things that go on in Shrine initiations and everything else, but most of it's a mental thing, and that's the reason you don't want to tell somebody, see, because you *think* things are happening, but nothing's *really* happening. That type a thing, you know. It's like when you go to Disney World and you ride in that space ship and you get all that sensation like yer flying through space but yer not doing anything but settin' there in that chair."

I say, there's a lot of things in this world like that.

He says, you know that's right.

He says that the Hillbillies have really taken off and become one of the most popular of all Shriner sideline degrees. One of the reasons, he says, is that the Hillbillies let the gals do stuff. The Shrine doesn't let women do anything, but the Hillbillies let them do stuff like run for Possum Queen. "We let 'em to ride in the parades and everything, too.

"See, there're certain rules the Shrine has, and they have to have it for in*shawnce* reasons and so forth, that you can't have kids riding in the parades, can't have women riding in the parade." Here he shifts into a lightly ironic and weary can-you-belive-this tone, and says, "Or you can't even dress *up* like women 'cause you don't want to offend anybody, or you can't even put *black* on your face anymore, you know, 'cause you don't want to offend anybody at *all*, so because of that you end up having rules that maybe seem like they're superstrict or something like that, but I'm sure there's good reasoning behind it. But whenever they have just Hillbilly parades, my man, they don't care about nothing! Bring your wife, your dog, your neighbor!"

He flings out his arms in joyous release.

*   *   *

The idea of the "hillbilly" sprang from a moment of cultural tension: upon their "discovery" after the Civil War, the Appalachian mountaineers were welcomed into the national fold as hardy exemplars of pioneer stock, but their reluctance to embrace middle-class values soon caused their self-sufficiency to be recast as backwardness and their traditions to be labled crude, their dress ludicrous, their language degraded. The public image of a depraved hillbilly culture became a means of rationalizing the poverty of an exploited region. The argument went like this: hillbillies are poor because they are ignorant and degenerate, and they're ignorant and degenerate because they're poor hillbillies.

The self-sufficient lifestyle of the mountain people was vilified by middle-class reformers, and a caricature of mountain culture became a major justification for the ruthless acquisition of land and resources. Ironically, just as the hillbilly stereotype justified social engineering, other aspects of mountain culture—handicrafts and ballads—provided in iconographic form a set of consumable objects that served to supply a semblance of rootedness in an increasingly fast-paced, neurasthenic, industrializing world.

The discovery of Appalachia took place in the new middle-class magazines that began to flourish after the Civil War—*Harper's, Lippincott's, Scribner's, The Century, The American Review of Reviews, The Atlantic Monthly*—in which the mountains were described according to the conventions of local color writing as the repository of a pioneer stock that had been common to America a hundred years earlier. Word of Appalachia's discovery was spread through articles with titles such as "A Strange Land and Peculiar People," "Our Contemporary Ancestors," "Our Kindred of the Boone and Lincoln Type," and "The Retarded Frontier." The middle-class magazine readers in the cities wanted reminiscences of the olden times before industrialization, before the homogenizing, compressive and accelerating effects of the railroad, stereoscope, penny press and federal national administrative system. The self-sufficient mountaineers provided the right stuff, not only as objects of nostalgic consumption, but as an untapped supply of white, 100 percent American labor to counter the increasing immigration of black-haired southern European anarchists (Shapiro 1978).

The mountaineers had a different sense of time from that of the capitalists; they would work at the mines in the winter, but would return to their farms in the spring and summer. If the mountaineers felt slighted, they simply walked off the job. They had alternatives. They had gotten by without the coal mines before, and they could do it again. But this was not acceptable to the bosses: "They make good woodsmen and guides, but their shiftless methods of living have not accustomed them to continuous and sustained labor and very little suffices. In short, they resemble the negro in their desire for frequent periods of 'laying off' . . . never having known or dreamed of anything better than the wretched surroundings of their everyday life, they are supremely unconscious of their own misery" (Eller 1982: 166).

Around the turn of the century, settlement schools in the mountains were part of a national trend; they were places where America's new middle class taught manners and comportment to the different, the unwashed, the exploited. In 1891 there were six social settlements in the United States; by 1897, there were seventy-four and by 1900, more than a hundred. The number doubled in each of the next five-year periods until there were more than four hundred by 1910. In 1902, some women's club members opened the Log Cabin Settlement School at Hindman, Kentucky. Around that time, one of the teachers at Hindman recorded in her diary that she could hear the crash of the great trees on nearby mountains where men were cutting the virgin poplars.

In 1920, the Hindman newsletter reported on the activity of coal company speculators who were coming into the mountains and buying land and mineral rights from the isolated mountaineers: "For lack of a milder term, it will have to be called commercial exploitation. It is a certainty that the rich mineral holdings of this section passed out of the hands of the original owners for the merest fraction of their real value . . . This is commercialism. These people shut in here for a century and a quarter are not prepared to cope with it. They must be trained to meet the changing order of things rather than be picked up in its vortex and swept on—or destroyed. Far be it from us, however, to give the impression that the coal operators are ruthless. Many of them fully appreciate the problems to be met. A number of them realize their obligations to this section and at least a dozen companies contribute to Hindman Settlement School" (Whisnant 1983).

The pauperization of the mountaineers was an accepted, foregone conclusion, so the culture workers in the mountains settled for teaching the hillbillies how to tell the salad fork from the dinner fork and how to decorate a Christmas tree: "Their wealth has passed into other hands," the newsletter concluded, "but they still have their splendid possibilities of personal development" (75–76).

The low-country Hillbilly is telling me that "real hillbillies ain't so far in the past. You can still get a jug of moonshine around here just like that!" He snaps his fingers to the side, a motion like flipping playing cards into a hat. "And not only that. You can ask a policeman and the police'll tell you where to get it. That's true! You wouldn't think it would be so, but they want people to have a good time. I don't know they'd do it with *every*body, but if they know you're a Shriner . . .

"When we came up here, first year we come up here, we wanted to get a jug of moonshine and asked one of the police, said, 'Where can we get us a little bit of moonshine,' and he said, 'Go over to the back of that truck and get whatever you want out of the back of it, and just drink out of there!'

"You know, it's like us, we all come up here and we all want to take a jug home with us. Part of the hillbilly tradition kinda thing. I'll tell you, one time down there where this ol' boy was selling that moonshine, he musta had, I don't know *how* many cases. But that's the only time he said he made it, was for this week. You can go to the store and get the bonded kind a helluva lot cheaper, and if you don't make it real, you know, *right*, it's pretty bad stuff. But most these ol' boys who make it for Hillbilly Days, they know how to make it right."

Dirty Ears reaches into his truck and cranks the volume on *Jerry Clower Live!* until I can't hear people talking anymore.

I sit within the din and think, *Real hillbillies ain't so far in the past.* Real hillbillies? The blurred spinning postmodern two-step ghost dance of simulation and authenticity has kicked up dust to sting my eyes.

If you have ever ambled through the gift shops up in the mountains, I'm sure you've seen them. Amid the cowhide bullwhips, rubber toma-hawks, black bear ashtrays and souvenir shot glasses is a class of roadside goods that reflects a tradition as old as the moniker "Appalachian" itself: hillbilly gags. Examples include a sack of Cheerios labeled "hillbilly donut seeds," a cut-out of a hand with fingers numbered one through five and labeled "hillbilly calculator," the "hillbilly flashlight" (a clothes-pin on a stick and a box of matches), the "hillbilly fishing pole" (a stick of dynamite), and the "hillbilly toilet paper" (a dried corncob).

While politically correct multiculturalism has banished many cultural stereotypes (Chinky Chinky Chinaman and Little Black Sambo) and has laid seige to others (Redskins and Braves), the white mountaineer-as-moron has not only survived, but shows signs of a renewed vogue. Once Arkansan Bill Clinton was elected, bare feet, floppy hats and corncob pipes began popping up in political cartoons.

The word "hill-billie," of unconfirmed Scots etymological heritage, first appeared in print in 1900. A writer for the *New York Journal* defined a Hill-Billie as "a free and untrammeled white citizen who lives in the hills . . . has no means to speak of, dresses as he can, talks as he pleases, drinks whiskey when he gets it, and fires off his revolver as the fancy takes him" (Green 1965: 204–28). The word "hillbilly" spread along with Victrolas and radio, being first popularized as part of the phrase "hillbilly music." Hillbilly came to refer to a hybrid of genuine folk elements commercialized for southern whites. While "race" records were sold to blacks, "hillbilly" music was sold to the southern whites who found themselves migrating from the country to the city. Hillbilly became a general reference for all types of music popular among southern whites: Dixie, old time, mountain, country, western, country-western, and the more or less perfected iconic form, bluegrass. It also became a general term for the poor white southerner, along with woolhat, peckerwood, linthead, redneck, ridgerunner, clayeater, tarheel, appleknocker, and turdkicker.

In 1958, *Harper's Magazine* ran an article entitled "The Hillbillies Invade Chicago," which read, "The city's toughest integration problem has nothing to do with Negroes. . . . It involves a small army of white, Protestant, Early American migrants from the South—who are usually proud, poor, primitive, and fast with a knife." Hillbillies were described as "the prototype of what the 'superior' American should be, white Protestants of early American, Anglo-Saxon stock; but on the streets of Chicago they seem to be the American dream gone berserk. . . . their neighbors often find them more obnoxious than the Negroes or the earlier foreign immigrants."

Four years later, in November 1962, *The Beverly Hillbillies* premiered. Currently, the hambone antics of "America's most lovable hillbillies" can be seen each weekday evening on TBS. What's missing is the historical context in which the show was born. Instead of moving to the slums of Detroit and Chicago, these hillbillies moved to a mansion in "Californy." If this sounds familiar, it's because the same pattern is found in many black-based TV sitcoms where racist mythologies are used both as mask and as justification and salve for economic exploitation.

The term "hillbilly" has by now been boiled down to a few icons: floppy felt hat, corncob pipe, jug with three X's, and words as misspelled by Li'l Abner and Snuffy Smith. Hillbilly imagery has been internalized, the cartoons sublimated to become part of history. Dirty Ears and Shady Grady tell me that Hillbilly Days celebrates the heritage. Here's what that heritage means to Dirty Ears: "See these old bibbed overalls? Me and Grady, we was raised in 'em. Outhouse tawlets? I was fifteen years old before I seen a bathroom. We went to two-room schools, walked to school."

It was this internalized image of mountain heritage that Jim Harris, the Imperial Remand of the Hillbillies, used to create his sideline degree. He lives in Ashville, Kentucky. He tells me how it came to pass that he created the Hillbilly Shriners, whose numbers have now reached fifty thousand. "Once you get in the Shrine they got what you call sideline degrees. That's where they want you to come on up and be a member of the Horse Traders or be a member of the Mandarin degree, be a member of this, be a member of that, be a member of something else. That's what they call a sideline degree and they got 'em all over Shrinedom.

"I joined some of those. And they didn't do much for me. They left me kind of cold. I joined one that was called the Mandarin degree and that was one of the most filthiest things I'd ever seen in my life. I mean it was filthy. It was vulgar. I told a buddy of mine, I said, that's dumb. We can do better than that. And one thing led to another and he said, If you're so smart why don't you do better than that. Well, I let it go, but they wouldn't let it go, those buddies of mine, they kept on me. Well, we had us a little wager going that I could do better, so I said, Okay, I'll write a hillbilly degree.

"I didn't start out to write a hillbilly degree, I started out to write a sideline degree about something, and I thought maybe I'd write an Indian degree. But I don't know anything about Indians. But I am a hillbilly, I was born in the hills, raised in the hills, and I do know about hillbillies. So I wrote a hillbilly degree. I sprung it on 'em and they couldn't believe it.

"Then, it just grew like Topsy. We'd initiate fifteen to twenty people locally, and when other Shriners would come into town, we'd ask them if they wanted to join, and they did. Then a guy said Hey, I know where we can get hillbilly hats wholesale. He was a truck driver and he'd been out on the road and he found out where we can get 'em, and we did. That was about 1969. We bought the hillbilly hats at thirty-five cents apiece when bought by the gross. Then we took some hats down to Miami and put on the degree work down there and it just grew like Topsy.

"So I wrote the degree about things that are hillbilly. Like, our honored symbols are the corncob and the crescent. If you know anything about hills and outhouses, the crescent is famous for being on that little outhouse. But in the Shrine we have a crescent that is a very honored symbol in our emblem. So it has a double meaning. The ritual they go through to get in, everybody loves it. It's a secret, but it's all based on the code of the hills. It involves a little corn likker.

"Women don't belong to the hillbilly degree, but we have the ladies auxiliary, sometimes called the Mountain Mamas, and they run for Possum Queen. I tell you, it's quite an honor for them. Some of these women are out for blood on this thing. They have a little performance. They get out there and strut around like at Miss America, only hillbilly style. They give her a plaque, a crown, a burlap robe and bouquet of wildflowers.

"That's the kind of activities that make the thing an ongoing success.

"Well, hillbilly is a derogatory word to a lot of northerners and big-city people. They call us hillbillies because we live in Appalachia and because we have a little different method of talking, a little different method of belief. In fact, a fellow named Al Capp made a very famous comic strip called *Li'l Abner* based on the culture of the so-called hillbillies, so we decided we'd just use that heritage and go ahead and stir them up!

"Well, nobody got upset about it until we had our first convention, in Cincinnati about twelve years ago. There was some minister up there and he had a piece in the paper, and he said these people are coming up here making fun of our poor neighbors in the South. Well, that is not true at all. I went up there to see that fella and I told him that I'm from the South and I don't feel like I'm making fun. We're pulling the wool over some of the big city people's eyes. There's a few people that actually believe we live like that, go barefooted all year round, and that's not true. We're just having a little fun. Our purpose is to have fun and raise money to help the crippled children."

"Mountain heritage comes home again" the *Appalachian News-Express* headlines at the beginning of Hillbilly Days. But what I notice about this version of Appalachian heritage is that it is media-made. The stories of cartoon stereotypes have been around so long that they have become a widely accepted version of the culture. The hillbillies have blurred history and hokum. The lead editorial "Head for the hill (billy days)," for example, is written in the contrived dialect of a lazy Ma and Pap:

> "Ay, God, womun, watsa matter wuth you? Hit ain't even good 'n daylight yit. Leave me alone. We ain't lost nuthin' in Pikevul."
> "But, Pap, I 'on't us to git a good start. Hit's time fer 'em ther Hillbilly Days . . .'em kids'll be wontin' to ride them rides and watch that ther p'rade with all 'em people all dressed up 'n lookin' purty. It brangs a ter to ma eyes ever time I see 'em men wuth 'em ol' stills 'n sich. Lordy, hit puts me in mine of the olden times when a man didn't haft to wurry 'bout no revnuers and laws ner nuthin'. I ain't ashamed ta tell ye, I miss 'em days."
> " 'At's me, too, Pap. I shore do miss 'em times we usta have 'fore everthang got s'all-farred fancy 'n what they call 'modern."
> "Ay, life wuz hard, but we shore had a good time, ain't no denyin'."
> (April 14, 1993)

The mountain heritage celebrated at Hillbilly Days is one of degradation and depravity, the legacy of the exploitation of the mountains' human and natural resources. To commemorate Hillbilly Days, some seventh graders at Elkhorn City Junior High wrote poems. This is the image of the mountain heritage being taught—not one of self-sufficiency and independence but of derangement:

> *Hillbillies are a rare breed*
> *They are the funniest creatures I ever seed*
> *With ole lazy dogs and a jug of liquor*
> *When cops chase 'em there ain't nuthin' quicker . . .*

The Hillbilly trucks are lined up along the parade route. Each clan has a truck which they take to the gatherings. The trucks are the old frames of anything from Model T's to pickups, vans, Volkswagens, and dune buggies, built over with boards, rigged with mismatched fenders and bumpers, headlights hanging like something freshly dead, and actual dead things themselves dried to discs of roadkill and nailed on. The trucks are hung with animal hides, rusty buckets, broken lanterns, plastic army men, tool blades, ax heads, skulls, horseshoes, auger bits, broken jugs, smashed buckets, horse jawbones, horns with squeeze bulbs, pulleys and broken ropes, tin cans, large neckties, rodentia taxidermied in basements—their wilted mouths and lips stitched with cord as on the necks of zombies—Raggedy Anns nailed to boards, legs from Barbie dolls, chamber pots, toilet seats and simulated outhouses. The trucks are painted with slogans: Cracker Clan; Maw and Paw; Hoosier Hillbilly; Kiss Me I'm Hillbillie; James Ratliffe: King of Concrete; Eat More Possum, Less Coon; Hillbillies Like Big Jugs; Old Shriners Never Die, They Live on in the Hearts of Crippled Children; My Heart Is in Farming but My Ass Is in Debt; Ugly Strikes One Out of Three; I'm Looking for the Perfect Woman—a Nymphomaniac with a Liquor Store; Honor the Cob; Respect the Crescent; This Car Is Constipated: It Won't Pass Anything.

There's a big flatbed of a coal truck for the Kentucky Black Lung Association float. It's a coffin surrounded by five or six folding chairs. There are Styrofoam-flowered memorial wreaths. One has a crossed black shovel and pick in the center. This year's float is dedicated to an old miner who died during the past year. In the middle of the greenery on one of the wreaths is a framed color picture of the miner riding on the Black Lung Association float in the parade the year before. The photograph shows him sitting among miners who are sitting around a coffin surrounded by flowered memorial wreaths; in the greenery of one is a picture of an old miner who had died—an endless chain of deaths and remembrances.

A man who has given me his hand to help me up onto the back of the coal truck tells me that coal is in trouble—not only that, but all Kentucky is in trouble. He says that if any sin taxes or energy taxes get passed the state will be hit hard. "Kentucky's got four sources of wealth: coal, whisky, tobacco and horse racing. We are going to hurt."

Among the arts and crafts booths in the park I meet a man named Sherd Maynard. He's an unemployed coal miner from Beckley, West Virginia. He is selling paintings of old outhouses. "Work got tight, a lot of miners got laid off back home, so I started picking this stuff up, something to make a living." He isn't doing too well. "A lot of these people are out of work, too." He copies his pictures from a magazine called *Good Old Days*. It's a special issue on outhouse memories. He says, "People like to get together and reminisce about their outhouses." He doesn't want to sell me the issue because then he wouldn't know how to paint more outhouse scenes. But he says I can tear off the back cover and keep the address so I can order one for myself.

I read it, and it's like a handbook for ghost dancing. The back cover says, "Take a monthly, nostalgic trip to the past! Your money back at once! If the first issue you receive doesn't please and entertain you beyond words! . . . For about the cost of a good movie, you can receive this big entertainment value each month for the next 12 months!" The list of some recent special issues includes "Days of the Woodshed," "Early 1900's Shoe Repair," "Dry Goods Store—1910 Style," "Thank Heaven for Biscuits!" and my favorite, "I Remember Butchering Day."

Hillbilly Days is all about remembering, but it's a ghost dance done not to perpetuate a specific, localized community—the Hillbilly Shriners come from across the continent—but to perpetuate the existence of an imagined community; it is a carnivalesque altered dimension where the hillbilly stereotypes exist as part of our shared mythologies, the collection of representations that make up a national history. This stereotype endures because the hillbilly is one of our culture's fools, a body of unrestrained impulses and unchecked appetites. The "mountaineer" resides in our collective memory as the person of quilts and dulcimers and natural wisdom, but the hillbilly remains as a creature of violence and ignorance, a part of industrial debris, just like the debris left in the valleys when the logging operations ended, and like the debris that decorates the trucks in the parade.

In 1938, a mountain farmer named William Wirt in Epperson, Tennessee, a remote cove in the Smokies near the Carolina line, wrote a friend about the effect of logging and the TVA:

> One day we were the happiest people on earth. But like the Indian we are slowly but surely being driven from the homes that we have learned to love, and down to the man we are not a friend of the Government for the simple reason that every move they have made has increased our poverty.
>
> We were told that if we kept the fire out of the forest that we would have plenty of range for our cattle, but we found that after a few years that there is no range left. We were also told that we would have plenty and increasing flow of water in our mountain streams, furnishing an abundance of fish for sport and food. But I've found that our streams are drying up and the fish in the ponds that are left are all dying, and at times you can smell them as you pass along the highway. Fifteen years ago you could have seen in the forest here thousands of cattle, sheep and hogs. Today you never see one out of the forest, and if you do his head and horns is the heaviest part about him.
>
> Now what are we going to do, move on and try to fit in where we do not belong or undertake to face the situation and gradually starve to death? In the little mountain churches where we once sat and listened to the preaching of the gospel with nothing to disturb us, we now hear the

84

roar of machinery on the Sabbath day. After all I have come to believe
that the real old mountaineer is a thing of the past and what will finally
take our place, God only knows. (Eller 1983: 241–42)

I am walking down the street in Pikeville during Hillbilly Days when
I find out what has taken the place of the "real old mountaineer." I hear
someone saying Hey, buddy. I turn around. There is a Hillbilly Shriner
with a necktie hanging four feet long and two hands wide, draped over
his swollen belly, his eyes hidden behind glasses on each lens of which is
painted a spiral spinning into a small flat pupil. As he speaks, the heavy
must of respirated alcohol obscures any sense. He holds in front of my
face a bright red wiener shrink-wrapped in plastic. He wants a dollar for
it, for the Hillbilly Shrine. "F'th cribblt kizzz," he says. For the crippled
kids. I shake my head no thanks and duck around him, the weiner and
its red brightness having burned a scar onto my retina, his breath having
fogged my glasses.

I have seen the politics of representation played out in the streets of
Pikeville. To complete my investigation of pop-culture hillbilly portrai-
ture, I get my car and drive across the river into West Virginia to find
the grave of Devil Anse Hatfield.

If someone says the word "feud," probably the first thing that pops
into most people's heads is the Hatfields and the McCoys. There's a
reason for that.

For more than a hundred years in American popular culture, in
between sporadic outbursts of square dancing and moonshining, clans
of barefooted, floppy-hatted hillbillies have been exchanging fire with
their squirrel rifles. They've been carrying out blood feuds, ancient
cross-generational combat, redressing grievances no one can quite recall,
but feeling nonetheless compelled by some visceral, undeniable animal
memory to hunt down anybody with another name. The violence that
took place in the Appalachian Mountains at the end of the nineteenth
century—violence expressed through the trope of the family but actually
caused by greater forces—has left its trace in the common culture, and it
shows up in the stories told in comics like *Snuffy Smith* and *Li'l Abner*,
in the roadside iconography of items for sale in gas stations and gift
shops, and in events like Pikeville's Hillbilly Days.

It is said that we make sense of the world by telling ourselves stories,
that narrative makes chaos coherent. In Psalms 90:9, it is said that "we

spend our years as a tale that is told," and that is how it is; each life is a life lived within the wrath of the Word, each life participates within many stories, and each story adds shape and contour to the landscapes which we occupy, landscapes conjured into physical reality by our stories and their versions. Stories, therefore, are part of politics, because to tell stories is to contribute to the construction of knowledge, and it is the structure of knowledge that simultaneously reveals, determines and serves the structures of power. Proverbs 26:22, "The words of a talebearer are as wounds, and they go down into the innermost parts of the belly," is true for local rumormongers, and also for history itself, which has been called the gossip of the winners.

Like gossip, history is interpretive, inevitably incomplete, and motivated by a desire to change people's beliefs. The problem is that rather than computing a complex calculus of cause and effect, people often choose to understand the world around them through simple mathematics, ipso facto logic that streamlines and simplifies the multiple patterns of determination. We prefer our understanding of the world to come to us through stories, and we prefer them to be inflected with theatrical effects.

Much work has been done to debunk the hillbilly stereotypes and restore dignity and integrity to the history of mountain cultures and to the people who occupy them today, but in the body of collective pop cultural representations, the hillbilly has a firm position—witness the harvest of hillbilly imagery deployed against Arkansan Bill Clinton after his election in 1992. Such imagery continues to reside in our national imagination, which consists of the collected works, stories and representations that are created, consumed and contemplated in everyday life. Increasingly, the national imagination resides in the vaults of broadcasting and cable networks. A common lore of symbols, icons and stories that once were perpetuated through sermons, songs, face-to-face encounters and popular speech has been usurped by mediated productions. We remember now in new ways, through the lens of popular culture.

We don't usually think about it, but culture-making storytelling takes place all around us, day and night: narratives found in prime-time news, weekly magazines, best-selling novels, the banter of friends, newspapers, and reruns of old TV shows like *The Andy Griffith Show*.

It was *The Andy Griffith Show* that I was thinking about as I drove out of Pikeville, curving on roads that wound along beside the river, at the foot of sheer rock faces, and heading toward the West Virginia line a dozen miles to the east. I had been a fan of the reruns for years. I liked the tones of black and white, the pacing of the dialogue and storylines, the inimitable antic comic stylings of Don Knotts as Barney and Jim Nabors as Gomer, the sweet bathos of the archetypal old maid matriarch-manqué Aunt Bee as portrayed by Francis Bavier, and the "aw shucks" sweetboy truth of Opie, the cosmic TV-land soulmate of Shirley Temple. Once I started reading cultural studies and rethinking the world around me, I began to see how *The Andy Griffith Show* was actually a rich repository of politicized cultural narratives.

I started to watch the show more closely and to notice that it isn't just slapstick and saccharine stories. More complex than I had first thought, the episodes resonate with historical references and cultural politics. In one episode Ellie, the female druggist and, for a while, Andy's gal pal, wants to give a box of makeup to a country girl whose father makes her wear pants and chop wood. The farmer doesn't want his daughter all sissied up because she's his only source of labor. Sheriff Andy solves the problem by showing him how, if he let his daughter paint her face, she could sucker in some big country boy who would be three times the labor. Everybody's happy.

In another episode, the landlord, old Ben Weaver, is going to evict the Scobie family because they owe him $52.50 for the mortgage. They can't pay it because Mr. Scobie is out of work. In the end, Andy gets Mr. Scobie a job at Weaver's Department Store so he can pay the bills he owes to Mr. Weaver. We find out this happy news when the sheriff comes by and Mr. Scobie tells him he can't go fishing because he has to go to work.

I realized that Sheriff Andy not only *enforces* hegemony, he is the very *symbol* of hegemony. Recall that "hegemony" refers generally to a form of control exercised not by direct coercive force but through the more complex process of presenting a certain view of the world and its social relations as natural and inevitable. Since people create symbolic universes in order to make life coherent and understandable, if you can convince somebody that the order of things in your symbolic universe is the best one, then you've got hegemony. In one episode, for instance, the isolated farmer Rafe Hollister doesn't want to be innoculated. Using his traditional logic, he says, "I ain't sick!" But another of Andy's gal pals, Nurse Peggy, insists that she fulfill her state mandate and give him a shot. Andy connives, and, through storytelling, tricks Rafe into believing that if he's not innoculated, he will die. He doesn't order Rafe explicitly or command him to submit to the shot, he just sings dirges, leading Rafe to make up his own mind. Rafe grows anxious with fear; his world disappears. His logic of health is replaced by Andy's and Peggy's and that of the scientific state. A good boy, he rolls up his sleeve.

*That* is hegemony: Andy Taylor—the sheriff without a gun.

The eighth episode made is called "A Feud Is a Feud," and the fact that so early in the show's history the writers focused on one of the most well-known legends of the southern mountains, the Hatfields and the McCoys, indicates the endurance of the story. In this TV version, two families, the Carters and the Wakefields, keep shooting guns in the general direction of each other (the fathers are stubbornly standing in the way of a romance between their two kids). When Andy tries to get to the bottom of the feud and stop the fighting by rooting out the first cause, he finds that the hillbillies are mentally limited to a redundant, circular logic. The exchange goes something, but not exactly, like this:

"Why are you shooting at them?"

"Because they're Wakefields."

"Why are you shooting at the Wakefields?"

"Because I'm a Carter."

"Why are the Carters shooting at the Wakefields?"

"Because we're a-feudin'."

"Well, why are you feuding?"

"Because they're shooting at us!"

This episode illustrates the most widespread belief about Appalachian feuds—that they were the result of irrational family hatreds and an innate tendency toward depravity and violence among mountain people. That explanation, however, obscures the economic forces and social tensions behind the feuds. Stories such as that of the Hatfields and McCoys— racist tales retold in innocence today but derived from imperialist capitalist origins—are, largely, wrong.

It was the encounter with this episode of *The Andy Griffith Show*, combined with some research into the actual facts of the Hatfield-McCoy feud, that led me to think about the manipulation of historical images in popular culture and their uses in the lives of ordinary folks, people not usually considered susceptible to the forces of postmodernism. This line of thought would lead to my epiphanic moment of understanding the ghost dancing movement on the cracker circuit. Telling the Hatfield and McCoy story is important because of the widespread misunderstanding of the facts behind the feud, because the economic forces at work during that time are similar to those in effect on the cracker circuit today, and because looking at this situation contributed to my approach to the final phase of my explorations. The story illustrates how the links from subject to subject are made and what constituted the chain of understandings that would lead me to my conclusions, foreshadowing my ultimate perspective regarding the pop rewriting of culture.

Leaving Hillbilly Days and driving over the ridge from Pikeville into the Tug Valley, I see small frame houses sitting close to the roads like litter. Coal trucks in low gear negotiate the mountains. Every time one passes, it drags a tail of eight or ten cars, impatient and creeping, waiting for a straightaway that never comes. The roads curve constantly, always turning, overhung with trees and cut rock; some curves are cupped by guard rails, beyond and below which is deep grey steaming space. Strings of lights trace conveyor belts. Open pits are surrounded by chain-link fences. Metal signs nailed to trees say "Ambulance Entrance"; the signs are trimmed around their edges with a corroded filigree of rust, like lace.

In a corn patch is a scarecrow made from plastic pipes and tubes, a plywood cutout Angus grazing at the end of a leash tied to its PVC arm. Along the flat roads in the bottom of the valleys, trucks rip past me like bullies in a narrow hallway. Nicknames in cursive are painted on the lips of their hoods and the crowns of their cabs: Big Tom. Walking Tall. Slick. Puppy Power. King Bird. Rolling Stone. I pass a place where men with red arms in tank tops and sleeveless T-shirts are leaning together over the hoods of cars while a gigantic tow truck hauls into the muddy graveled lot of a garage the crushed cab of a coal truck, its windshield sprung and riven like the spine of a well-read book, its hood painted with the name Raw Possum.

It was in this country that the Hatfield and McCoy feud took place—along the Mates, Thacker, Beech, Sulphur and Grapevine creeks that drain into the Tug River, the border between Kentucky and West Virginia. The Tug Valley is flanked by two ridges. Over the ridge to the north is the Guyandotte Valley and the county seat of Logan Courthouse. Over the ridge to the south is the Levisa Fork of the Big Sandy and the county seat of Pikeville. Among the first settlers

Statue of Devil Anse Hatfield at his West Virginia grave

in these mountains were William McCoy and Valentine Hatfield, who came around 1800. Valentine begat Ephraim in 1811, and Ephraim in 1839 begat Anderson, who, for reasons unknown except maybe because of his boyhood habit of capturing bear cubs and wrestling catamounts, was ever after known as Devil Anse.

When the first settlers came into the mountains, they staked claims to vast tracts of land, most of which was mountainside used for hunting or grazing. The tillable bottom lands filled up fast, and, over a couple of generations, the lands were divvied and divvied again among the huge families, until there was no more useful land to be had. The families were big. Valentine Hatfield had twelve kids. His son Ephraim had ten, and one of Ephraim's sons, Devil Anse, had thirteen. Daniel and Margaret McCoy had thirteen. One of their sons, Randolph, and his wife, Sarah, had sixteen.

Game in the mountains was already getting scarce, and after the war the federal government began passing conservation laws restricting hunting and fishing. It also started enforcing liquor taxes, and the treasury department began waging an undeclared war against mountain distillers to collect the revenue owed to the state, a war sometimes compared to the war on Filipinos taking place around the same time across the Pacific. The pressure was on.

Devil Anse never got any land from his father. He got some from his wife's family, and, with a brother-in-law, decided to go into timbering, which was a dubious practice that encouraged dishonesty and corruption and challenged the mountaineers' worldviews. Once, the woods had been open and used as a commons, but, as the valleys filled with farms, boundaries were policed, and court dockets filled with complaints of trespass. In 1872, Devil Anse accused two brothers, Perry and Jacob Cline, of illegally cutting timber on Hatfield land. Perry Cline settled by deeding to Devil Anse five thousand acres along Grapevine Creek, land willed to Cline by his father.

Things looked good for Devil Anse. He was making deals, hiring men. He hustled. He was an entrepreneur, a man of the new age who used his profits to buy frock coats and fine boots for himself and bonnets and combs for his wife and daughters. But Devil Anse was also a man caught between the market economy and the life of the mountains. He was a dealer, but he also came out of a culture of mutual obligation and interdependence where the motives of shame and honor were strong. Devil Anse couldn't read, kept no books, and trusted verbal contracts. To merchants in the growing towns, he was a bumpkin to be bilked. He was not, as legend holds, a violent man. Altina Waller's remarkable book about the Hatfields and McCoys, *Feud* (1988), shows that Devil Anse, when cheated by a merchant, took the offending party to court. Devil Anse went to court often, and he frequently won.

Randolph McCoy was jealous of Devil Anse's increasing success. Called Old Ranel, McCoy lived on the Blackberry Fork of Pond Creek in Pike County, Kentucky. Although the McCoys had come into this country before the Hatfields and secured big land grants, Old Ranel had had to marry into land. His father, Daniel, had been considered an idle layabout who, after fifty years of marriage, was divorced by his wife. Ranel married Sally McCoy, his first cousin and daughter of Samuel, Daniel's brother, and one of the most successful McCoys. Ranel was like the old man—morose and irresponsible. Ranel and his wife were once sued by their cousin Pleasant McCoy for spreading gossip that she had had intercourse with a cow.

In 1878, Old Ranel McCoy, irritated by the award of the Cline land to Anse six months earlier, accused Floyd Hatfield of stealing some pigs. Floyd was Anse's cousin. He and Ellison Hatfield, Anse's brother, had married sisters. Floyd named one of his sons Anderson. The case of the stolen pigs, which Old Ranel lost in court, and a murder that followed, reveal some of the economic forces which weave through the family metaphor that dominates the traditional narratives of the

Hatfield and McCoy feud. On *The Andy Griffith Show*, the feudists fight simply because they are Carters and Wakefields, but the real ones fought for much more complex reasons, a main one being economic tensions caused by the disruption of the way of life in the mountains.

A man on the jury named Selkirk McCoy might have been expected to vote in favor of Old Ranel in the hog dispute, but he didn't. He voted against him, even though he was the nephew of Ranel's wife, Sally. Selkirk McCoy and two of his sons had worked for Devil Anse's timbering crew since 1872. Two years after the hog trial, in June of 1880, there was a fight between a man named Bill Staton and two of Ranel's nephews, Paris and "Squirrel Hunting" Sam McCoy. Bill Staton was the son of Ranel's cousin Nancy, so he should have been a McCoy, but he lived on the West Virginia side of the Tug and was best friends with Floyd Hatfield and Devil Anse's brother Ellison, each of whom married one of Staton's sisters (who were daughters of Ranel's cousin Nancy), so Staton actually was considered a Hatfield.

Sam McCoy was known to shoot a hundred squirrels in a day and donate them for church suppers, but he was nonetheless still considered "queer." In the fight, Staton, the Hatfield loyalist, was killed. Eventually both the McCoys were acquitted on grounds of self-defense. Showing admirable forbearance, Devil Anse had asked his brother Valentine, who was president of the county court at the time, to let the boys off to prevent more trouble. He had enough problems already with his timber business.

Later in 1880, Roseanna McCoy and Johnse Hatfield flirted during election day and began living together at Devil Anse's. The relationship was not the Romeo-and-Juliet-in-homespun that legend suggests: the two separated six months later with Roseanna pregnant. Johnse, who was notoriously priapic, married Nancy McCoy, the daughter of Asa Harmon McCoy, who was a Union sympathizer killed during the Civil War by Devil Anse's Confederate guerillas. Pregnant Roseanna returned home to the McCoys. Victorian morality had not yet ridden the trains into the mountains, so Roseanna's brothers had greater reasons to feel shame than the unwed mother: the men had no land and were forced into wage labor and sharecropping.

A month after Paris McCoy was acquitted for the murder of Bill Staton in the fall of 1880, Tolbert McCoy got himself appointed special deputy in Pike County and, with the help of his brother Bud, arrested Johnse Hatfield on a trumped-up charge of carrying a concealed weapon.

Roseanna, although separated from Johnse, warned Anse. Anse rescued Johnse, and captured the McCoys. Tolbert went back to Pikeville, got more warrants, and three months later arrested Elias and Floyd Hatfield. Still, Devil Anse relied on the courts. Two McCoy cousins even testified in support of the Hatfields.

Two years later, on election day 1882, Tolbert McCoy started demanding that "Bad Lias" Hatfield pay him money owed for a fiddle. "Bad Lias" was a Pike County Hatfield. Devil Anse's brother Elias was a Mates Creek Hatfield and was called Good Lias. Bad Lias said he had already paid the debt. Tolbert kept badgering Bad Lias all day long. Squirrel Huntin' Sam McCoy would later say that on that day strife and ambition were high. Finally, Ellison Hatfield, brother to Devil Anse, intervened. Ellison was a tall, strong, landowning war hero. Tolbert, a useless punk, went crazy. He pulled a knife. He stabbed Ellison more than a dozen times. Spilling blood, Ellison still managed to raise a rock to crush Tolbert, but McCoy was saved when his two brothers, Pharmer and Bud, intervened. Pharmer got a gun and shot Ellison down.

The three McCoys were taken to the Pikeville jail. Good Lias, Ellison's brother, sent word to their other brother Devil Anse that Ellison was nearly dead.

Devil Anse had finally had enough. He said the McCoys would be kept in the Tug Valley and not returned to Pikeville. The Hatfields seized the McCoys, tied them to a corn sled and hauled them down Blackberry Creek to the Tug and across into West Virginia. Devil Anse said that if Ellison died, so would the McCoys.

During the night, Ellison died.

Devil Anse and about twenty others took the boys back across the Tug to the Kentucky side, just across from present-day Matewan, tied them to some pawpaw bushes and filled them full of lead.

I see evidence I'm on the right roads: there's the McCoy Elkhorn Coal Company and Hatfield Salvage. I also see Vanessa's Fashions, Gowns, Tuxedos; Shoes for Sale; Lost Beagle Pup; Pizza N More, with Garfield the Cat. Nailed to a tree is a small handlettered poster: Typing by Karen. I stop for gas. Inside the Meta Produce and Fresh Meats I wedge two dollars into a mayonnaise jar taped with a piece of notebook paper that reads "Minerva Stone Has Lung Cancer. Family Needs Help. Please Donate." In the grassy ditches along the road are rusted chunks of machine, old sofas, a Chevette on blocks with a copper body and blue doors, and a house busted up, walls tilting and insulation spilling from holes. There's Sunny Sands Tanning and Beauty Salon on the edge of Blackberry Creek. These deep valleys don't get much sun, so there are lots of salons: Tropical Sands Salon, Nu Image Beauty Salon, Moonlight Tanning Salon, Fantastic Judy's, Ti-Tan-Ic Beauty Salon, and House of David Hairstyling. I saw old fifty-gallon drums welded onto posts as shelters for gamecocks.

The McCoy boys were executed where the Buskirk Cemetery is now, just below the Nu Image Beauty Salon and across the street from the Honest Injun Outlet, a small strip mall anchored by the Family Dollar and Bargain Basement Tobacco. Matewan is just across the Tug, on the West Virginia side. Two wet dogs, a boxer and a dalmation, run and circle with me through the cemetery. They each keep grabbing plastic bouquets off the graves and plunging back and forth, diving, their wet coats steaming, celebrating the flowers, tearing them up. Coal mining sucked all sorts of immigrants into these hills, and on the headstones are their names: Hamb, Dado, Phaiano, Chafin, Hager. I try to get the dogs to pose beside Sid Hatfield's headstone, but they won't. Sid Hatfield was the police chief in Matewan who fought on the side of the miners during the coal mine wars of the 1920s.

Although the Pike County court indicted Anse and the others for the killings, there was a tacit acceptance in the Tug Valley that justice had been served. No attempt was made to extradite the Hatfields. Nobody outside the region had yet heard about the Hatfields and the McCoys, but Appalachia was just being discovered by capitalists and local color writers.

The best years for Devil Anse had been from 1870 to 1881. He had served as deputy, and his brothers had been constables and judges. He had power and influence. In 1881, though, West Virginia restructured its county court system, disrupting the traditional webs of kinship. The county courts were replaced with circuit courts covering larger territories, with the justices and commissioners now chosen from the new urban middle class, the land speculators, merchants and lawyers, who wanted to stamp out the rustics and attract development on a national scale. In 1881, Anse lost a case in the new circuit court. After that, he never won again.

\*   \*   \*

These changing conditions contributed to Devil Anse's demand for local justice. When Ellison was killed by the McCoy boys in 1882, Anse was becoming aware of his threatened status.

Nothing happened regarding the McCoy killings until four years later. From the beginning, Old Ranel McCoy had been trying to get Perry Cline, a powerful figure in Pikeville, to take action against Devil Anse for the murder of his three boys, but there wasn't enough reason until 1886, when the Norfolk and Western began looking for a route for a rail line linking Virginia and the Ohio River. The two best choices were the Tug Valley and the neighboring Guyandotte Valley. While everybody was waiting for news about the Norfolk and Western route, Anse's creditors began a flurry of claims against him, hoping to get the five thousand acres along the Grapevine Creek, the old Cline land.

Meanwhile, in the fall of 1886, Cap Hatfield and a farmhand whipped some McCoy women with cowtails for telling Ranel about Hatfield activities. Jeff McCoy, one of the new class of landless—therefore dangerous—young men, tried to avenge the whipping but was killed by the Hatfields. Since developers had an interest in showing potential investors that the mountaineers welcomed industrialization, any flare-up of feud activity was bad publicity, so, after the killing of Jeff McCoy, Perry Cline went to Frankfort, Kentucky, to revive the old warrants against the Hatfields. The fact that the Hatfields were West Virginians would make Kentucky look progressive. The governor of West Virginia refused to extradite the Hatfields. At the end of summer in 1887, the governor offered rewards for the Hatfields. Private detectives and bounty hunters made forays into the mountains. The journalists were right behind them.

On December 12, Cline and Bad Frank Phillips rode with a posse to raid the Hatfields, but the only Hatfield they could capture was Selkirk McCoy. The following January 1, 1888, Cap Hatfield led a raid on Ranel McCoy's home in Pike County, killing two of Ranel's children and beating his wife. Ranel escaped by hiding in the pigpen.

Old Ranel hauled his wife and dead children into Pikeville on a wagon. By the eighth, the *Louisville Courier-Journal* had picked up the story. It ran across the country. The Hatfields became murderers and desperadoes, their crimes unmotivated and brutal. Bad Frank Phillips and his posse began raiding Hatfield territory. What had started as a dispute between neighbors over timber rights ended as a symbol of clashing historical forces and the struggle for economic and political power.

Ironically, this phase of the feud, the one which was widely publicized, was carried out by different people. The analysis presented by Altina Waller in *Feud* shows that, of the thirty-seven Hatfields, only four were new to the feud. Of the "McCoys," only one third were related to Old Ranel, and the number was up from eight to forty, all brand new to the feud. They were mostly Pikeville area residents, not Tug River folk. Forty percent of the recruits Cline gathered to hunt down the Hatfields were among the wealthiest people in town. The bottom half of the group were dependent on wage labor. Half of Cline's group were from Unionist/Republican families who favored industrial development. The elite of Pikeville—the forces of commerce and industry—were aligned against the traditional culture of subsistence farming and small-scale timbering. Devil Anse was not only an old Confederate but an obstacle to development.

On January 30, 1888, eleven days after a battle between the Hatfields and the group from Pikeville, Devil Anse sold the old Cline land along Grapevine Creek to a group of Philadelphia capitalists for seven thousand dollars. Later that year, railroad surveyors broke a path along the Tug River. By 1890, two years after Devil Anse was forced to sell it, the Grapevine Creek land was worth seventy-five thousand dollars.

Devil Anse moved away from the Tug Valley, up a mountain where he built a barricaded house. He was never arrested. He hadn't done anything wrong. Some of the Hatfields were finally tried in August of 1889. Valentine Hatfield died in the penitentiary. Ellison Mounts was the only person hanged as a result of the Hatfield-McCoy feud. Mounts, who is today considered a mentally deficient scapegoat, was executed on February 18, 1890, only weeks after the massacre of the Sioux at Wounded Knee in South Dakota.

The reputation of the Hatfields and the McCoys, and of other hillbillies in Kentucky and West Virginia, was one imposed upon them by people with an interest in getting rid of the mountain cultures that conflicted with new industrial capitalist values. On February 18, 1888, the *New York Times* reported that "the latest vendetta in the backwoods of Kentucky shows the purely savage character of the population more strongly than almost any previous instance." Claiming that Valentine Hatfield had five wives, the report went on to say that "it is evident that a strong course of common schools, churches, soap and water, and other civilizing influences is required before these simple children of nature will forbear to kill a man whenever they take a dislike to him."

Mountain folk interfered with development. The *Wheeling Intelligencer* complained: "Capitalists refuse to come and prospect because they say they are afraid of our outlaws. You cannot get them to go into the interior to inspect our timber and coal lands for fear they will be ambushed."

Johnse Hatfield went on to become an agent for the United States Steel, Coal and Coke Company. Cap Hatfield learned to read and became a lawyer. Good Lias Hatfield, Devil Anse's brother, became chief of police in Logan. One of his sons became governor of West Virginia in 1913. The governor's daughter married the president of the United States Steel Corporation. The Tug Valley is now the heart of one of the nation's richest coal fields. Where there were no towns, two were built: Williamson was laid out by a group of investors, and Matewan was founded and named for the hometown of one of the railroad engineers, Mattewan, New York. (The local residents, exercising what little autonomy they had left, deleted a "t" and changed the pronunciation of the town's name.) Grapevine Creek ran red with the sludge from mines.

Devil Anse died in 1921. That same year, Sid Hatfield, the chief of police in Matewan, along with the mayor, Cabal Testerman, tried to stop some Baldwin-Felts detectives from evicting striking coal miners from their company homes. Sid killed seven agents. The mayor and some bystanders were killed. A year later, Sid and his wife were assassinated in nearby McDowell County. The killing sparked the West Virginia mine wars, which were quelled at the battle of Blair Mountain.

On the edge of Matewan is a red caboose with the word "Matewan" painted in large letters on the side, complete with stylized bulletholes. A sign posted nearby says Blasting Zone. They're widening the road. On a track above the town along the edge of some hills, an endless series of coal cars pass. There are picnic tables in deep wet grass on the edge of the Tug. The historic marker reads: "The Hatfield McCoy Feud. The death in 1882 of Ellison Hatfield, brother of Devil Anse, from wounds he received during an election day fight in Pike County, Ky., with three sons of Randolph McCoy, and their subsequent killing by the Hatfields, triggered America's most famous family feud. The feud continued 6 years across the Tug River and brought death to an unknown number of Hatfields, McCoys and their kinsmen."

I drive through Matewan and into West Virginia looking for the grave of Devil Anse. I stop at a place selling baseball cards, paperbacks and

Bruce Lee posters. The two young men inside don't know where the Hatfield graves are. I go up the road and stop at a gas station. Inside, one wall is covered with pictures of local babies. The cashier doesn't know, says, maybe up the road some, she thinks there's a cemetery. Next door is a headstone retailer, so I walk over there, thinking they must surely know, and they said keep going this way and then that way and it'll be on my left. A small TV is on and they're watching what looks like a soap opera or spice channel porn—a sweaty guy with no shirt is pitching hay. A woman is watching him from a horse's stall. The man sitting at a desk covered with shattered pieces of mirror tells me the cemetery is easy to find. There's a marker by the side of the road. You cross the creek and walk up the hill.

In the Hatfield cemetery, empty twelve-pack cartons and wine cooler bottles lie in the gravel around the historical marker. It has begun to rain lightly, and there's a mist coming off the trees. I cross the creek and climb the hill. The Italian marble statue of Devil Anse, erected in 1921, stands above his own grave, as well as those of his wife, his sons, his grandsons, his nephews, and his daughters-in-law. There is no moonshine jug marked XXX, no corncob pipe, no floppy hat. There is dignity in the luminous stone and the rugged visage that stares out toward the misted hills. Back in beneath the trees are the graves of some Greeks who had come to work the coal mines. They died in Appalachia and were buried in the hillsides under short blankets of cement; ball jars embedded in the cement as permanent vases are now filled with leaves. The names of these dead Greek miners are scratched on the crosses in the alphabet of Socrates.

I take a picture of Devil Anse's statue. I think to myself that he don't look nothing like they say.

# CHAPTER FOUR

# THIS YEAR'S HERNANDO

## The De Soto Celebration at Bradenton, Florida

I'm standing on the hot plaza in front of the Manatee County court-house in Bradenton, Florida, on the southern side of Tampa Bay, when a slim, jumpy reporter from a St. Petersberg newspaper sidles up to me. He's wearing dark aviator sunglasses. He folds his arms in front of himself, across his chest, looking like De Niro as Travis Bickle in *Taxi Driver*, when he edges up to the secret service man and asks him what size gun he's packing. The reporter doesn't look at me directly; we're both watching the little bunch of protesters standing at the curb along Manatee Boulevard. They are wearing bright yellow T-shirts that declare "De Soto Was a Slave Trader" and waving at the traffic with their signs reading "De Soto Equals Rape," and "De Soto—Pioneer in Ethnic Cleansing."

The reporter asks me, "Who ya with?"

I tell him I'm not really sure how to answer that. I say I used to be a freelancer, used to write for a paper, but that right now I was just looking around to see what I could see, driving around checking out weekend expressions of public culture. I tell him I have been to events like Rattlesnake Roundup, Swine Time, and Hillbilly Days, and that now I have come to Florida to see what goes on during the representation of Europe's first contact with the people of America's Southeast. I tell him I am in Bradenton for the De Soto Celebration, which has been happening for more than fifty years, and that I just happened to read about the protest in the newspaper so I thought I would check it out.

I ask, "Are the Indians really going to block the parade like they say?"

The reporter's mouth is set and grim. He lights a cigarette with a zippo. The women along the side of Manatee Boulevard begin to shake rattles made from beer cans painted neon yellow and orange and filled with gravel. Some men bring rawhide drums out of the back of their VW van, while others get plastic buckets and turn them upside down. They all begin, in some confusion, to set up a rhythm. The reporter answers my question with the prideful exhausted confidence of a flatfoot hack who knows his beat.

"Oh, sure," he says. "Sure, sure, sure." He's a fast talker. "I'm sure. I'm sure. They've had their little classes in civil disobedience. They'll get out there and get hauled in and that'll be it. They'll get arrested and get bailed out and that's that." He pauses, glints a peek sideways at me from behind his shades. He says, "Yeah, they're just going to sit in the road. But there's rumors about a militant faction that promises they're going to run around through the parade route and disrupt. But the skinheads will probably put a stop to that."

Skinheads?

"Yeah. You know, you never know. You hear rumors. Those fuckers. Just rumors. You know, I've heard it all. 'The skinheads are gonna kick some ass.' Right now I'm sure there's some rednecks drinking beer saying, 'We're gonna kick some Indian ass.' "

I had been hearing about "the Indians" and their planned protests against the De Soto Celebration since I got to Bradenton the day before.

Protesting the De Soto Celebration

I point out to the reporter that very few, if any, of the group along the sidewalk are Indians. Or, at least they don't *look* like Indians.

He says, "Yeah. But you know, they all say they've got some Indian in 'em somewhere. They say they're three-sixteenths or four-fifths. Everybody's got some Indian in them."

I say, "They could be. Maybe they're getting into Indian heritage."

He says, "Yeah. You know, you never know. Could be. You're right. I don't give a shit. It gives them something, some meaning in their lives." He grimaces, nods, snorts, and imputes a simplistic motive to the protesters, explaining their behavior by saying they're a bunch of losers who don't fit in. To illustrate his point, he picks out a woman: "See that, uh, heavyset lady?" He gestures toward a woman who is indeed very big. "She's here because she finally gets to hang out with some people. She has a reason to get up today because the fat bitch gets to go downtown and beat a drum. Fucking shit."

I tell him I see what he means.

He says, "I think I'll go over and ask some Anglo chick why she's here."

He goes, and I'm relieved to be left alone to watch the cops and the TV crews while the crowd of protesters grows larger. I had already talked to some of the Anglo chicks. One was wearing a black hooded sweatshirt, the hood up over her head despite the heat. She was passing out leaflets detailing some of Hernando de Soto's crimes. She told me that her group was part of a peace coalition, and, yes, it was true, they were not all Indians. I said I thought it was funny that everybody called them Indians anyway.

"I know," she said. "We don't mind, though. It's good. We're all Indians in a way, I guess." The sun was hot and intense and my forearms were getting burned, so I told her I didn't get the hood. She said it represented death. Just like de Soto. *De Soto Equals Death!* She said de Soto had dogs that killed Indians.

"He was really horrible," she said. "He was worse than they thought. De Soto wasn't an explorer, he was a conqueror. He came here looking for slaves and gold. He shouldn't be celebrated. And that's all we want— we just want them to change the name of the celebration. They could call it the Manatee Festival. Call it the Save the Manatee Festival." She handed me a flyer that explained why de Soto, once thought to be a tragic hero of European conquest, was now considered the scourge of the Southeast.

This was a Saturday in May of 1993. On the previous Wednesday, the Native People's Information Exchange had filed a suit with a federal judge in Tampa asking that the parade be stopped. The theme of the parade was "A Celebration of Our Heritage, Our People, Our Present, Our Future." The petitioners argued that the celebration of Hernando de Soto was an incitement to commit genocide. "The parade devalues Indian life," said Sheridan Murphy, executive director of Tiyospaya American Indian Student Organization. She explained how they had concluded that the Grand Illuminated Parade—a nighttime, brightly lighted caravan of floats for Busch Gardens and Minute Maid orange juice—would constitute a threat to life. "It's undoubtedly a form of advocacy, and advocacy is a form of incitement." Darryl Barking Dog, the executive director of the American Indian Issues and Action Committee in St. Petersberg, said his group was going to block the road because "De Soto was considered the scourge of the earth. That certainly isn't the kind of man who should be celebrated. This is insulting to us."

David Goyette, of the Florida American Indian Movement, said, "We will stop the parade. We plan on being arrested." Sheridan Murphy said, "We expect to be hurt." David Wilcox, the president of the De Soto Celebration, said, "If they insist on being arrested, they will have that opportunity." The mayor of Bradenton said that history, "awful as it may be," cannot be erased. He said they wouldn't stop the event, but they might change the name. "Maybe the word celebration isn't the best word. Maybe they should call it a festival," he said, with bizarre logic. A longtime resident of Manatee County wrote the local newspaper: "As a child I sat on Manatee Avenue and watched the parade go by and had a great time. I have never considered the De Soto Celebration to 'celebrate genocide.' I never got that message growing up."

In the shifting cultural landscape, however, the meaning of Hernando de Soto's adventures was being refigured. The De Soto Celebration was the site of yet another battle over public memory, and the historical society was losing the struggle over meaning. The pressure from Native American activists had already begun to chip away at the celebration. In earlier years, the De Soto Historical Society would restage the conquistador's landing at the De Soto National Monument on the edge of Tampa Bay, complete with victorious sword fight against the natives. But the park service denied the permit this year, fearing bad publicity and the costs for extra security to deal with the promised and inevitable protests. The Shriners used to ride in the parade, but this year they too pulled out, fearing "violent Indian attacks." I read in the newspaper that the grand marshals for the parade were the characters from the movie *Aladdin*, who would be riding in Mickey Mouse's Li*mouse*ine, in spite of the potential hostilities. Friday evening before the De Soto Ball, I watched the report on a local TV station's six o'clock news, which said: "The century-old De Soto Celebration is part of Manatee County's history. But some American Indians say it celebrates a man who killed their people. City officials term the objections ludicrous, and say they won't drop the celebration, although they may consider changing its name." Without remarking on the difficulty of celebrating something without mentioning its name, the anchorperson cut to Bill, with the weather.

Hernando de Soto was from Xerez, Spain. When he was nineteen he captained a troop of horsemen who rode with Pizarro to sack the city of Cuzco and capture Atabalipa, the lord of Peru. De Soto returned to the Spanish court, rich with Inca gold, decked in silks and served by slaves. He married Dona Ysabel de Bobadilla, daughter of Pedrarias Davila, count of Punonrostro. Pedrarias Davila was the man from whom de Soto learned how to handle man-eating dogs.

In 1513 Juan Ponce de León, while commanding two caravels in search of "the fountain which converts old men into youths," had been blown by a storm to the coast of a new land, which he named La Florida. When de Soto returned from the plundering of Peru, he asked the emperor Charles the Melancholy to let him conquer La Florida. In May of 1539, de Soto and an army of six hundred sailed from Cuba in five ships, two caravels and two pinnaces. The men wore helmets, breastplates and coats of mail. They armed themselves with arquebuses, crossbows, shields, swords, Biscayne lances, one piece of artillery, and packs of killer dogs—greyhounds, bloodhounds and mastiffs.

The use of killer dogs has contributed heavily to the bad reputation from which the conquistadores have since suffered. Dogs had been used in wars against the Moors in Spain—often eating the bodies of Moorish children—and the subjection of the Canaries, Peru, Panama and Nicaragua. After combat, the dogs frequently gorged on human flesh, which trained their tastes, served as a reward and was cheap dog food. Spaniards were known to kill Indians in the West Indies and Central America just to feed their dogs; butchered quarters of Indians were sold in the markets. Sometimes when the Spanish armies marched, they had Indians carry the huge mastiffs in hammocks so the dogs wouldn't bruise their feet or get tired. By the time killer dogs were loosed in Tampa Bay, they had already been used when the Spanish searched South America for the fabled Land of Cinnamon. In Nicaragua, Pedrarias Davila staged man-dog combats in the plaza to train puppies how to kill. When he served with his future father-in-law in Panama, de Soto became addicted to the *monteria infernal*, the man hunt (Varner and Varner 1983).

Marching into Florida, the Land of Flowers, de Soto's army carried portable forges and lots of cheese. They carried raw iron for making chains and collars for captives. They brought along alchemists with crucibles for refining gold. They herded a drove of hogs which would grow during the expedition to number in the thousands. They had 213 horses. They had twelve priests, eight clergymen and four monks, who toted holy relics and a stockpile of sacramental wine and bread for administering communion. When the army landed at Tampa Bay they thought they might find flying monkeys or unicorns or a cyclops.

It's hard to know exactly what the southeastern Indians were like before contact with Europeans, but anthropologists have come to this conclusion: without their horses, the Spanish would not have had a chance. The Indians could fight with clubs, darts, slings and sticks of various lengths, but they preferred to use the bow and arrow. Indian boys as young as three practiced with bows, shooting mice, lizards and insects. The bows were strung so tight that a Spaniard could barely pull one back to his face, while the Indians easily pulled the weapons past their ears. In the time it took a Spaniard to reload a crossbow or an arquebus, an Indian could shoot six or seven arrows. Once an Indian arrow that was nothing but a fire-hardened reed nailed a Spaniard to his horse, running through his thigh, the wooden saddle, the quilted saddle blanket and into the horse. The Indians could sometimes shoot an arrow through a horse from stem to stern. If the supply of arrows ran out, the bows were used as clubs and were heavy enough to split skulls.

When warriors travelled they were nearly naked. Before they headed for a fight, they fasted and drank button snakeroot; some would eat deer meat for speed. They would sometimes paint themselves red and black, the colors of conflict and death in the Southeastern Ceremonial Complex. They carried bows and arrows, knives, war clubs, sometimes blankets, some parched corn meal, dried cornbread, leather and cord to repair their moccasins, and sometimes armor and shields made of leather and woven cane. Once on the trail, the warriors would never lean against anything while sitting or standing. Sometimes if a man snapped a twig, he had to pick it up and carry it until dark. The warriors might divide up into groups, travel in single file, and step exactly in each other's tracks. If somebody had a bad dream, the whole group would turn around and go home.

Scalping was an old southeastern practice, and de Soto's men were often so treated. To get the scalp, the warrior would make an incision around the top of the head, plant his feet on the dead man's neck, and pull. In later wars, one Creek warrior became famous for pulling scalps off with his teeth. Sometimes instead of scalping, they would cut the heads off and take them home to mount on posts and the tops of their public buildings. The Timucuans in Florida were known to cut up dead men and hang pieces from the trees, and the Natchez to tie captives to a frame, scalp them alive, and poke them with burning cane. Sometimes it went on for days. The scalp was given to the dead man's relatives, who were supposed to wipe their tears with it. More commonly the person was tied to a stake, with his arms lashed down, and he would run on a leash of grapevine tied to his neck. Wet clay would be put on his head to protect his scalp. Women and children would beat the captive with sticks and burning cane. If he showed fear, everybody howled with laughter. If he fainted, they splashed him with cold water. When he finally died, they scalped him and chopped him up (Hudson 1976: 240–57).

In 1934, Congress passed Public Act No. 440 authorizing the creation of the United States De Soto Expedition Commission to locate the landing place and route of de Soto's army as part of the commemoration of the four hundredth anniversary of his landing in 1539. The commission, headed by the Smithsonian's John R. Swanton, met with archivists, local historical societies and representatives of the Spanish government. They consulted old maps, made surveys, got help from the department of agriculture and the war department, and, after motor car tours and exhaustive readings of the earliest retellings of the de Soto story, designated Shaw's Point, on the southern edge of Tampa Bay, as the place where, in 1539, de Soto and his army first touched ground (the most recent archeological evidence suggests a landing site deeper in the bay).

A section of mangrove swamp has been set aside as park land at the De Soto National Monument. A looping trail cuts through the cabbage palm, sabal palmetto, strangler fig, prickly pear, yucca, black mangrove and button mangrove (which makes a smokeless fire), and the sea grape, the leaves of which were used for stationery by the conquistadores. An eight-ton granite marker was donated by the Society of Colonial Dames of America and put at the point on May 30, 1939.

The genealogy of the De Soto Celebration is different from that of the festivals like Rattlesnake Roundup and Swine Time. While those events derive from the fragmented traditions of agricultural festivals, the De Soto Celebration is related to the nineteenth-century tradition of historical pageants, at which inspirational vignettes of heroic triumphs would be restaged as public civics lessons. In 1941, the Colonial Dames repeated their commemoration, and this time Manatee County staged the De Soto Pageant Spectacle, which was a costumed reenactment of the first landing of the Spanish. As the 1993 celebration booklet put it: "Volunteer actors portray the native Indians when de Soto and his Conquistadors come ashore in search of gold and glory . . . A terrible battle ensues. Although the Indians fight fiercely, they are no match for the better equipped Conquistadors, and de Soto is soon triumphant . . ."

Inside the air-conditioned gift shop at the De Soto National Monument is a display of some Spanish weapons and armor. For sale are copies of Garcilaso de la Vega's *The Florida of the Inca*, the book from which most people, including me, get the fullest (and often wildly exaggerated) portrait of the expedition. Also for sale are decks of Great Explorer cards—"Fifty One Adventurers Who Changed the World"—and "The Easy to Make Columbus Discovers America Panorama." A movie narrated by Fernando Lamas runs in a screening room; the ranger guessed the movie was made in about 1970. I watched it with some small families and two teenage boys who kept making squeaking noises, like imitations of trapped animals. At the end of the movie, Fernando Lamas got his biggest laugh with a line uttered in all sincerity but today received, even by the mom and pop and kids behind me, with involuntary chuckles and disbelieving chirps of "Did you hear that?" Speaking in the voice of an anonymous Spaniard, Lamas said, "Fifty men were lost. Many died of fever. The Indians fought for every mile of river to the gulf. They never could understand that we came in peace, that all we really wanted was their gold."

The ranger told me that the park service didn't have enough money to make a new movie.

When de Soto landed in Tampa Bay, his army had to fight. A conquistador named Narvaez, the captain of a failed Spanish expedition to the area eleven years earlier, had cut off the nose of the local chief and had his mother eaten by dogs. When de Soto's ships entered the bay, plumes of smoke rose as warning signals. Horsemen sent to capture guides found deserted villages. In the villages the Spaniards (who, in most of the oldest works about the expedition are usually called "Christians") found carved statuary draped in strings of pearls.

De Soto's most enormous break was finding Juan Ortiz. Ortiz was a survivor of the Narvaez expedition who had narrowly avoided being killed by the Indians, and had been living with them. When the Spaniards came again into the land, Ortiz was allowed to go meet them. Being heavily tatooed like the Indians, Ortiz again narrowly escaped death, this time at the end of a Biscayne lance, when Spanish soldiers bore down upon him, pulling up only at the last moment when Ortiz shouted "Seville!" and the name of the Virgin Mary. Ortiz had learned much of a local Indian language and was able to act as de Soto's translator. With Ortiz's help, de Soto soon heard about a place where there was so much gold that the people wore golden hats. The Spaniards marched toward that country.

De Soto fought Indians all the way through middle and north Florida. The narrow trails through the swamps barely allowed two men to walk abreast. When captured guides led them astray, they would in turn be disemboweled by dogs. The army, always running out of food, was forced to eat unripe corn, watercress and palmetto cabbage. The Spaniards considered themselves lucky when they could catch Indian dogs, which looked like guinea pigs and were raised for food. It is said that these dogs did not learn to bark until they came into contact with European dogs. Some people think the animals were actually herds of domesticated possums.

The only way the Spaniards could manage communication with the Indians was through a chain of translations. Ortiz knew only the language of a people from middle Florida. As they moved north, the Spaniards had to find Indians who were bilingual and could understand both Ortiz and the Indians of the next region. As de Soto moved deeper into the continent, eventually making it as far as North Carolina, communications sometimes went through more than a dozen voices; simple information took hours to decipher, and then, more likely than not, was wrong.

The Spanish soldiers were picked off one by one. A man would walk off a short distance and never come back; those looking for him would find only a headless trunk. If they buried the body, the Indians often came back, dug it up and dismembered it, cutting the flesh at the joint with cane knives, then busting the bones with clubs and carrying the chunks on the ends of spears.

The Indians encountered, almost always described as well formed and muscular, could be very tough. Some could outrun a horse and run down deer. Once when an Indian was fighting with an ax, the Spanish cut one of his hands off, but he still gripped the ax with his other hand and the bloody stump. He kept fighting until he was sliced in half, and even then, before his body flopped in two, he managed to shout a curse. Another time a guide led some Spaniards astray, and before they could kill him, the guide, who was in chains, attacked them. The Spaniards slashed and stabbed him, but his body was so tough the weapons barely cut—"the many strokes given him left no more wounds than did the lashes which they customarily inflicted with a rod of quince or wild olive." One man used two hands to impale the Indian on a lance, but could only stick it in a few inches. Then they loosed a greyhound to gut and eat him; thinking he was finally dead, they heard the dog start howling. They rushed back and found the Indian with his thumbs in the dog's mouth, tearing its head apart. The Spaniards finished killing the Indian, cutting off his hands because they could not be pried loose from the dog's jaws.

On Friday night I went to the De Soto Ball, held at the Bradenton Municipal Auditorium. The male members of the De Soto Historical Society wear black trousers, red satin shirts and gold cummerbunds; their wives wear evening gowns. Those who aren't members can sit in bleacher seats in a balcony if they have paid five dollars to play an observer's role in this class spectacle, to look down on the women in gowns and the men in satin as they drink cocktails. Before each celebration the members elect one of their number to serve as Hernando de Soto throughout the next year, dressing in the cuirass, helmet and pantaloons of the Spanish conquistador and making appearances in parades and publicity events. Anybody who has been a Hernando in the past wears a gold satin shirt and red cummerbund. At the ball they install this year's Hernando.

In the bulletin, the outgoing Hernando wrote his message:

> It's been a challenge for me to portray Hernando De Soto as a discoverer, a man of vision, but obviously a man who to our modern eyes had some shortcomings. Civilization was completely different in those days, and we don't necessarily commend all the things De Soto did. But we do commend that he came here, and we try to spread the word about the great life here.
>
> So many people come here from other places, and they don't know our history. It's everywhere—in our street names, for example—and we try to bring those names off the street signs and to life. It's extremely rewarding and extremely fun.

He offered this advice to all future Hernandos: "Sit down with your wife and make sure she's happy with the situation. Being Hernando is a joint effort by the spouse and you; you cannot do it without her. . . . The wife is Hernando as much as you are. Hernando is really all of us who put in thousands of hours on the Celebration."

In a spooky, undoubtedly apocryphal yet unintentionally predictive threat, one Indian chief in northern Florida named Vitachucho is said to have chastised the Spanish for coming into the country. He said if the conquistadores were virtuous they never would have left their homes. They would have stayed in Spain, planted their gardens and practiced their virtues, instead of wandering the globe committing robberies and murders shamelessly. Vitachucho said the Spanish lacked virtue because they went from land to land, plundering, taking the wives and daughters of others instead of bringing their own with them, and maintaining themselves off the labor of others. Vitachucho then told de Soto that flocks of birds were going to swoop down carrying corrosive poison in their beaks and that the poison would cause the men's bodies to mortify while they were still alive. He said the air and water and herbs of the land would be so poisoned that neither horse nor rider could escape with his life.

At one point Vitachucho reportedly planned an ambush of the Spaniards, but de Soto struck first. De Soto's horsemen broke the Indians and drove hundreds into a nearby lake where all night long the warriors treaded water. Once in a while three or four would cling together, one would climb up, shoot an arrow and drop back into the lake. When the Indians sneaked under lilypads to the shore, horsemen drove them back. All the Indians gave up. The last ones were dragged from the lake by their hair.

Vitachucho was captured, but he spread the word that he would lead an uprising. One day while eating with de Soto, Vitachucho stood up, cracked all his joints (an Indian practice when one was preparing for a fight), and lunged at de Soto. He grabbed de Soto by the collar and crushed his face with his fist. Blood spurted from de Soto's eyes, nose and mouth. Vitachucho could have killed him with one more slug, but the Indian was run through by Spanish swords.

The chained and captive Indians exploded. They grabbed pots of hot food, large animal bones left over after supper, stools, benches, tree branches. More than a thousand Indians were killed. Only four Spaniards were killed, but almost all the rest had cuts, bruises, broken arms and legs and knocked-out teeth. The young kids were divided up as slaves, and the rest of the prisoners were tied to stakes. The Spaniards made their Indian allies kill the captives so that the Indians would dare not abandon the conquistadores. De Soto could not eat solid food for twenty days. This episode occurred fifteen miles west of Micanopy. The Spaniards marched north and spent their first winter near Tallahassee.

North Florida was extraordinarily fertile. The Spaniards marched through miles of squash, bean and corn fields; the pumpkins and plums were better than any in Europe. They found a young Indian boy who said he knew of a land where yellow metal was taken out of the ground, but one night the boy woke up foaming at the mouth, saying that a demon with a giant face accompanied by imps had come and forbidden him under pain of death to guide the Spaniards. The boy, bruised and scared, said that the imps had pulled him from the hut and beat him until he couldn't move. To solve the problem, the Spaniards baptized him and named him Pedro.

In March of 1540, the Spaniards moved on. Most of the Indian slaves had died during the winter. They found more Indians who stored maize in raised cribs, made shawls from the inner bark of trees, wore black deerskin shoes and dressed deerskin so well it looked like fine broadcloth. The Spanish put iron collars on the Indians and made them grind corn and carry luggage. They said that the women and children would be upset at being captured until they got a hundred leagues from home; by then they would be as lost as the Spanish and could go about unbound.

The Indian boy named Pedro guided de Soto through Georgia but kept leading the army astray. They wanted to dog him but he was the only one Ortiz understood. In South Georgia de Soto made friends with a chief who enlisted their help to destroy some neighbors. The Indians rampaged, scalping men, women and children and burning huts and temples. De Soto, fearing retribution, sent the Indians away, but for two days the Spaniards marched through an abandoned land of scalped corpses.

At Cofitachequi on the border of Georgia and South Carolina, de Soto met a woman who was queen of her people. She gave de Soto a string of pearls that wrapped around three times and hung to her waist. In the village temples he found hundreds of pounds of pearls, baskets of furs and skins, Spanish weapons from an earlier, failed, expedition, wooden statues twelve feet high, figures of babies and birds made from pearls. The Lady of Cofitachequi gave the Spanish food and pearls. De Soto then chained her up and used her as a ticket for safe passage through her lands.

The Spanish marched through Cherokee land, across the Appalachians and into north Georgia where they found bear fat stored in calabashes, drawn as fine as olive oil. They found walnut oil, honeycomb, and grapevines that climbed to the tops of trees and hung out over clear rivers. They stayed for thirty days to fatten their horses.

In August of 1540, the Spaniards met Tuscaloosa, the greatest Indian they would ever see. Tuscaloosa was, they say, broad at the shoulder and small at the waist, a foot and a half taller than any other Indian. They met him sitting under an umbrella of deerskin dressed as fine as taffeta. While they were in Tuscaloosa's province, a malady caused by a lack of salt broke out among the Spanish. The illness, starting with a fever, caused the Spaniards' bodies to turn green; after a few days, they would begin to emit a stink that could be detected at a distance of several paces. The Indians showed them a remedy made from the ash of a certain herb. Those who used the remedy lived; those who rejected it died of a general mortification of the intestines.

De Soto took Tuscaloosa with him as they traveled into Alabama to the town of Mauvilla, which is reckoned to have been near the junction of the Alabama River and the Tombigbee. The town was on a plain and was surrounded by a high wall made from the trunks of trees woven together with branches and plastered with a smooth mortar of clay and straw. Windows ran along the walls, and every fifty feet was a tower.

The tree trunks that formed the palisade had taken root and sprouted, and an arbor had grown up that shaded the village. There were about eighty houses, some of them so large they could hold as many as fifteen hundred people.

Once they got to Mauvilla, Tuscaloosa told de Soto to go on without him. Instead, de Soto put Tuscaloosa's house under guard and after a few days began to suspect a plot. The grounds outside the fort had been picked clean of all plants and roots, making a massive killing plain. There weren't any women or children around, except for the young girls who had danced as part of the welcome party. They noticed that the houses were packed with thousands of armed men.

Finally the Indians struck, pouring from the houses. The Spanish were overwhelmed and forced to retreat from the city, abandoning all their supplies. They fought for three hours on the plain. The Spanish eventually hacked through the walls of the palisade and set the town on fire. The cavalry rode up and down between burning buildings, killing Indians with their lances. De Soto was shot through the thigh but kept fighting for several hours standing in the saddle. Tuscaloosa's warriors lay dead in heaps. Hundreds of women hiding in the houses were burned to death. The fighting didn't stop until all the Indians were dead.

Dozens of Spaniards were killed, and, even worse, forty-two horses were dead. Eighteen of the dead men had been shot through the eyes or mouth because the Indians had adjusted their fire to avoid the body armor. Every Spaniard left alive had a wound of some sort. They had no shelter, clothes, or bandages. They flayed the bodies of dead Indians and used the body fat as ointment. For the next month while they recuperated, they ate their dead horses. When they foraged for food, they kept finding dead Indians in thickets and ravines. While some sources say eleven thousand Indians died, the figure is probably closer to three thousand.

I was milling among the members and guests, leaving my seat in the bleachers. One man, a visiting member of the Minnesota Winter Carnival, was dressed in the chilled blue satin of a czarist sleigh captain, with rope decor on his chest and shoulders, and a tall, stylized fur bonnet. The bartender at the cash bar must have remembered him from a function held the night before, because when the Commander of the North Wind walked up, the bartender said, "I remember you. Let's see . . . A screwdriver?" And the Snow King laughed, har har, and said, "You screwed me to the ground last night!" Within the historical society, there is a subset, the Conquistadors, who wear the helmets and garb of storybook characters. In the restroom two Conquistadors were standing at the urinals, working through the folds and secret passages of their pantaloons and tights. One was telling the other about the time he used the women's restroom and how, when someone protested, he said, "Hey, look, I'm wearing pantyhose, aren't I?" As they did quick bends at the knee to complete their projects, their swords clanking against white porcelain, the other Conquistador said, "You're making a lot of additions to your house, aren't you?"

To start the evening the Conquistadores march in and form an honor guard, between which guests will walk as they are introduced. As they took their places, the emcee for the evening, Vernon "Mr. De Soto" DeSear said, "You look great, guys."

The room, full of Manatee County business people, erupted with the De Soto Historical Society's signature cheer: Olé!

Mr. DeSear then announced that the federal judge in Tampa has refused the Indians' petition to stop the parade.

Olé!

When the cheering subsided, Mr. DeSear kicked it up again. "We have one message for those Indians—get a life!"

Olé! Olé!

Among the guests were the mayor of Bacarrota, Spain, where Hernando spent his childhood; the reigning Miss Mexico; and John de Soto, a lineal descendent of Hernando. Also present were the Queen of Ice and Snow and King Neptunius the Fourteenth from a St. Petersberg party society.

Olé! Olé!

The evening's fun had an aggressive edge to it, as though the partying were being done under siege, while outside the ballroom the city was being threatened by infidels and an age was passing, an era over. The society has been and still is the power structure of Manatee County—store owners, cops, lawyers, dentists, sales managers, realtors, executives of banks and Coca-Cola bottlers (the very first Hernando was played by Sergeant Bill Sheetz, chief radio operator of the Bradenton police department)—but they have since collided with the righteous indignation of what David Wilcox, the president of the Hernando De Soto Historical Society, called in his annual message "politically correct multi-culturalists":

"The times, they are a' changin'. . . . The complexities of our modern world and the pressures of the politically correct multi-culturalists are here to stay. You will recall that the De Soto Historical Society dove head first in to the 90's a few years ago when we brought in our first black and female member. . . . [W]hile we want to expand our understanding of all peoples and cultures, such understanding should not come at the sacrifice of our rich Spanish heritage. The 450 years since Hernando de Soto stepped onto our shores, has given us a historic past that is worth preserving."

(My unscientific data indicated that families of Spanish descent were not the bulk of the historical society's members: in the bulletin I read names like Heitmuller, Anderson, Corali, Pickering, Hildebrandt, Levy.)

An unsigned statement in the bulletin declared: "Modern Conquistadores have the same dedicated spirit as their predecessors did in 1539. Today's Conquistadores, however, are not seeking treasure in the new world. As members of The De Soto Historical Society, their dedication is to the enrichment of our community in general. . . ."

I saw an advertisement in the fiftieth anniversary bulletin from 1989 which rephrased that sentiment more succinctly: "Hernando explored it—but to 'BUY OR SELL IT' Call G— L—, Broker Salesman."

After the slaughter at Mauvilla, de Soto's men had had enough. They wanted to march to the sea and meet their ships. De Soto refused to give up. He had a lot invested; his reputation was at stake. If he quit now, La Florida probably would never be conquered: first there had been Ponce, then Ayllon, then Narvaez. De Soto marched north, away from the ships. The Spanish moved on to the land of the Chickasaw, to the banks of the Yazoo.

In March 1541, a surprise attack against the Spaniards while they occupied a town led them to lose all their supplies again. The Indians blew conch shells, whirled braided cords with embers at their ends until they flamed, then shot burning arrows into the houses. Half the town was in flames before the Spaniards woke up. Their wounded burned in the huts; horses burned to death in their stalls. De Soto was one of only two who were able to get mounted, but in the smoke the stampeding horses on the loose scared the Indians and they were beaten back. Eleven more Spaniards and fifty more horses died. Many Spaniards were naked because they had to crawl from their beds to escape the burning huts. During the following nights they huddled around bonfires. De

Soto's army would have been destroyed if the Indians had returned, but they did not. In eight days, the Spaniards had made new saddles and lances out of ash trees. The Spaniards were harassed all through the winter, fighting Indians whose legs and arms were painted with stripes of red, black, white and yellow, who wore feathers draping their bodies and horns on their heads and had blackened faces and eyes circled in vermillion.

Finally the Spaniards reached the Mississippi River, bestowing upon de Soto the credit of being the first European to see it. On the river the Spaniards saw an armada of two hundred canoes maneuvering with the efficiency of a school of fish. Across the river, in what is now Arkansas, the Spaniards easily surprised the Indians there, who had not heard of the advancing army. Near the Mississippi the Spaniards cut down a pine tree so big a hundred men could barely lift it and used it to make a cross. They set it on a hill and had twenty thousand Indians kneeling before it. The chief asked for rain, and rain came that night. The chief then asked if the cross worked in warfare.

The Spaniards found a town where a canal had been dug alongside where the chief kept a supply of fish. They saw catfish weighing 150 pounds and otherfish the size of hogs. The Spaniards made cloaks, jerkins, stockings, cassocks, and gowns from bear skins, cat skins, and deer skins. They made waterproof cloaks from the bear skins and armor for their horses from raw buffalo hides. They heard that to the north there was a cold, thinly populated land where buffalo were so thick it was impossible to protect any planted field, so the Indians in that country lived largely off meat. They saw people with tatooed faces and heads flattened in infancy; these people were called Tula, and their name was used to scare children.

In 1542, Ortiz died, leaving no interpreter of any sort. De Soto finally agreed to head toward the sea. The Spaniards wandered through the Mississippi Delta, finding nothing but impassable canebrakes. Fish were so plentiful that they could be killed with clubs. As the Indians in leg irons dragged their chains through the mud, sluggish bottom feeders would rise to the surface, where they were easily taken. On May 21, 1542, de Soto himself finally died of fevers. The Spaniards buried him, telling the Indians that de Soto had just gone to talk with the sun (he had been saying to everybody they met that he was an immortal child of the sun). Seeing the Indians toe the earth over de Soto's grave and fearing that the body would be disinterred, the Spaniards did so themselves. Sealing it in a green log, they sank the body in the middle of the Mississippi River.

For a while, the Spaniards tried to go overland to Mexico. They entered the Southwest, where it was said that Indians wandered like Arabs, had no settled place of residence, and lived on prickly pears and plant roots. They began to find turquoise and cotton, which were supposed to be signs that they were near fabled cities of gold, but, being without food and water, they decided to retrace their steps and to try sailing on the river to the sea.

Back at the river, in an incredible survival feat, they set up a furnace and a forge. They took what chains and shot were left, as well as the stirrups from their saddles, and melted these down to make spikes. There was still one man who could saw timber, and one who knew how to build brigantines. They had four or five carpenters, two calkers and a cooper who, although almost dead, was able to make two half-hogshead casks for each of the seven brigantines. They made ropes and cables from the bark of mulberry trees and sails from Indian shawls. In March of 1543, the Mississippi flooded, and for two months they could do nothing. They lived on the roofs of Indian houses. They finished the boats in June, jerked the flesh of horses and the last of their hogs, and released more than five hundred Indian captives, many of whom had learned Spanish and been converted. Just as an Indian alliance was making plans to crush them once and for all, the river rose again, lifting the boats and floating them out into the current. Seventeen days later they reached the gulf, and, fifty-two days after that, they sailed to the River of Panico. About 150 men survived. Some went to Peru, others stayed in New Spain or went back to Old Spain, and others eventually joined later expeditions that returned to the Land of Flowers to establish a Spanish presence in the American Southeast that would last for about 150 years, until they were finally driven out by the southern warrior hero Andrew Jackson.

In the lobby, after the honor guard of pantalooned Conquistadores was dismissed, I spoke with the first woman ever elected to be a Conquistador. Her name was Martha, and she worked for a firm that did personnel management. Her husband was a Conquistador, too. She said all the guys had been just great to her. When I asked her about the planned protest, she said, her small face framed in a white Elizabethan ruffle, "To tell you the truth, we just wish the Indians would go away."

While I sat in the bleachers watching the members of the De Soto Historical Society mingle and chat, I looked through some newspapers I had picked up. I found an editorial in the April 21, 1993, edition of a small weekly called the *North River News*. I tore it out and put it in my notebook. It was by a man named Art Schofield, and it was surprisingly brusque, refreshingly politically incorrect and antique: "One statement often made is that we don't understand 'them.' Is it our duty to 'understand' them? Or should they try to understand us?"

He said that if you listen to the "strangers" in Manatee County, you might get the boneheaded impression that all the Indians were kind and gentle—"always trying to help the colonists and would not harm a fly." He said if you wanted to know the truth, read Mrs. Lillie B. McDuffie's *Lures of Manatee* and you would find out about burned-out homes, kidnapped kids, murdered girls. "Why isn't someone weeping over their remains? Not a single soul mourns the death of a single person killed during the many Indian uprisings."

The next day, Saturday afternoon, I walked around the high school stadium parking lot where the floats were being prepped. There were floats from Busch Gardens, Tropicana, Disney World, assorted civic associations and school groups. In a corner of the parking lot, where slabs of ribs cooked on a smoking grill, were the Anna Maria Island Privateers. The Privateers are the unshaven, beer-drinking counterpart to the bourgeois, cocktail-sipping historical society. When the Conquistadores got their new float—a half-scale replica of one of de Soto's own caravels—they gave their old ship to the Privateers, who hoisted the Jolly Roger and painted the vessel black. Once a year, the Privateers host a Kids' Day at the beach on Anna Maria Island and give free hot dogs, Cokes and Domino's pizza to any Manatee County kid who shows up.

A big, hearty, bare-chested guy told me to get a rib. While I ate, I asked him to give me his opinion on the controversy.

"Doesn't much matter to me," he said. "What's done is done in the past. We're here to celebrate history. That's all what it is. History. It's history. He was here. That can't be helped. He came and that's history. That's all what it is. What's done is done. We're just here to celebrate history and have a good time."

I asked him if he really thought the Indians would try to block the parade. He hesitated until I promised not to say he was the one who told me. Then he said, "Oh yeah, they're going to be arrested. If they protest like they say they are, they will most definitely be locked up. And they won't be out in no forty-five minutes, either, like they might think. We won't have a court hearing until Monday. They'll have a seventy-two-hour maximum. They'll stay in there till Monday morning till the next judge comes in. Yeah, that guy, what's his name, Barking Dog? Barking Dog and the mayor had a meeting and the mayor basically told them to go to hell and eat shit on the way, that if any one of them protested they'll go to jail. Reason I know is 'cause I'm friends with a guy who dates one of the mayor's daughters.

"See, since the blacks aren't going to protest the David King thing . . ."

David King?

"You know, that . . . *Rod*ney King, *Rod*ney King. You know, after *Rod*ney King was de*tained*, so to speak, since they're not going to protest that, I'm sure the Indians will be down there.

"If it's not one thing, it's another. Get you another rib and I'll show you the float."

Later, full of ribs, I am back along Manatee Boulevard. Pulses of cars whiff down the one-way street, timed to the rotation of the lights. The protestors, whose crowd has grown larger, now numbering maybe fifty, no longer cluster and then disperse as the bursts of cars come past; having reached a critical mass themselves, they occupy their space along the sidewalk with the confidence of numbers. More drummers have shown up. Some are punks, some hippies, and a few are the sort of skinny guy I see at all kinds of rallies and protests—guys with hard tans, truckers' wallets and thin grey pigtails, packing personalized leather carrying cases studded with turquoise and silver for their Bic lighters, and who eat the purple pickled eggs and microwave mustard dogs from the Seven-Eleven and wear short-brimmed leather Harley-Davidson beanies.

One drummer is a mod ska in a porkpie hat. There are a couple of skate dreds, and somebody with a big set of Ricky Ricardo congas, and a ska punk who is working over a plastic lard bucket with heavy-gauge sticks like there's no tomorrow—which of course, there will be, because at tonight's parade they will line up in the street and avoid arrest. The drummers are pounding and excited about maybe getting their heads bloodied, but they will instead (they don't know this yet, but I know it now) run out in front of the parade and unhindered will lead the procession down Manatee Boulevard, being unmolested except for a few who will be pelted with raw chicken and a few who will be arrested in minor arguments, arrested just because they want to be. All in all, they will have an untroubling night.

But they don't know that yet, so they're still at it with plastic buckets and bongos and stretched hides, with beer can rattles and even rings of keys that set a high sharp edge to the sound. The din has a driving rhythm and a momentum of its own, steady, loud, sounding back off the building across the street, and then back again off the marble Confederate memorial and the granite Vietnam memorial in the courthouse plaza. The cars passing are no longer the cause of a timid rattling, but are now becoming victims of it, which is the point of the gathering in the first place, the acquiring of power by the mass. And they do now have power. They are getting what they wanted. They are local news, and they will be mentioned on TV, and, without diminution of their collective pulsing throb, whenever the cameras roll on Darryl Barking Dog, the Ojibway, a crescent of protestors closes in behind him like an arc in the ring of the Whos down in Whoville when the Grinch comes down on his sled, and they hold up their "Dump De Soto" signs and keep drumming and nobody can hear what Barking Dog says, but that's okay because just being there is the point of it all anyway.

I walk around to the side of the courthouse. Since it is a Saturday afternoon, most of the streets in this hot flat Florida town are empty. I see a woman in her fifties sitting under the shelter at a bus stop. Her purse is on her knees. I say hey. We start to talk. I ask her what she thinks of the protest and the protestors.

She winces, squints over her shoulder toward the drums, rattles and TV cameras.

The drumming continues to throb.

"*That* shit get on my *nerves.*"

# CHAPTER FIVE

# DESTINY IN DAYTON

## The Scopes Trial Play and Festival at Dayton, Tennessee

*Your name is Harry Shelton?*
*Yes, sir.*

*Did you go to the high school up here?*
*Yes, sir.*

*Study under Prof. Scopes?*
*Yes, sir. . . .*

*Did Prof. Scopes teach you anything about evolution during that time?*
*He taught that all forms of life begin with the cell.*

*Begin with the cell?*
*Yes, sir. . . .*

*That's all I want to ask you.*

[Cross-examination - By Mr. Darrow]

*How old are you?*
*Seventeen.*

*Prof. Scopes said that all forms of life came from a single cell, didn't he?*
*Yes, sir.*

*Did anybody ever tell you before?*
*No, sir.*

121

*That is all you remember about biology, wasn't it?*
Yes, sir.

*Are you a church member?*
Sir?

*Are you a church member?*
Yes, sir.

*Do you still belong?*
Yes, sir.

*You didn't leave the church when he told you all forms of life began with a single cell?*
No, sir.

*That is all.*

*[Witness excused]*
Scopes trial transcript (*State of Tennessee v. John Thomas Scopes* [1971/ 1925], 128–29)

The judge is dead, and so are the members of the jury. Clarence Darrow, William Jennings Bryan, and John Thomas Scopes himself are dead, as are all the witnesses except one. This is the summer of 1993, and the only surviving participant of the world's most famous court trial—*State of Tennessee v. John Thomas Scopes*, better known as the "monkey trial"—is Harry Shelton, a retired bookkeeper for textile mills who was seventeen when he testified that John Scopes taught his Dayton, Tennessee, high school class that all forms of life begin with the cell. Harry Shelton is the last living link to the media spectacle that, more than any other episode in the twentieth century, cinched the Bible Belt firmly around the reputation of the South.

"Most of 'em are gone. I don't know if there's anybody around older than I am who remembers the trial just as a citizen of Dayton, but I know the jurors are gone and the lawyers are all dead," Harry says when I meet him. "I'm the last student witness."

Harry still lives in Dayton, in a neighborhood called Pine Henge, a subdivision on the edge of town built upon hills claimed from the woods. Pastures and cornfields stretch over the bottomland across the road. His house is a modest ranch-style with a partial flagstone facade and a clipped, green lawn. A small red card hangs on his front door:

"Oxygen in Use." Harry has emphysema. His hair is thin, mostly gone. His eyes have the preoccupied, distant look of a person who can't get enough air and has resigned himself to it. On the bookshelves in his living room are volumes like Time/Life's *Gunslingers* and *Ghost Towns*. On top of the television are videocassettes of home-recorded episodes of *Wild America*. Harry tells me he likes to watch programs about the way things used to be.

Harry's wife, Miriam, says hello and then steps into the kitchen to fix her lunch. She says Harry doesn't eat much. While Harry and I talk, I hear a bell from a microwave, and I don't see Miriam again until an hour later, when it's time for me to leave.

His body is sunk deeply into an easy chair, his emphysema temporarily relieved by medication, and his breath coming comfortably for the moment. He tells me his story as the last student witness from the great monkey trial.

"I wasn't born here," he says. "I've lived here since about 1920, but I was born down in Rome, Georgia, in 1908. My father was a railroad man. He was a brakeman, conductor, yard master, depot agent. He was with the Southern and Central of Georgia, the Missouri and Kansas, and Texas Pacific. My father was depot agent in the little town of Supply, Oklahoma, up near the panhandle. We moved up there about 1910. I was only about two years old. We lived there until about 1915 and we came back to Tennessee."

Dayton, the seat of Rhea County, sits on the southern end of the Sequatchie Valley, between the Tennessee River and Walden's Ridge, about forty miles north of Chattanooga, in part of the same range in the southern Cumberlands that includes Lookout Mountain and Rock City, of painted-barn-roof fame. After leaving Dayton, the Tennessee River runs north for about a hundred miles, where it empties into the Ohio River at Paducah, Kentucky. The town was first called Smith's Crossroads, named for a store built there in the 1820s at the junction of the Kiuka War Trace through the Cumberlands and the main north-south Indian trail that linked the southeastern Indians to the Great Lakes. In 1838, as a result of Andrew Jackson's Indian removal policies, the Cherokee crossed the Tennessee Valley near here on their forced march to Oklahoma. After 1870, the town was renamed Dayton, and mining became the big business in the area. All the elements needed for the manufacture of steel were available in nearby mountains: iron, coal and lux, limestone. Northerners and the British provided the capital.

It was the railroad and the iron mines that brought Harry Shelton's folks to Dayton, Tennessee: "My father's father, he was an old country doctor, and he ran a drugstore there in Graysville and he became in ill health and he wanted my father to come back and take over the drugstore, although he wasn't a pharmacist. My father wasn't. Of course my grandfather was; he could write prescriptions. He was in the Civil War and was the type that 'read medicine.' That's what they called it. Said they 'read medicine'; in other words, he didn't finish at any college or school, but he did a lot of doctoring in that little town of Graysville."

Harry pauses and breathes in slow, unhurried, shallow sighs. "My mother was a Jones. She was born in Kansas. My grandfather Jones from England came over here and settled in Pennsylvania and then Chattanooga. He was kind of a wanderer, wound up in Lawrence, Kansas. After my mother was born, they went back to England. She was about fourteen when they came back to this country, come back mostly to Dayton because the furnace was being constructed at that time. Her name was Jones and she married a Shelton, my father, Walter Raleigh Shelton.

"The folks on my mother's side of the house, they were all brickmasons from England, most of 'em, who came here to work the furnace they were building in the 1880s at what they called the Durham Coal and Iron Company. That furnace made pig iron, but it closed in 1913, went bankrupt. It was a English concern and they went bankrupt in '13 and closed up. If they could have held on till '14 they could have sold all that pig iron and gotten back into production. What happened was that, a bit later on, a man named Jack Robinson sold most of it to Japan as scrap iron, and they threw it back at us during the war."

Harry again stops for a minute; he looks out the window, breathes, then continues.

"I was about six or seven years old and I started school there in Graysville and later we moved to Chattanooga in about 1917 when my father went to work for the Central of Georgia. My grandfather had passed away and they closed up the drugstore. From Chattanooga we moved to Dayton, and from Dayton to Crossville and the Tennessee Central, and when we came back to Dayton my father left and traveled around a little looking for work. He wound up in a munitions plant in Erie, Pennsylvania, at one time, and then came back to Dayton and worked up at the coal mine. He wasn't a miner, though. Then he went back to Chattanooga and finally, with us living in Dayton, he got back with the Central of Georgia."

In 1925 Harry Shelton was a seventeen-year-old sophomore at the county high school. One day he and some other students from the general science class were asked to testify that John Scopes, the school's math teacher and basketball coach, while serving as a substitute in the science class did, in violation of Tennessee state law, teach them the theory that man descended from apes. In thirteen lines of testimony, Harry said "Yes, sir" eight times and "No, sir" twice; his only full sentence was "He taught that all forms of life begin with the cell."

Harry says of the trial: "I took the stand, but I didn't contribute much. I wasn't at that time and am still not much interested in evolution. 'Course, I know there's some forms of evolution that are acceptable, but as far as springing from monkeys, why, I don't really go for that at all."

Later this afternoon some townspeople and folks from the local nondenominational Christian college, which was named after William Jennings Bryan, will be restaging an abbreviated version of the Scopes trial downtown at the Rhea County courthouse. The play, *Destiny in Dayton*, is the main attraction at the Scopes Trial Play and Festival, which began in 1988 and is held every year in July. The play is performed in the original Rhea County courtroom where Clarence Darrow and William Jennings Bryan went baldhead-to-baldhead as part of the titanic struggle between traditional fundamentalist biblical creationism and modern scientist Darwinian evolution. The play's organizers from Bryan College encourage descendents of trial participants to attend because their presence—like the display of relics in the courthouse basement and the original hard, wooden chairs that have been restored in the original courtroom—adds an additional legitimizing authenticity to the production, which has been constructed from excerpts of the trial transcript.

Harry has been to the Scopes Trial Play and Festival before and likes it okay, but he's not going this year. He's not up to it. This emphysema has kept him sitting down for the past couple of years. Even though he's not going to the play, they still keep free tickets for him at the door.

Karl Marx once said that all great events and persons in history occur twice: the first time as tragedy, the second as farce. He was referring to a pattern he saw in the history of French revolutions, particularly the

February Revolution of 1848 and the counterrevolutionary coup d'etat of Louis Bonaparte, nephew of Napoleon Bonaparte, in 1851, in which the costumes and slogans of past great episodes were resurrected to give legitimacy to, in his opinion, tawdry contemporary doings.

Marx wrote, "The tradition of all the dead generations weighs like a nightmare on the brain of the living. . . . they anxiously conjure up the spirits of the past to their service and borrow from them names, battle cries and costumes in order to present the new scene of world history in this time-honoured disguise and this borrowed language." Marx's clever adage has since found its way out of his classic *The Eighteenth Brumaire of Louis Bonaparte*, and into my handy little red book of glib cultural studies sayings. To call it glib, though, is not to diminish its rhetorical effectiveness. Episodes of public memory, where history is invoked in celebration, are almost never merely about the past. Instead, occasions of public memory focus on contemporary issues, such as power and money, presenting new scenes in a time-honored disguise. Detaching Marx's analysis from its specific object, and setting aside the phrase's origins in the class struggle, "the first time as tragedy, the second as farce" is a wry, eerily appropriate way to discuss a lot of the history being restaged these days on courthouse squares. The tragedy-farce coupling was apparent at the De Soto Celebration when Bradenton's hegemonic bloc dressed in polyester conquistador outfits, sipped cocktails and shouted "Olé!" It was there at Hillbilly Days when skewed imperialist stereotypes were celebrated as "heritage." I notice it again at the Scopes Trial Play and Festival, which is, I will discover, more than simply a nod to the past, being instead another skirmish in the war over stories, with the tradition of dead generations weighing like a nightmare on the brains of the living.

The original Scopes trial was the inspiration of a Yankee mining engineer working in Dayton in the 1920s who hoped the publicity from a sensational trial would attract developers to invest capital in this small Cumberland town. The trial—the first to be broadcast nationally on radio—was indeed a spectacular battle for America's soul and got unprecedented media coverage, but the local boosters reaped no reward for hosting it: their plan succeeded only in attracting international scorn.

That was the tragedy. The farce is that the 1990s re-presentation of the trial, *Destiny in Dayton*, along with the Scopes Festival, is an attempt by William Jennings Bryan College to rehabilitate the reputation of their namesake—the main spokesman for the prosecution—whose performance in 1925 was pickled by H. L. Mencken's corrosive spleen and later preserved in grotesque caricature in the 1960 movie *Inherit the Wind*. The college has an interest in revising the popular history because Bryan's bad reputation, as well as the lingering tainted reputation of Dayton and the entire South as the region of rabid fundamentalist hillbillies, sometimes, it turns out, makes it hard for the college to recruit students and solicit donations.

Frustration with the unflattering portrait of Dayton and the South perpetuated by Mencken and *Inherit the Wind* is nothing new. For decades after the final gavel in the 1925 Scopes trial, this small town in the Tennessee Cumberlands tried in vain to shake that monkey (so to speak) off its back. Branded by the national and international press as a backwater hotbed of fundamentalism, for almost seventy years Dayton has felt wrongly accused.

"Most people think that Ted Kramer's movie *Inherit the Wind* is true," Harry Shelton says firmly. "I suppose it had to entertain, but it was a gross exaggeration."

Dayton and the South had been mocked during the trial, but it got worse after the 1960 movie. In the film, the character modeled on William Jennings Bryan is portrayed as a Bible-beating bunco artist, alternately stuffing himself with fried chicken and belching sanctimonious platitudes. The denizens of Dayton and surrounding hills are depicted as unlearned fanatics, a lynch mob in the making. Gene Kelly plays the Menckenesque reporter. When a resident asks him if he needs a nice, clean place to stay, the reporter responds, "I had a nice, clean place to stay, but I gave it up to come here." Although Jerome Lawrence and Robert E. Lee, who wrote the original play, claimed their version was fiction, the movie version of *Inherit the Wind* is widely considered to be accurate and is often still used in classrooms to teach the lesson of the great clash between reason and religion.

In the movie, the story of the monkey trial begins when a goon squad led by a stiff-collared preacher marches into a high school classroom to roust the young, idealistic, bow-tied science teacher in the middle of a lesson on the descent of man. The earnest educator (played by Dick York) is hauled off to jail. Howling mobs call for his head. The roaring preacher condemns the young man to hell, much to the dismay of his girlfriend, who just happens to be the preacher's daughter.

Jail doors clang, tears flow . . .

*Cut!*

That's not at all what happened. Scopes never went to jail. There was no preacher's daughter, no howling mob.

And, Harry says, the alleged crime never even took place. "Scopes never taught me any evolution. He was just substituting and the portion of the textbook, pages 197 and 198, had already been taught by our regular teacher, Ferguson, before he got sick. In fact, when he was here during the premier of *Inherit the Wind*, the Ted Kramer film, Scopes told someone then that he hadn't taught evolution. And I think there was a story out at that particular time, in '25, that he'd gathered a few students and got in a taxi cab and went out to the country and sat down under a shade tree and taught 'em some evolution just to make sure he'd broke the law, cause the whole point of it was to have him declared guilty so the ACLU could take their challenge of the law to the Supreme Court."

From the last living witness of the Scopes trial: "It was all a set-up."

The same mines and furnaces in Dayton that brought Harry Shelton's mother to Tennessee also brought George Rappelyea, the man whose bright idea led to the Scopes trial, but, by 1925, the mines in the surrounding mountains had shut down because the ore was too lean. The valley had become a place for truck farms growing fruits and vegetables for Chattanooga, the booming city to the south. In the hills around town, fires were regularly set to mask the smell of stills brewing corn liquor.

Rappelyea was a young engineer in his thirties. His black hair was streaked with gray. He wore thick glasses and had a quick walk. He had been brought to Dayton to oversee the disposal of the properties belonging to the Tennessee Coal and Iron Company, mines full of water and surrounded by barbed wire. When John Thomas Scopes first met Rappelyea, the young school teacher thought the engineer's accent was Cajun. It turned out Rappelyea was a New Yorker.

By 1925, the public clash between traditionalism and modernism was coming to a crisis point. The 1920 census showed that for the first time in American history more of the population was living in cities than in the countryside. The infallibility of the Bible was being challenged by the rise of science and mass society. Sociology was replacing theology; reason was replacing faith. Up north it was the Jazz Age. One of the biggest best-selling books at the time of the Scopes trial was *The Man*

*Nobody Knows*, in which author Bruce Barton reinterprets the story of Christ as an instructional tale about the most successful business executive in history.

After World War I, science became the dominant intellectual force in an increasingly secular, industrial America. In 1921 the newspaperman E. W. Scripps, founder of Scripps-Howard, helped finance the Institution for the Popularization of Science. But postwar anxiety inspired a fundamentalist backlash against the most visible target: the teaching of evolution in schools. Antievolution bills began popping up around the country. The most prominent opponent of evolution was William Jennings Bryan.

As we have seen, one of the key sites of culture and power is the story, since it is through stories that we perceive the world, and the stuff of our surroundings rises up through layered webs of narrative. Seeing how this really works can be complicated. While it's usually the turf of literature scholars to analyze stories, the cultural studies approach adds another dimension. In addition to paying attention to the plot, characters, or structure of a story, cultural studies situates a story in the social and political context in which it is created.

Stories are important because they provide a way for inspiring thought or motivating behavior. Stories embody social codes that govern mobility and constraint; they are active representations, cognitive maps of how the world works, part of a symbolic economy of signs that excite human desires, fears, and aggression.

William Jennings Bryan was a firm believer in the power of storytelling, and he didn't much care for the stories told by modernists like Charles Darwin. Since the 1890s, Bryan, who was known as the Great Commoner, had been one of the most popular leaders of the Democratic party. He was nominated for president three times and served as Woodrow Wilson's secretary of state (before resigning on the eve of World War I). He is considered one of the greatest orators in American history, a stump speaker who could hypnotize crowds for hours. He was a populist hero, with legions of fans in the West and the South. During his career, Bryan, who was from Nebraska, fought for women's suffrage, independence for the Philippines, currency reform, progressive income tax, world peace, prohibition, the direct election of senators, public disclosure of newspaper ownership, workman's compensation, minimum wages, an eight-hour day, a prohibition against injunctions in labor disputes, pure food acts, public parks, government regulation of railroads and public regulation of political campaign contributions.

He said good things like: "Mankind is made up of two distinct types of people: those who are so busy producing they have no time to collect, and those who are so busy collecting they have no time to produce."

He said bad things like: "The black people in the south have the advantage of living under a government that the white people make for themselves. The laws apply to everyone and are better laws than the black man would make for himself" (Levine 1965: 257).

To get to the college named after the Great Commoner, one crosses Little Richland Creek and follows the signs pointing toward the Coon Club and the B&B Paintball Range. The college is at the top of the hill. The person at Bryan College who knows most about the school's namesake is Dr. Richard Cornelius, whose small office is stacked with cardboard boxes of leaflets, flyers, pamphlets, reading lists, and reprints of Bryaniana, which he sells at the Scopes Festival. These items include copies of *William Jennings Bryan: He Kept the Faith* for twenty-five cents and copies of *In the Hands of God: A Historical Novel Based on the World Famous Monkey Trial of Dayton Tennessee in 1925* for two dollars each. There are copies of Richard Cornelius's review of *In the Hands of God* for ten cents and of Bryan's famous "Cross of Gold" speech. There is a street map to famous monkey trial sights.

Dr. Cornelius, an English professor in his fifties, is neatly and comfortably dressed in a short-sleeved shirt tucked into gray slacks. Although calm and focused, he can still get worked up defending Bryan, even after having been an advocate for more than twenty years. Dr. Cornelius works diligently to battle the unfortunate legacy of the Scopes trial.

"Bryan was ahead of his time," Dr. Cornelius tells me, rebutting the verdict of historians who claim that Bryan was actually a relic, ghost dancing to the tune of "Gimme That Old Time Religion." He continues, "He was for women's suffrage. He promoted higher education. And he wasn't even against the teaching of evolution. He just felt that evolution should just be taught as one version of creation, not as the only truth. It was just one theory among many. He knew you couldn't trust the scientists. Scientists at the time were arguing using Piltdown man as evidence for evolution and it turned out to be a hoax."

Dr. Cornelius picks up a copy of the biology textbook from which John Scopes allegedly taught evolution. "And the *Civic Biology* text was blatantly racist." He shows me the book. He tells me this with a slight edge of tired indignation slipping into his voice. He points out the passage and I copy it into my notebook: " . . . the highest type of all, the Caucasians, represented by the civilized white inhabitants of Europe and America . . ."

By the time of the Scopes trial, Bryan had fallen from greatness. A diminished legend, he had been battered and rebuffed, reduced to being a rural hero in a world that worshipped urban values. Bryan, though, never abandoned his sense of mission. He felt confident that he knew how to save the increasingly godless nation where college boys thought it smart to be skeptical. Only a return to the traditional old-time religion could make the center hold, keep things from falling apart. He found many like-minded believers in the vanishing culture of the rural, agricultural South.

The 1920s were a bad time for the South, as well. The memory of the Civil War and the legacy of the failed populist revolt at the end of the nineteenth century still contributed to strong sectionalist feeling. Attacks on the grotesqueries of the South in the 1920s were, as George Tindall wrote, "the high road to the Pulitzer." Three Pulitzers went to newspapers for articles attacking the Ku Klux Klan: in 1923, the *Memphis Commercial Appeal*; in 1926, the *Columbus Enquirer-Sun*; in 1928, the *Montgomery Advertiser*. In 1929, the *Norfolk Virginian-Pilot* won for a campaign against lynching. In the middle of all this came the Scopes Trial.

H. L. Mencken wrote this about Bryan at the time of the Scopes trial:

> He has these hill billies locked up in his pen and he knows it. . . . He can never be the peasants' President, but there is still a chance to be the peasants' Pope. . . . It is a tragedy, indeed, to begin life as a hero and to end it as a buffoon. But let no one, laughing at him, underestimate the magic that lies in his black, malignant eye, his frayed but still eloquent voice. He can shake and inflame these poor ignoramuses as no other man among us can shake and inflame them, and he is desperately eager to order the charge. . . . Once he had one leg in the White House and the nation trembled under his roars. Now he is a tinpot pope in the coca-cola belt and a brother to the forlorn pastors who belabor half-wits in galvanized iron tabernacles behind the railroad yards. (Tompkins 1965: 35–51)

Dr. Cornelius insists that Bryan wasn't as insane as all that. Bryan had objected to "Darwinism" as early as 1904, but by the 1920s he felt that

131

the threat to his version of America was imminent. Increasing numbers of kids were going to public schools where they would be vulnerable to virulent rationalism. There were statistics to prove it. In 1916 a professor at Bryn Mawr published a study claiming that 40 to 45 percent of college students lose their faith by the time they are through college. To Bryan, that was the road to national ruin.

Bryan believed that God was necessary to inspire sublime behavior in human beings, that the ideas of Darwin and Nietzsche weakened democracy and strengthened the power of the wealthy, and that, whereas Christianity makes the strongest the servants of humanity, Darwinism makes them the oppressors.

Bryan was a progressive politically but a fundamentalist culturally. He felt that science had no morality—that scientists were demanding freedom in the classroom while at the same time manufacturing the technology of mass death, that they were producing weapons but providing no moral logic for their control.

Nor was Bryan a big fan of literary interpretation. "Give the modernist three words, 'allegorical,' 'poetical,' and 'symbolical' and he can suck the meaning out of every vital doctrine of the Christian Church and every passage in the Bible to which he objects" (Levine 1965: 281).

After the 1925 session of the Tennessee General Assembly opened, an antievolution statute was snuffed by the senate judiciary committee. But John Washington Butler, a farmer from Macon County and a member of the Primitive Baptist Church who had been elected to the house in 1922 on a platform opposing the teaching of evolution in schools, drafted a bill which would make it unlawful for any state-funded school "to teach any theory that denies the story of the divine creation of man as taught in the Bible, and to teach instead that man has descended from a lower order of animals" (Levine 1965: 326). Other legislators tried to pass similar bills that would require water to run uphill and have the climate and temperature remain even the whole year round, but their strategic use of scornful irony failed. The Butler Bill was passed seventy-one to five in the house, twenty-four to six in the senate. The law was considered to be symbolic, a protest against the antireligious exaltation of science. The governor didn't want to sign it, but he did, writing at the time: "Right or wrong, there is a widespread belief that something is shaking the fundamentals of the country, both in religion and in morals. It is the opinion of many that an abandonment of the old-fashioned faith and belief in the Bible is our trouble in large degree. It is my own belief" (Levine 1965: 327).

Bryan had suggested that the law not carry any penalties, but it went into effect threatening fines of one hundred to five hundred dollars. Despite that, Bryan was pleased. He wired the governor: "The Christian parents of the State owe you a debt of gratitude for saving their children from the poisonous influence of an unproven hypothesis. . . . The South is now leading the Nation in the defense of Bible Christianity. Other states North and South will follow the example of Tennessee" (Levine 1965: 327).

When he signed the bill, the governor wrote to the legislature: "[I]t will not put our teachers in any jeopardy. Probably the law will never be applied." But he was wrong. The American Civil Liberties Union, which had been founded only five years earlier, wanted a test case. Ironically, the state itself never undertook to investigate any curricula or teachers. The only attempt to enforce the bill was instigated by the ACLU, which notified Tennessee newspapers that they would cover the expenses for anybody willing to test the law.

When George Rappelyea saw the notice in the Chattanooga paper, he got a bright idea. Why not have someone in Dayton break the law? Such a case would shine national attention on the town, and maybe spark economic revitalization. All the hot issues were present: church and state, parents and children, religion, academic freedom. It was not fanatical southern persecution of some righteous prophet that led to the Scopes trial. It was all a stunt, a staged spectacle, cultural performance in the service of capital investment.

Rappelyea talked with F. E. "The Hustling Druggist" Robinson, who was the head of the county board of education and the local dealer in textbooks. Robinson agreed that it was a great idea. Then they talked John Scopes into saying he had taught evolution when he substituted in a biology class. Scopes went along partly because of the inspiration of his father, an Englishman who had immigrated to America in 1883, landed in Galveston carrying a Bible, a Church of England hymnbook, Carlyle's *The French Revolution*, and a copy of *Origin of Species* (published in 1859), and who had worked as a fireman, roundhouse foreman and machinist for railroads in the Midwest. Scopes's father was a socialist and friend of Eugene V. Debs, and he had helped found a machinists' union. John Scopes had enrolled in the University of Illinois in 1919 and transferred to the University of Kentucky when his father retired and moved to Paducah. He graduated in 1924; the job in Dayton was his first. He coached football and taught math and physics.

The Hustling Druggist called the paper in Chattanooga and said, "This is F. E. Robinson in Dayton. I'm chairman of the school board here. We've just arrested a man for teaching evolution." At one point, Chattanooga tried to get the trial moved to the memorial auditorium in that city, and, when that failed, they tried to set up their own case with a Chattanooga teacher, but the boosters in Dayton arranged a special session of the grand jury rather than wait until the regular session in August. When it looked like attention was lagging, Rappelyea staged a fight with the local barber. "There are more monkeys here in Dayton than there are in the Chattanooga zoo" was Rappelyea's line. "You can't call my ancestors monkeys!" was the barber's. A fake fight ensued. Rappelyea told the *Chattanooga Times* that H. G. Wells had volunteered to help with Scopes's defense. When reporters called Wells in England, Wells said he had never heard of anybody named Scopes. By the time the trial ended, Rappelyea had collected a trunk full of press clippings.

Once Bryan agreed to aid the prosecution, Clarence Darrow, once a Bryan supporter but now a harsh critic, volunteered for the defense.

On Tuesday, July 7, Bryan's train was met by an enormous crowd. That night, citizens honored him at a banquet, and, after the meal, Bryan drove around Dayton in a truck mounted with the first loudspeaker the townspeople had seen. He wore a pith helmet, hawking some Florida real estate that he was trying to sell—the first road to Miami Beach was just being built—and munched radishes out of a paper bag.

Darrow arrived the next day, followed by Mencken, then by hundreds of farmers, preachers, showmen, and reporters. The train into Dayton was nicknamed the Protoplasm Special. The Scopes case was the first trial broadcast live across the country by WGN. Sixty-five telegraph operators worked nonstop, cabling more words to Europe, Australia, China, Russia and Japan than had ever been cabled about a single American event. Along with the press came the sideshow that has since become a tradition with sensational American trials.

They crowded into the small, east Tennessee town: circus performers, free silverites and exponents of flat-earth geology. A handler brought a chimp named Joe Mendi to be used, if needed, as an exhibit for the defense. When the townspeople heard about it, the animal's trainer had to search half the night to find a boardinghouse that would let him in.

Someone named Zack Miller came to Dayton with a man he claimed was "the missing link" in the transformation of monkeys to men— a man named Jo Vlens, who, according to the *New York Times*, had formerly been the mascot of the Burlington, Vermont, fire department. He was fifty-one years old and only three and a half feet tall. The reporter described Jo Vlens as having "a receding forehead and a protruding jaw not unlike a simian's, and a peculiar shuffling walk which is described as that of an anthropoid" (July 11, 1925). Mr. Vlens was kept secluded at the Mineral Springs Hotel in the hills outside of town, where he sat alone smoking a pipe, held back as a potential surprise witness to aid the prosecution with an argument that man didn't evolve from apes, but that apes devolved from man, and that, with Mr. Vlens as an example, man "may go down now even as he went down ages ago into the anthropoid." A man who ran a meat market displayed two kittens with the hind legs of a rabbit. Calling them "cabits," he said that their grandmother had both rabbit blood and cat blood and that they were examples of the Mendelian law of inherited characteristics. Another man who lived outside of town brought a chicken with one side marked like a barred Plymouth Rock and the other a Rhode Island Red. The local movie being shown at the time was *The She-Devil*. There was a man tattooed with Bible verses. The best-selling pamphlets were "God— Or Gorilla?," "Jocko-Homo Heaven Bound," and "Hell in the High Schools." One day an Independent Free Thinker from Michigan came to Dayton and began to speak on the corner of Main and Market streets. The crowd grew large and restless as he lambasted Jesus. The town's only policeman, Sid Strunk, pushed through and hustled him off. "He wasn't talking right," Mr. Strunk told reporters. "And I was afraid some of the boys'd take hold of him. I guess 'disturbing the peace' is the charge." The majority of the crowd consisted of plain people in plain clothes, who came in wagons rigged with settees and chairs, drawn by horses and mules. They were "sober faced, tight lipped, expressionless." There were blind minstrels and street preachers; a banner on the courthouse commanded "Read Your Bible." Peddlers sold watermelons, roasting ears, early harvest apples and tomatoes. On the courthouse lawn were set up "strange pipes, where one pressed a button and bent to drink for relief from the sun which beat down upon the village" (water fountains). The greeting used by "out of town iconoclasts" was "Brother, thy tail hangs down behind," with the response being, "Thy tail hangs down behind, brother." Blacks mingled freely in the crowds. One Georgia preacher

135

drove a wagon into town and tried to sell a pamphlet arguing that the Negro was not human. But, the July 9, 1925, *Times* reported, "The Tennessee mountaineer is no 'nigger hater.' In fact, he fought in the Union Army to help free the negro, and since he is a man of fixed ideas he shows no desire to listen to attacks on the negro." John Washington Butler, the farmer/senator, came to watch one day, letting someone else do his threshing. He was "large boned and slow of motion and speech, brown as an Indian from work on his farm." The two daughters of the presiding judge were noted to have rolled their stockings in the approved fashion of the effete. The Hustling Druggist sold a Monkey Fizz down at his soda fountain. During the trial, the courtroom was packed beyond capacity, and the people outside on the grounds moved along with the sun in an effort to keep in the shade.

The trial opened on Friday, July 10. During the first days of the prosecution, witnesses testified simply that, while substituting for an ailing biology teacher, Scopes had taught from the book called *Civic Biology*, in which appeared the theory of evolution. During the trial Bryan raged against evolution, arguing that without God, society would degenerate into barbarism. Defense attorney Dudley Malone won over the crowd with a speech about truth and reason. Finally, Bryan himself took the stand. It was a very bad move. Darrow hammered the old man. First, Darrow got Bryan to say that he believed the whale swallowed Jonah; however, he then admitted that he also believed that the earth moved around the sun, so that when the Bible referred to Joshua having made the sun stand still, it was a matter of using language that the people of the time would understand.

Next, Bryan admitted that the six days of creation didn't necessarily mean twenty-four-hour days. Then Darrow wanted to know how, if Adam and Eve were the first humans, it was possible for Cain to take a wife. And if the snake only crawled on its belly after God commanded it to do so, how did it move before that?

Bryan was flummoxed, his admirers aghast. Court was adjourned as Darrow and Bryan, both on their feet, shook their fists and hollered at each other.

Bryan's image was irreparably harmed, his fundamentalist fan club stunned at his backtracking on a literal interpretation of Scripture. Mencken had quipped that "one accused of heresy among them is like one accused of boiling his grandmother to make soap in Maryland" (Tompkins 1965: 35–51).

The trial ended on Thursday, before Bryan could give his final speech or get Darrow on the stand. The jury took only eight minutes to find Scopes guilty. The show was over. The fine of one hundred dollars was paid. The town began to empty. Over the next few days, Bryan finished writing his speech and visited Chattanooga. On Saturday, he gave a speech in Winchester, Tennessee, spent the night in Chattanooga, and was back in Dayton by Sunday morning with proof sheets of his undelivered final speech.

On Sunday, after dinner, Bryan lay down for a nap and died in his sleep. His personal physician said he died from fatigue and exertion and diabetes melitis. His supporters said he died of a broken heart. Upon hearing that, Clarence Darrow said, "Broken heart nothing; he died of a busted belly."

During the trial, Scopes got so much mail it had to be delivered in no. 3 washtubs. Afterwards, he was offered movie deals (including two thousand dollars a week to make *Tarzan* movies) and large sums of money to lecture on evolution from the vaudeville stage. He turned it all down. He accepted some scholarship money for graduate school; when that ran out, he was offered a fellowship to complete his doctorate. But the president of the university (which was not in the South) administering the oil company endowment nixed Scopes, saying, "As far as I am concerned, you can take your atheistic marbles and play elsewhere." Scopes went on to work for oil and gas companies in South America until he retired in 1963.

George Rappelyea, the Yankee eccentric whose original idea had resulted in Dayton's bad reputation, moved on as well. In Cuba he developed an anti-mildew roofing process and in Canada an extra-hard airstrip pavement made from blackstrap molasses.

The people of Dayton did their best to forget about the whole thing. But other people wouldn't let them.

After Bryan died in his sleep in 1925, the Bryan Memorial University Association was formed to raise $5 million to build and endow a college. An eighty-two-acre site was found in Dayton. Classes began in September 1930, held at the old Central High School, where Scopes had taught for one year. In 1935, the college moved to its current site on some hills above the town. With most of its faculty and students coming from elsewhere, the college for years had the reputation of being aloof from the town, and was referred to as "that college on the hill."

Then, in February of 1988, an itinerant entertainer in his mid-forties named Frank Chapin, who was guest directing at a community theater in Oak Ridge, Tennessee, decided to visit Dayton. Chapin had long had an interest in the play *Inherit the Wind* and, when he realized that Dayton was less than an hour away, he got the idea of staging the play in the original courtroom. A little research and a conversation with Dr. Cornelius at Bryan College led Chapin to realize that the real story of the Scopes trial differed considerably from the fictional version presented in *Inherit the Wind*. Chapin, whose earlier gigs had included playing the piano at Shakey's and staging showcases for the U. S. Army's Division of Morale, Welfare and Recreation, decided to edit the actual trial transcript into a workable play.

Chapin found enthusiastic supporters at the creationist Christian college on the hill. When he spoke of adapting the transcript, the college jumped at the chance to work toward setting the record straight. Chapin didn't find much interest among the townspeople, who had been doing their best to ignore that part of their history. But he found plenty at the college, which had been finding it hard to recruit students to a school named after a man whose final historical reputation was that of a senile fundamentalist buffoon. "I have absolutely no desire to do an 'Inherit the Wind' hatchet job," Chapin wrote in a statement to the town that Dr. Cornelius showed me. "I therefore tried to have each side of the case presented as factually and impartially as I know how."

After Chapin put together *Destiny in Dayton*, he moved on. People at the college think he's now somewhere in California.

"He wasn't a Christian," Dr. Cornelius says, sotto voce, leaning toward me as a waitress at the Golden Monkey pours iced tea. "But I don't think that's hurt the play any. I'm not totally happy with it, but it's pretty balanced. If anything, it favors the evolutionists' side."

The Golden Monkey is the first business in Dayton to make an explicit effort to capitalize on the legacy of the Scopes trial. The restaurant was built at the new Best Western motel in 1992. Dr. Cornelius and I drove there in one of the college's vans, along with two other men who help with staging the Scopes Trial Play and Festival. Inside the Golden Monkey, toy chimps hang in cages, wired to toy swings amid plastic greens. Instead of a menu, customers order from "The Docket," and appetizers are referred to as "Opening Arguments." We have the buffet.

Dr. Cornelius says that when the Golden Monkey was getting ready to open, he was asked to help them out by providing mementoes of the trial. He loaned them copies of newspaper articles with big banner headlines that were laminated to table tops. As we eat, he lowers his voice, looks both ways and says, "I didn't know they were going to use them in the *bar*." He says they used to have the tables from Scopes's old classroom. "We had the wood saved from the original science table, but now I'm afraid it's been tossed out. I still bemoan the fact that one day we cleaned house too well." He puts his finger to his chin and drifts into thought. "I'll bet you I know when it was. I think it was probably that time in 1966 . . ."

After lunch we go downtown to visit the Scopes Evolution Trial Museum in the basement of the courthouse. The museum is small and the displays dog-eared, some of the glue dried, various items fallen from their mounts. There are big blown-up photographs, sheet music for the hits "Bryan Believed in Heaven, That's Why He's in Heaven Tonight" and the "Darwin Monkey Trot," and a picture of Harry Shelton as a seventeen-year-old being sworn in.

Local residents of Dayton are beginning finally to take an interest in the Scopes museum, which they neglected at first, being ambivalent about celebrating the South's greatest public relations fiasco. Now, almost seventy years later, as the last of the living memory dies, people are recollecting their associations with the monkey trial. Newly added to the exhibit are various objects donated by local people and placed in a glass cabinet of curiosities called The Monkey Case. There is a coin bank shaped like a schnauzer and labeled "Metal Animal, Now Considered an Antique." Other items include "Door Keys from an Old House," "Sewing Basket with Sewing Notions," "Dress Worn to Scopes Trial by Mrs. Jess Goodrich Whose Husband Was a Juror," "Moustache Cup to Keep the Moustache Out of the Coffee," and "Miscellaneous Flat Ware."

Upstairs in the records room of the courthouse, Dr. Cornelius finds the death register. We look up Bryan: "65, White Male, Illinois, July 26, 1925, apoplexy." He's listed between an eighty-year-old who died of tuberculosis and a seventy-six-year-old woman who died of uremic poisoning.

Dr. Cornelius asks one of the clerks to make me a photocopy of Bryan's entry in the death register. She hands me the sheet and I fold it, slip it into my notebook. As we leave the courthouse, I mention the movie *Planet of the Apes* and ask Dr. Cornelius if he knew that Cornelius was the name of one of the apes who was friendly to Charlton Heston once they found out he was a talking human. "I didn't know that," he says.

I ask him if maybe one of the screenwriters did it as a joke, since he, Dr. Cornelius, was a Scopes trial specialist. He said he didn't think so, but it would be pretty funny if that were true.

These days, Dayton is quiet, hot. If not for the McDonald's sign on the back fence of the baseball field and the Cavaliers driven by the sheriff's deputies and the Wal-Mart out on the bypass and the high-tension powerlines sucking juice from the nearby nuclear power plant, this could be the same still, placid Dayton of seventy years ago, with the mountains blue in the west, strawberry fields across the valley floor, and the grass grown deep in unmowed orchards.

I walk through town with a small mimeographed trifold leaflet as my guide to the notable sites. I look at the house where the Hustling Druggist used to live, the house where Scopes roomed and where members of the defense team slept. I walk by the house where Joe Mendi and his trainer stayed, which is marked by a small fading sign stuck in the corner of the yard. There is an empty Mountain Dew can near the steps, a stroller and a broken ironing board in the front yard. I pull leaves off a fig tree and slip them into my notebook, writing on the undersides "House where Joe Mendi stayed" and the date.

Downtown, everything is closed. The only real sign of economic life on this Saturday are the kids' bicycles left fallen at the curb in front of a video arcade. Looking in the window of Rogers Pharmacy, I see a rack of faded greeting cards, with the categories Juvenile Boy, Sorry Haven't Written, Secret Pal, and Masculine Relative. The shelves in the drugstore are bare (customers favor the Rite Aid and Wal-Mart on the bypass). I see only a stack of female urinals and crutch tips. In town, there are a few businesses like Sleep City, the Pastime Q Room, and the Crisis Pregnancy Center, but the bigger ones have left this downtown for the edge of the highway.

In 1990, the college started including a festival along with the play to better reproduce the atmosphere surrounding the 1925 spectacle. So now, on the courthouse lawn, arts and crafts vendors sell yarn-haired dolls, candy apples, cutout plywood monkeys. Bluegrass is being played, and there are hamburgers, beekeeping and ham radio exhibits, and, in a nearby parking lot, some guys shooting black powder muskets. The money raised from concessions is used to support missionary efforts by William Jennings Bryan College.

I can feel the festival's tentativeness; unlike Rattlesnake Roundup or Swine Time, it's not attended by thousands. Rows of show cars are parked on the courthouse lawn, their owners sitting apart from the cars and eating off chinette paper plates. A limp, plastic banner saying "Read Your Bible" hangs on the courthouse.

Inside the hallway of the courthouse, tables are set up holding boxes of Dr. Cornelius's Bryaniana; you can buy, for example, a copy of the stenographic court record (twenty thousand copies were sold one month after the verdict in 1925).

The play is held in the courtroom where the trial took place. I watch a matinee performance. I'm no drama critic, but the play seems slightly choppy, which I suppose is inevitable given that the script is a court transcript edited down from seven days to an hour or so. Neither side is emphasized over the other, but it's obvious that the sentiments of the crowd are with Bryan, who appears as a righteous but beleaguered defender of the faith. The play includes the element of audience participation, and we are encouraged to hiss at Darrow if we like, just as the original audience did. The performances are admirable, considering that the entire cast—all men—is drawn from townspeople and Bryan College faculty. Mr. Darrow works at the La-Z-Boy factory, the judge teaches music, and Mr. Bryan teaches at the college. Darrow and Bryan, neighbors, practice their lines while mowing the grass. Darrow and the judge go to the same church and sing in the choir together. Everybody, in the cast and the audience, is white.

After the play I talk to Ray Legg, an instructor at Bryan College who has played the role of William Jennings Bryan for four of the play's five years. He says, "The greatest challenge for me is to try to change the public perception of Mr. Bryan. What I've tried to do with the character is to demonstrate his forcefulness, both in his convictions and in the dynamic nature of his personality." There are signs that Mr. Legg and the rest of the cast are succeeding a bit in their revisionist mission and are winning unlikely converts. "We even got a fan letter from a group of atheists."

Besides staging the annual play, *Destiny in Dayton*, Bryan College is remembering William Jennings Bryan in another way, through the work of the school's Center for Origins Research, which is dedicated to fighting yet another battle over storytelling. This one concerns versions of the story of the creation of human beings.

"Bryan was probably known for two things," says the head, and the only member, of the center, Dr. Kurt Wise, when I meet him in his office one afternoon. "First, he was a great orator. Second, his participation in the Scopes trial. So the college added a communications major and established an origins research center for the Southeast."

Now in his thirties, Dr. Wise was hired straight out of Harvard, where he had studied under one of the world's foremost evolutionists, Stephen Jay Gould. Dr. Wise's idea is to try and reinterpret all the data of the physical world in terms of a creationist model. He has the manic energy of a man who is trying to redescribe the world and the unstoppable conversational style of an evangelical.

While he was growing up, on each birthday his father gave him a present that would introduce him to a different area of science. By the time he graduated from high school, he had thirty-six hobbies and collections. He got his bachelor's in geology from the University of Chicago and went on to Harvard. His four disciplines were macroevolutionary theory, invertebrate paleontology, paleobotany and stratigraphy.

In his office at Bryan College is a broad table covered with his utility belt, sacks of rocks, small picks and hammers. He pulls apart a big broken piece of rock and reveals fern prints and lizard tracks in the Tennessee shale that he's dug out of the gaps and coves up in the low Cumberland Mountains. He's using the fossils to help him date Noah's flood.

A cow skull that he found when he was a kid in Illinois has been made into a lamp and now sits on his desk. His bookshelves hold chunks of quartz, limestone, and bone stacked between biblical concordances. Scriptural notations are chalked on the blackboard, near taped construction-paper love notes from his daughters. In the hallway outside his office is an informal natural history collection: stuffed heads, insects, cigar boxes of gems, grocery sacks of stuffing materials, jars of chemicals, wings and feathers. Little photos of alumni missionaries are thumbtacked to dry beehives and mounted fish they've sent back from their posts in Africa, Asia, and South America.

Dr. Wise says, "It's been traditional in the creationist community and the catastrophist community, rather than spending time working on your own model, to attack conventional geology, attack the status quo, attack evolution. Our neocreationist position is that we want to build our own positive creationist model, to reinterpret all of the data of the physical world in terms of a creation model.

"Our position is that Scripture, the Bible, contains truth. And it is true. So there's data there. There's data from the Scripture. And the physical world is true, too. I mean, it's there. What we observe about the physical world is data, is truth. So we've got the physical world and we've got scriptural data, and we take all those data, truth units, and we try to construct a theory which makes sense of both of them.

"It can be done, but it's not real easy. Reinterpreting the entire archeological and geological record is a lot of work."

# CHAPTER SIX

# "HEY, BARNEY. HEY, ANDY."

## Mule Day at Calvary, Georgia

I had my epiphany at Mule Day.

Calvary is a small town deep in south Georgia. The population consists of a widely dispersed three hundred souls, and the downtown is little more than a handful of houses, a farm supply warehouse, an old decommissioned one-pump gas station, and two or three stores, all of which cluster at a crossroads on Highway 111 like a node on the root of a legume. A dozen miles to the northeast is Whigham, the home of Rattlesnake Roundup. A dozen miles to the northwest is Climax, the home of Swine Time. Calvary is an unincorporated community, but it does have a Lion's Club, and on the first Saturday in November each year, the Lion's Club sponsors the annual Mule Day.

It had just gotten dark. The street was busy. Pick-up trucks drove slowly through the crowd hauling horse trailers and tarp-covered carts toward the Mule Day grounds, and couples and families and clubs of folk walked back and forth from the Seven Kings General Store to the nearby fields, from which rose campfire smoke, the sweet white steam of boiling cane syrup, and the chipped, metallic sounds of hammer blows and bluegrass.

Under cold lights at the end of the Seven Kings, men and women sat on overturned bushel baskets, bellied up to temporary tables of pine planks and sawhorses, eating bowls of washpot pilau—chicken and rice—and wearing windbreakers with stitched, silk-screened, air-brushed, or ironed-on designs and patches and decals that announced memberships in the Jaycee and Kiwanis and Rotary clubs, the First Coast

Christian Bass Fishing Society, and the State Park Campers. Most of the people in town this night before Mule Day would the next morning open their booths and spread their wares across the muddy pastures where maybe seventy thousand people are expected to come.

I was just getting geared up, figuring the lay of the land, following three teenage boys, two in jeans jackets, the third wearing a black bootdragging Marlboro-man duster—Sam Peckinpah a la J. Peterman via Dixie Westernwear—and flicking in the dirt a multicolored foam rubber lizard tied with fishing line to the end of a plastic stick. I was planning, as an exercise, to track their route, eavesdrop on their conversation, map their stops, see what kind of girls they nosed out, and what food, if any, they chose to eat. But I lost them when I got distracted by a gigantic and unpatronized ride called the Bavarian Ski Slope.

Crackling speakers blared mariachi music. Next to the Bavarian Ski Slope was the House of Mirrors. These two attractions had been set up near the volunteer fire department's fire truck shed, well away from the Mule Day grounds, but still I was puzzled by their very presence in Calvary this weekend. The Ski Slope and the House of Mirrors were more like midway attractions for a traveling fair and seemed inappropriate for Mule Day's nostalgic festival of country living. The shrill contraptions were little carnival-in-a-can portable erector-set spectacles, the kind that are unfolded, plugged in, lighted up and amplified—fifty-cents-a-head introductions to fractured modernism and technological reconciliation—screeching, howling gizmos that shake the ground beneath your feet and turn you inside out through the multiplication of reflective surfaces, then set you down safely in the end. They didn't seem to fit in with Mule Day's clogging, slingshot turkey shoot, cakewalk, syrup boiling, and plowing contest.

I was considering the chilly thuggishness of the female ticket taker who was silhouetted against the white glitter of the House of Mirrors, wondering what metaphors I could make out of this stark, expressionist sight, when I realized I had let the subjects of my surveillance slip away. They cut off the road behind a truck of onions, heading into a dark grove of trees.

But it turned out to be better for me: if I had kept following the boys I probably would have ended up watching them smoke cigarettes and listening to them tell me how they were gonna move to Tallahassee when they got out of high school. Instead, I paused within the vortex of strobing lights and trebly mariachi music, and that put me in place to experience a fieldworker's moment of grace.

For it was then, there by the volunteer fire department shed, in front of the feed and seed store and near a parking lot strewn with rusted loops of barbed wire and dried, broken gourds, that I received my epiphany, my critical hermeneutic vision: it was a 1964 Galaxie 500, painted black and white. It had a red light on top. A star decal was on the driver's door.

At first I just thought, Cool old squad car. Wonder whose?

I knew it wasn't Calvary's. Calvary is nothing but a small half block of old brick ghost town in the pine barrens on the swampy edge of south Georgia's wiregrass plain. There's no town hall, no charter, just a Presbyterian legacy and a blinking yellow light. Maybe the Galaxie belonged to Whigham, the only other Grady County town besides the county seat of Cairo that's incorporated. I thought that surely Cairo, a big city of ten thousand and home of the Cairo Syrupmakers, one-time state Triple-A high school football champs, would equip its law enforcers with speedier vehicles.

Maybe the patrol car was a relic from a nearby vanished or dwindled town: Amsterdam, Reno or Climax. If I could find out what retro ville there in the pine barrens and swamps of the South's coastal plain maintained antique Galaxies for their police force, maybe I could also discover barns filled with old farm equipment—corn shuckers, mole traps—or stores on Main Street still stocked with bow ties and lilac toilet water and unintentional folk art that I could buy cheap and sell dear, or some big-bellied small-town corruption, echoes of Jim Crow, that I could expose and sell freelance, or maybe—and I'd settle for this—just some good fried chicken and sweet potato pie.

That's what I was hoping for when I first saw the patrol car. But the opposite happened: instead of cluing me in to an unplundered old-time town, the Galaxie sideswiped me, nudging me into that headspace nicknamed "hyperreality" by theorists like the semiotician and novelist Umberto Eco and the hallucinating Frenchman Jean Baudrillard.

I read the star on the Galaxie door: Mayberry Sheriff's Department.

It stopped me in my tracks.

For a split second I thought, this can't be real. I looked up. I couldn't stop a grin of joy, that rictus inevitable when a serendipitous discovery occurs, a grin most easily simulated by exaggerating the second syllable in a silent enunciation of the searcher's sacred word, Eur*eee*ka.

MULE DAY

On the other side of the car, I saw Barney Fife hitching up his gunbelt. Standing next to him was Andy Taylor, the High Sheriff of Mayberry. I was, as best I can recall, flummoxed. They weren't *really* Barney and Andy; they were look-alikes. *Were they simulacra?* My heart began to race. These weren't just *any* celebrity look-alikes. These were *Barney and Andy* look-alikes, ultimate icons of the mythified train-depot-and-post-office small town white crossroads South. These were *serious* simulacra: *copies of a copy for which there is no original.*

I could hardly contain myself. Was this what I had been studying in school? I was nonplussed: how do you respond when you've just gotten smote by the sight of a dazzling textual clue? When you're in deepest Dixie, looking forward to the next day's mule show, plowing contest and pork rinds, and suddenly the snide presence of a fugitive postmodernism begins to choke you like the smoke from goateed cigarettes?

What do you say in a situation like that?

"Hey, Barney!" I said, doing my best Gomer Pyle. "Hey, Andy!"

I have said that seeing Andy and Barney at Mule Day was a hermeneutic vision. Hermeneutics is a Greek word which refers to the craft of interpretation, the practice of unweaving meaning and explaining things to others, of bringing what is hidden out into the open. The word is derived from Hermes, the messenger among the Greeks' Olympian gods, and the one who invented language and speech. I wasn't concerned with the rigorous specifics of formal hermeneutics, a field of philosophy and criticism developed around the interpretation of the Bible; instead, I had invoked Hermes as the perfect logo for what I was doing there at Mule Day, pondering the secular scripture of public culture. Of all the gods, Hermes (called Mercury by the Romans), the wing-footed deliverer of flowers, was my hero, and I had stuck him like a magnetized personal Jesus on the dashboard of my car.

Hermes is the god of travelers and luck, of roads and doorways, dialogue, discourse and words, of boundaries and places of departure and arrival. He's the god of going between. He is associated with the markers and signposts along the roadside that define routes, contain myths and symbolize places. As the patron of interpretation, he's a raider across borders, a traveler of depths, a trickster who trades in riddles, who privileges that which is latent over that which is manifest, that which is unarticulated over that which has been said. Hermes invented scales, weights and measures. Treasure casually found is

considered a gift of Hermes. And Hermes is related to the stones used
to mark graves.

Hermes conducts the dead to the underworld and brings dreams after
sleep, dreams in which things are switched from their places, turned
into their opposites and appear in disguise, just as under the gaze of
interpreters clear things become murky, and dark things become light.
It is therefore fitting that, just as Hermes is the patron of interpreters and
the craft of interpretation, so too is he something of a saint to perjurers
and thieves and tourists. He's a perfect icon for tourists like me; by the
time I got to Mule Day, measures, boundaries, and the dead were on
my mind.

I had been out on the cracker circuit visiting public festivals for two
years, and I had fingered the texture of the web, wrestling a pig, hunting
rattlesnakes, witnessing the agonies of the Banana Festival and the
Tobacco Festival, watching Floridian business leaders drink screwdrivers
and shout Olé! to honor a neglected conquistador. I had set out on the
road with a desire to track names, reveal unsuspected linkages, unpack
the cultural politics, and decode the meanings that are wired within the
shaped behavior of public ritual. I was going to reckon with some stories
written within festivals and parades, to sense their resonance with the
separate histories of certain Souths, and everything I found was shot
through with themes of death and remembrance. So, just as my trek
was something of a secular vision quest via rental car, it came to pass
that the god of interpretation would finally appear to me in the form
of two pop simulacra from Mayberry. Andy and Barney inspired my
hermeneutic vision because they were treasure found along a roadside;
their identities marked the boundaries of a certain South; and they were
specters returned from the underworld.

"Hey, Barney!" someone twanged from up the dark street. "We got
Otis down here throwing a drunk!"

It was Wayne, the chairman of the Mule Day parade committee. He
was bracing himself with one hand and clutching a clipboard with the
other as the driver of their small, green, balloon-tired all-terrain utility
vehicle wove between folks in the road and revved to a stop near me
and the Mayberry look-alikes. Barney tugged his hat and chuckled at
the Otis joke like he'd heard it all before but he would still be tolerant
and good-natured about it.

Wayne said he'd been waiting all day for them to show up. He said, not really expecting an answer, "Where's Aunt Bee?" and while he chucked his head at what he assumed was his own wit, Andy and Barney grinned again, clucked a little and looked off around Wayne and down the road toward the smoke and lights and banjo music coming from the pasture.

"We'll have you coming at the head," Wayne said, checking the list on his clipboard. "And behind you we'll have the mules carrying the flags. You got a si-reen on that car? You can run the si-reen if you got one."

Barney and Andy both seemed a little overwhelmed and distracted, like it was all happening a bit too fast. They had just driven into Calvary from Alabama and stepped out of the patrol car, and they were immediately the center of attention.

Barney started getting cranked up, getting into it, saying Yeah, yeah, yeah, yeah, and nodding his head while Wayne showed him the order of march and the timetable for starting the parade the next morning. I noticed that this Barney was an old Barney—not a period Barney, not a classic, lean Deputy Barney Fife circa 1962. This one was like Barney on a comeback show, Don Knotts off the Placidyls and working again, with long jowls and rheumy eyes, but still quick and spastic, still Barney, just old. This Barney kept hitching up his gunbelt, squaring his hat, looking up and down the road. He was jumpy and excited under the grins and gazes of people walking by.

Andy was quiet and subdued, smiling shyly and keeping his fists balled in his khaki trouser pockets. While Barney went over their instructions with the parade chairman, Andy leaned against the fender of the patrol car, crossed his feet at the ankles and didn't say much.

Andy and Barney had just driven the old Galaxie from Florence, Alabama, and the whole way over they'd been smelling something burning. Barney was thinking maybe it was the power steering leaking fluid, but he said he was not going to let a lack of easy steering stop him and Andy from driving at the head of the parade. No sir. As long as the car ran, he could hold it in the road. But he didn't really know about running the siren. "You think we should?" Barney again hitched up his gunbelt and settled the black leather around his stomach. "I mean, won't it spook the mules? We might want to think about that."

Wayne shrugged, spat. "Whatever." He said he didn't care one way or t'other; it was just an idea. Then he said, "You prob'ly right. You prob'ly right. What with all the animals we got here. We got a big jack mule right behind you, and you cut that si-reen on he'll prob'ly run right over ya!" Wayne laughed—he was quick with the laughs—braced himself and said See ya in the morning, as his driver popped the clutch on the utility vehicle and the balloon tires spun and spat gravel.

They mowed a U-turn through the crowds and headed through the cold nighttime lights back down past the House of Mirrors toward the glowing smoke of fires in the muddy fields.

Anyone who has ever played any sport will be familiar with this experience: a bat hits a baseball solid with no hand-buzzing shivered physics; a tennis ball thwoks firmly into the sweet spot of a racket; a basketball goes doosh, hitting nothing but net. I'd been playing this fast-paced jam of fieldwork, interpretation, name games and playful juxtaposition, exploring the hypertext links nested within the rituals and characters of public culture, so the gratification I experienced when I saw the Andy and Barney look-alikes was intense. *Nothing but net.*

There I was, in a little almost-not-town in the deepest corner of Georgia's wiregrass plain, and there were two men dressed up to simulate fictional characters from Mayberry, TV's classic southern Brigadoon. I had expected to come to Mule Day and work out a simple portrait of a rural celebration, something quaint and archaic, but instead I got swept up in a surreal shivari of poststructuralist spells. The critic Fredric Jameson is America's foremost theoretician of postmodernism, which, he says, is the cultural logic of late capitalism. Jameson (1991) has written that in this postindustrial information age, we exist within a new and original historical situation in which we are condemned to seek history by way of our own pop images and simulacra of that history, which itself remains forever out of reach. One overriding symptom of that "condition of postmodernity" is the rhetorical deployment of texts, images and discourse within an economy of sign exchange where simulacra and spectacle are the common coin. As I stood there in the cold night by the volunteer fire department's fire truck shed and spoke with the pop simulacra of a southern sheriff and his deputy, a bit more of the poetics of contemporary public culture confessed itself to me.

Barney, it turned out, was a retired employee of Florida's agriculture department. Andy was an Alabama carpenter. They had won a look-alike contest and were going to drive the squad car at the head of the Mule Day parade, fulfilling yet again the second half of the "first time tragedy-second time farce" coupling. On that cold November night in Calvary the presence of Mayberry's sheriff at the head of the parade brayed out a deep-bellied hee haw of history's irony.

Here's the tragedy: this land, which is drained by the Ocklocknee, the Chattahoochee and the Flint rivers, used to be the territory of the Muskogee Creek Indians. It was Andrew Jackson—the original southern hero, the seventh president of the United States, the man on the twenty-dollar bill—who led his hungry armies through the South's piedmont and coastal plain, crushing the Creeks, and, finally, when president, forcibly removing the Indians and opening the Southeast for settlement from the Chattahoochee to the Mississippi. Andrew Jackson, the South's premier Presbyterian Scotch-Irish cracker, cleared the ground for the great antebellum plantation economy. After Andrew Jackson, the Southeast would become The South.

Here's the farce: the full name of the High Sheriff of Mayberry, whose simulacrum would lead Saturday morning's parade of mules through this long-conquered landscape, is Andrew Jackson Taylor.

I can't remember what I said once the parade chairman left. I was still shaking my head in amazement at this encounter with the Andy and Barney look-alikes. While they talked to Wayne about rendezvousing with the caravan of mules in the morning, I kept trying to think past the tintinnabulation of the mariachi music from the House of Mirrors and figure out why I was so intrigued. I had come to Mule Day to rehearse a cultural diagnosis of wilted small towns, but these look-alikes were stirring something strange somewhere in my pretheoretical viscera.

I think I said something like, "You Barney?" or maybe, "Y'all really from Mayberry?" or maybe even, "Andy! Barney! What's up with that?"

Barney's and Andy's stories had that tremulous inevitability brought by hindsight to the narrative of any success. It turned out that the University of North Alabama in Florence, Alabama, each year was host to an event sponsored by George Lindsay, the actor who played Goober Pyle, cousin to Gomer, on *The Andy Griffith Show.* In 1991 the university held a Goober Festival. Officially it was called George Lindsay Day, but everyone called it the Goober Festival.

"My wife saw Goober on *Nashville Now* and she heard that they was going to have a Mayberry look-alike contest at the Goober Festival," said Barney, whose real name is J. T. Garrett. His voice was dry and pitched like a screen door hinge. "Since I been called Barney for more than twenty-five years, she said, 'We gonna set you up.'"

J. T. talked fast, in bursts between breaths, as if he were claiming his place in a story, telling it all quickly so it wouldn't be forgotten. "I'm a retired petroleum inspector for the Florida Department of Agriculture. Worked that for twenty-two years. I was the one checked the service stations, checked the pumps for the amount of gallons put out, calibration of the pumps, that sort of thing.

"When I was working for the state, a lot of the stations I inspected, they'd say 'Come in, Barney.' They wouldn't say, 'Come in Mr. Garrett,' or 'Come in, J. T.' They'd say, 'Come in, Barney.' At that time, you know, I was eatin' it up. I watched the show quite a bit, and my daughter, back when she was in high school, she'd bring the kids in, her friends, they'd come in and she'd say to 'em, 'Who does my daddy look like?' Some of 'em would look a little shy about saying it, and they'd snicker a little bit, and she'd say, 'He don't mind!' And they'd say, 'Barney Fife!' "

It was the same story with Andy. When I asked him how he ended up as Andy, he stood up straight from leaning against the patrol car, and, speaking slowly and drawling and pushing his fists deeper into his pockets and grinning to himself, said, "Aw, yep, well, back when I was first called Andy, I had a little ol' grocery store, and some of the kids would come in, you know, and when I did that store business I didn't have time to watch the show, but some of the kids there they'd call me Andy. . . . See, well, they was this little ol' girl at my church, where I go to church there back in Muscle Shoals, Al'bama, and she heard they were going to have an Andy Griffith thing, and she kept buggin' me to enter it. She'd say, 'Come on.' And I'd say 'Naw.' And she'd say, 'Aw come on,' and so finally I said, 'Aw, okay, I will.' "

Then the Andy look-alike told me his name. "Sterling White," he said, eliding the final 'g' to make it sound, to me, like "Sterlen."

I said, "Sterlen?"

He said, more sharply, "*Ster*-lung."

I said, "Oh. *Ster*-ling."

J. T. leaned in with his thumbs in his gunbelt, his cap set back on his head, his wet eyes wide and bugging and reflecting the bright white lights from the House of Mirrors and interjects a comment. He said something that brought me a leap closer to understanding the textual and historical significance not just of these Mayberry look-alikes but of the whole cracker circuit.

J. T. said, "Sterling White. It don't get much whiter than that! Get it? *Sterling White*!"

And there it was: once again, the coincidence of names coming together like pieces puzzled out from chaos and fitting one to another to compose a world and mark the edges of the sky and the earth.

A man named Sterling White plays Andrew Jackson Taylor in a cold morning ritual of conquest in Dixie's coastal plain. Andrew Jackson, Sheriff Andy, Sterling White—this coincidence of names, seemingly inconsequential and innocuous—is what smote me while I stood on the side of the highway in Calvary that night. Using the evidence of the histories buried within the tracery of namings, the allusions and pop simulacra that make up the public festival culture of the South at the end of the millenium, I would come to conclude that the Andy and Barney look-alikes weren't simply two guys dressed up like TV characters; they were accidental prophets of a postmodern ghost dance sweeping the countryside, inadvertent bearers of a message of salvation through persistent simulation. In 365 B.C., Antisthenes said that the beginning of all instruction was the study of names, and so it was that the linking of names took on even more poetic resonance when I realized that Andrew Jackson's victories over the Indians in the Southeast took place on the heels of a failed ghost dance.

*It don't get much whiter than that!*

I like Andrew Jackson because to this day he holds the record as the American president who had the most gunshot lead lodged in his body while serving in office.

Jackson's mother, Elizabeth, wanted him to become a preacher, but he preferred cockfighting. His father, the son of a linen weaver and merchant in Carrickfergus, Ireland, was also named Andrew Jackson, and he and his wife had come from Ireland to America in 1765, working their way through Pennsylvania and down the Great Wagon Road to its end in the valley of Virginia. From there they followed the Catawba Trading Path to Salisbury, and, after that, a royal post road westward into the Garden of the Waxhaws, a section of the Carolina upcountry where four of Elizabeth's sisters had already gone. In 1765, the year the Jacksons sailed to America, a thousand wagons passed down the Catawba Path and into the wilderness frontier on the edge of Carolina.

Already for thirty years settlers had been trekking down into the piedmont regions of Virginia and Carolina, filling Cherokee lands and establishing the largest white ethnic group in the backcountry of the South. In the years before the American Revolution, nearly 250,000 Scotch-

Irish migrated from Ulster to America, escaping British oppression and misfortunes including a system of rack-renting under absentee English landlords, economic sanctions against the wool industry, a collapse of the linen trade, anti-Presbyterian laws, forced taxation to support the Anglican church, bad crop years, and a vicious breed of corn speculator.

In 1767, the elder Jackson strained himself lifting a log and died soon after. Such was the life of a Scotch-Irish settler in Carolina. One month later, Elizabeth gave birth to her third son, and named him in honor of her newly dead husband: Andrew Jackson.

During the Revolutionary War, Andy and his brothers went to fight after 113 Americans were massacred and their bodies hacked to pieces by the British. The fourteen-year-old Andy was captured, and, once when a British officer demanded that the boy black the officer's boots, Jackson, a punk ahead of his time, refused, demanding his rights as a prisoner of war. When the officer slashed at Jackson with his sword, the boy managed only to block the death force with his arm, which was gashed, as were his skull and hand. Thus began the collection of hacks and bullet wounds that remain unequaled in presidential history.

Jackson's mother and two brothers died during the Revolution, and, after the British withdrew from Carolina, Jackson followed back to Charleston the wealthy low-country refugees who had fled to the Waxhaws during the war. Back in Ireland, Jackson's grandfather died, and, since the rest of his family was dead, he got the bankroll. For the next half decade Jackson read law during the day and partied at night. He threw dice, raced horses, sparked women, pitted fighting cocks, got drunk, smashed tables and set fire to the ransacked taverns. After he passed the bar in 1787, a gambling buddy appointed him public prosecutor in eastern Tennessee. There he met Rachel Donelson Robards and married her. Unfortunately, she was still married to her first husband. (Once Jackson confronted Rachel's estranged husband and tried to slice his ears off with his hunting knife.) When Rachel's divorce finally came through, she and Jackson staged another marriage, but the scandal would haunt him all the way to the White House and would drive Rachel to insanity.

Jackson was Tennessee's first member in the United States House of Representatives. In 1796, he helped write the Tennessee constitution. From 1798 to 1804, he was a judge on the Tennessee Supreme Court. When the House of Representatives passed an almost-unanimous vote to adopt a farewell tribute to outgoing president George Washington, Jackson voted no. He thought Washington was too soft on the British and too tolerant of the Indians. Tennessee was on the front lines, and Washington's war department would not lend support for a war against the Indians without provocation. Jackson wanted preemptive strikes to clear them out. "Andrew Jackson" and "Indian Removal" were to become synonymous.

Unlike his Mayberry namesake, Jackson loved duels. In a 1795 duel, Jackson and another man both fired wild. An 1806 duel took place after a man named Dickinson, who was mad about a horseracing bet, got drunk and said unkind things about Jackson's wife. At a rendezvous on the Red River in Logan County, Kentucky, Dickinson fired first. Onlookers saw a cloud of dust bang out of Andrew Jackson's coat. Jackson clutched his chest and clenched his teeth, then raised his pistol and blew a neat hole through Dickinson, who was thereby dead at twenty-seven. Dickinson's aim had been skewed by Jackson's ill-fitting clothes, and his shot had barely missed Jackson's heart. "I should have hit him if he had shot me through the brain," Jackson said, walking away with shattered ribs and shoes filled with blood (Remini 1988: 54). The bullet stayed in his chest the rest of his life.

For the next few years Jackson tended his crops in Tennessee, buying and selling land, slaves, and race horses. He asked thirty dollars in ginned cotton for a stud fee. During these years, Jackson went on a festival of naming. He and Rachel were occasionally asked to take in children whose fathers were dead. They named one of these boys Andrew Jackson Donelson and another Andrew Jackson Hutchings. When a relative gave birth to twins and could only afford to keep one of them, she gave the other to Andrew and Rachel, who legally adopted him and named him simply Andrew Jackson, Jr.

Andrew Jackson liked war. He once said, "Should there be a war, it will be a handsome theatre for our enterprising young men, and a source of acquiring fame" (Remini 1988: 54). Jackson was ready to fight anybody—Indians, French, Spanish, or British. When war was declared against Britain in 1812, Jackson was forty-five and running hot. Britain had been impressing American sailors and encouraging Indian raids, but the overriding motivation for the War of 1812 was a desire for national expansion. The young America needed to prove itself in war and at the same time take territory in Canada. Britain was allied with Spain, and the warhawks in Congress thought that a victory over Britain could lead to Spain being booted out of Florida. President James Madison asked Congress for a declaration of war. It came on June 18, 1812.

Jackson had earlier been made a general in charge of two thousand Tennessee militia. He had hoped to be called up immediately, but, because of politics, wasn't mobilized until the end of the year. Jackson and his men headed toward New Orleans but were forced to stop at Natchez. After weeks of delay, they were ordered to disband. Jackson refused to let his army dissolve in the middle of Indian country, so he headed them back to Nashville. A hundred and fifty men were on the sicklist; fifty-six couldn't raise their heads. Jackson and his officers turned their horses over to the sick. As an example for his men, Jackson would only eat the offal from the hogs they slaughtered. Even with that bullet still in his chest, Jackson showed no fatigue, hustling and herding his men successfully all the way back to Nashville. They gave him the nickname Old Hickory.

In June of 1813, a duel between one of Jackson's junior officers and the brother of Tennessee politician Thomas Hart Benton caused Benton to rage at Jackson for being party to a botched affair which had resulted in Benton's brother Jesse being shot in the buttocks and humiliated. Benton accused Jackson of incompetently managing an unnecessary duel. Jackson said he was going to horsewhip Benton the first time he saw him.

In September, Jackson and two friends rode into Nashville to the Old Nashville Inn. The next morning, on their way to the post office, Jackson and his friend John Coffee saw Benton standing in the door of the City Hotel. On the way back with their mail, they walked past the City Hotel. As Jackson passed the doorway where the two Bentons waited with loaded pistols, Jackson wheeled, drew his gun and pushed Thomas Hart Benton into the hotel. Jesse Benton ducked into a hallway and fired at Jackson, hitting him in the arm and shoulder with a slug and a ball. Jackson fired as he fell. Thomas Hart Benton fired twice at Jackson on the ground. More men rushed in. One tried to impale Jesse Benton with a sword cane, but the point broke on a button, so the man wrestled Benton to the ground and stabbed him with a dirk. John Coffee missed his shot at Thomas Hart Benton and tried to club him, but Benton fell down a flight of stairs out the back of the hotel.

The gunfight was over. Thomas Hart Benton and Andrew Jackson would not see each other for a decade; when they next met, they were both United States senators.

Jackson's shoulder was torn open and shattered. Before the holes were plugged, he soaked two mattresses with blood. The ball was embedded next to the bone of his left upper arm, where it would stay for the next twenty years, joining the chunk of lead already in his chest. His shoulder finally stopped bleeding when his wounds were dressed with poultices made from elm shavings. The life-saving remedy was a contribution of Native American medicine.

While Old Hickory was recovering from his wounds, he heard the news about a massacre of settlers by the Creek Indians at Fort Mims in a part of the Mississippi Territory.

Sterling White—"Andy"—is a carpenter. He works with two other guys, a fellow and his brother, building houses in Florence, Alabama. They do it all: framing, sheetrock, electric, everything but the plumbing. It's only because he works with this guy and his brother that he gets to go out on the road and travel with J. T. and do things as Sheriff Taylor. If he worked out of a local union, he couldn't just get off like he does to drive to Mule Day or wherever. J. T. can go anywhere because he's retired.

"We been to Opryland. Did three shows there," J. T. tells me. J. T. is sixty-five years old, but doesn't feel it; a lot of people say he doesn't look it, either. (He and Sterling are unaware that the showboat at Opryland U. S. A. is named General Jackson, a fact that, along with all the other name games going on, is making a clattering noise in my head.)

"We've been to *Nashville Now*. We were backstage guests at the Grand Ole Opry and in May we went to Branson, Missouri, with Goober and Charlene and Ernest T. Bass. We had six shows at the Lowe Theater in Missouri. In Opryland we had Otis with us, and Thelma Lou, and the Darlin' Boys. We went to Mount Airy, Andy Griffith's hometown, and they had a two-day festival there. Mayberry Day, they called it. We were there for two days and been in the parade. They put us up at the old jail. We just had us a big time.

"We go to schools, too. Man, I tell you what, those kids at schools, they go crazy over us. You'd be surprised. I never realized it, but they love Andy and Barney. I was at a school just last Thursday in Crestview, Florida, and man, them kids went wild."

J. T. tells me about Mayberry Days. "Biggest majority of the time we really had a blast. They had a big field like, like a camping area, and had it roped off and put Andy in separate."

After waiting patiently for J. T. to finish, Sterling tells me his impressions of the Mayberry Days. "Now, that's something else. They have shows on Friday and Saturday night. Usually the Darlin' Boys are on the bill somewhere. They have trivia contests. And they got Floyd's Barber Shop, too. They got Snappy Lunch. It's where Andy used to eat his lunch. They have got a tremendous pork chop sandwich there. There's no bone in them at all. They just as tender as they can be. It's called Snappy Lunch. And they have a Mayberry Motel, and a Aunt Bee's Restaurant, and they have the old Mayberry Restaurant. . . . Yeah, we're going up again. We're kind of making it a yearly thing."

Then Sterling toes the gravel by the patrol car and shrugs his shoulders and tells me his opinion of *The Andy Griffith Show*: "Oh, I like the show. That's something you can watch and you don't get tired of it. It's kind of a family show, you know. Clean."

In 1811, a half-Shawnee, half-Creek Indian named Tecumseh came south to gather the Creek, Choctaw and Seminole Indians into a great confederacy to stop the westward expansion of the Americans. Tecumseh visited a Creek village on the Tallapoosa River and spoke with a chief named Big Warrior, who was dubious about Tecumseh's activities. To prove he was sent by the Great Spirit, Tecumseh told Big Warrior he was going back to Detroit, and when he got there he would stamp his foot and shake down every house in Tuckhabatchee.

Tecumseh left. The Creeks counted the days. On the morning when he should have reached Detroit, the great 1811 earthquake, centered around New Madrid, Missouri, shook the entire Southeast. The Creeks prepared for war.

The Creeks were made up of fragments of peoples already displaced by the European settlement, and many of them were prime candidates to participate in what was to be the last serious, concerted effort by Native Americans to stop the conquest. It had been 270 years since de Soto rampaged blindly through the forests, swamps and plains of the Southeast, and 126 years since the Spanish started their first permanent settlement at St. Augustine in 1685, and the native populations had been decimated. Current estimates show that from 1685 to 1775 (the eve of the American Revolution) the number of Cherokee in the Carolinas, Tennessee and Georgia declined from 32,000 to 8,500 and of Choctaws and Chickasaws in Mississippi, west Tennessee and Alabama from 35,000 to 16,300. The number of Natchez near the Mississippi River dropped from 42,000 to 3,700 and of all Indians in Florida from 16,000 to 1,500. In South Carolina, what had been 10,000 Indians east of the Appalachians was 300. The population of Creeks in Georgia and Alabama held fairly steady around 15,000 only because their villages and towns along the rivers absorbed members from the other displaced tribes. In 1699 the Wando tribe near Charleston was hit with smallpox. It was written that the disease "swept away a whole neighboring nation, all to 5 or 6 which ran away and left their dead unburied, lying on the ground for the vultures to devouer." The governor said that "the Hand of God was eminently seen in Thinning the Indians, to make room for the English" (Wood, Waselkov, and Hatley 1989).

In the early 1700s, Virginia's governor, Robert Beverley, recorded the condition of the Indian towns within the dominion:

> Matomkin is much decreased of late by the Small Pox, that was carried thither.
> Gingoteque. The few remains of this Town are joyn'd with a nation of the Maryland Indians
> Kiequotank, is reduc'd to very few Men.
> Matchopungo, has a small number yet living . . .
> Chiconessex, has very few, who just keep the name . . .
> Wyanoke, is almost wasted, and now gone to live among other Indians . . .
> Appamattox. These live in Collonel Byrd's Pasture, not being above seven Families . . .
> Rappahannock, is reduc'd to a few Families, and live scatter'd upon the English Seats . . .
> Wiccocomoco, has but three men living, which yet keep up their Kingdom, and retain their Fashion; they live by themselves, separate from all other Indians, and from the English. (Wood, Waselkov, and Hatley 1989)

In 1716, an official in Charleston wrote of the Indians in the area that "several Slaughters and Blood Sheddings had lessened their numbers and utterly Extirpated some little tribes as the Congarees, Santees, Seawees" (Wood, Waselkov, and Hatley 1989). A few years before Governor Beverley wrote his remarks, a small group of Seawee had been so desperate to stop the destruction of their people that they went to sea in their canoes intent on reaching England. Most of them drowned. Those that didn't were picked up by an English ship and sold into slavery in the Caribbean.

The Indians in Georgia and Alabama had been spared direct contact during the sixteenth century, and when they first started trading with the English, the Muskogees were a loose association of towns along the Tallapoosa, Coosa, Chattahoochee and Ocmulgee rivers.

St. Augustine had been founded in 1685, and the British founded Charles Towne in 1686. The Spanish tried to drive the British out of Charles Towne but failed. The Spanish and their allies, the Guale (Georgia's coastal Indians), fled south of the St. Mary's River into Florida. In 1704, the British and their Creek allies burned Spanish missions in north Florida, killing hundreds of Apalachee Indians and making hundreds more slaves. By 1705, the Carolinians had destroyed thirty-two towns. When the Yemassee, in league with some Creek towns, turned against the British in the Yemassee War in 1715, the Indians almost succeeded in driving the British out of their coastal lands, but instead were destroyed. Refugees from this war drifted into the vacant north Florida that they had left ten years earlier, and later coalesced as the Seminoles, a name derived from the Spanish "cimmaron," which means "runaway."

By the time the languages of the southeastern Indians began to be documented, hundreds of linguistic groups, including Taensas, Koroas, Yamasees, Calusas, Tequestas, and Avoyels, had already disappeared due to the effects of European contact. By the time of the American Revolution, the displaced tribes in the Southeast had conglomerated into a confederacy primarily speaking Muskogean and calling themselves Muskogees. The English called them Creeks because they lived along the waterways. The Creeks absorbed some Apalachicola driven out of Florida by the Spanish, the Taensas from Louisiana, and the Natchez from Mississippi. By the beginning of the 1800s, about twenty years after the cotton gin was invented, the Creeks could field about six thousand fighting men.

It's not hard to understand why the Native American countryside was full of apocalyptic prophecies at the beginning of the 1800s. By this time the Cherokee had surrendered half of their original tribal lands. They had fought as allies of the British from 1776 to 1794, but they backed the wrong horse and had few friends among the victorious Americans. Their oldest towns and sacred places were lost. By 1808 some chiefs were trading their mountains for land west of the Mississippi. Their traditional life was over. Presbyterians were setting up missions in Tennessee, and itinerant Baptists and Methodists were out preaching across the land. Among the Cherokee, communal values were no longer rewarded, and class distinctions were taking shape. Wealth and favor went to those who put on European clothes and built American houses. In 1809, a census showed that the Cherokees had 583 black slaves, 13 gristmills, 3 sawmills, 567 plows, 429 looms, 1,572 spinning wheels, 1 powder mill, and uncountable numbers of hogs, chickens, sheep, cattle and horses, all of European origin (McLoughlin 1984).

Prophets wandered the land. In 1811 some Moravian missionaries in Cherokee country in Georgia were told about a vision recently experienced by some Cherokee travellers. A crowd of Indians on black horses appeared to them, and their leader said, "Don't be afraid; we are your brothers and have been sent by God to speak with you. God is dissatisfied that you are receiving the white people in your land without distinction. You yourselves see that your hunting is gone—you are planting the corn of the white people—go and sell that back to them and plant the Indian corn of your forefathers; do away with the mills. The Mother of the Nation has forsaken you because all her bones are being broken through the grinding of the mills. She will return to you, however, if you put the white people out of the land and return to your former manner of life" (McLoughlin 1984: 150).

The prophets all said that the Indians must give up white ways. They had to give up cattle, plows, spinning wheels, featherbeds, fiddles, cats and books. They had to revive their old dances and festivals. Some prophets said the Indians had to get rid of everything acquired from the Europeans; others said they could keep the horses and guns.

More prophecy went around in 1812 that God was coming to snatch away all the white people, and that he was going to take everybody wearing European clothes. After that, during the revival dances a frequent ritual involved throwing European clothes onto a burning pyre.

The apocalyptic prophecies reached a frenzied pitch from 1811 through April of 1812, during which time ten separate tremors from the great quake at New Madrid shook the Southeast. Despite the explosions of thunder, lightning strikes, wind storms, flattened houses and gigantic sinkholes that accompanied the tremors, the white people didn't disappear. The Moravian missionaries were told by a woman named Laughing Molly that in three months the moon would go dark and hailstones as large as hominy blocks would fall and kill all the cattle. Three months later, in June of 1812, the United States Congress declared war on England.

The War of 1812 was the culmination of postindependence conflicts between the British and Americans, as the young country was forced to assert itself to protect its maritime trade and to claim territory in Florida and Canada. Most of the "war hawks" pushing for a declaration of war were southerners whose agricultural exports had been harmed by naval harassment and who were hungry for land, and it was in the South that the War of 1812 saw its bloodiest fighting, beginning with the war against the Creeks.

Whenever the Creeks decided to go to war, the villages choosing to fight would hang a red war club in the middle of the town. After Tecumseh visited the South in 1811, half the Creek villages hung the clubs. The men were called Red Sticks, and were led by William Weatherford, a part-Scottish Creek who was also known as Red Eagle. When the War of 1812 broke out, the Red Sticks took arms from the British and mobilized. The first big engagement came after some Creeks who favored the Americans took refuge with white settlers at Fort Mims. The Red Sticks attacked the stockade, killing more than four hundred people. Word spread that the Red Sticks had killed children by smashing their heads against logs and had cut open pregnant women while they were still alive, letting the babies out of the womb.

The Americans sent three armies against them. Fort Mims had been destroyed in August. By October, Andrew Jackson was up out of bed, his arm in a sling, and marching his Tennessee army into the Mississippi Territory. At a village named Tallushatchee, Jackson's Tennessee boys killed 186 and captured 84 women and children. Davy Crockett, who was fighting with Jackson, described the battle against the Red Sticks at Tallushatchee with a classic simplicity: "We shot them like dogs" (Remini 1988: 73).

J. T. told me what it's like being a Barney Fife look-alike. "The main question I get asked more than anything else is 'Do you have your bullet?' And I keep a bullet in my pocket. I tell you, I never knew it was such a big thing, but boy!" He said this after I had asked him "Do you have your bullet?," a reference to the fact that on *The Andy Griffith Show* Barney was such an incompetent that the sheriff made him keep his gun unloaded, letting him keep one bullet in his shirt pocket in case of emergencies.

Sterling told me he had two children, a boy and a girl, and two grandchildren. I asked him if any of them looked like Opie, and he smiled quietly and again spoke slowly. "Aw, nope. None of 'em look like Opie. But my wife looks a lot like Aunt Bee. We thought about dressing her up. She considered it. She looks a whole lot like her. She's lost a little bit of weight lately. She was kind of heavy, but she still looks a lot like her in the face and the hair. A lot of people tell us when we go somewhere, 'Why, she could pass for Aunt Bee!' But that's about the only two things in our family.

"They's a lady in Nashville, now, *boy*, she'd sure pass for Aunt Bee's sister. She looks just like her. I tried to get her to go to Mt. Airy with us last year to the Mayberry Festival, but we couldn't talk her into it. She looks just like her and she got a dress just like Aunt Bee's too. We met her on the *Nashville Now* show last year, year before. . . . We had a Ernest T. this year. *Boy*, he knowed his part. I don't know if he didn't do it better than Ernest T. does it! He was a young fella, but boy I'm telling you . . ."

J. T. and Sterling keep up with what's happening on *The Andy Griffith Show* circuit by subscribing to *The Bullet*, the newsletter for The Andy Griffith Show Rerun Watchers Club. Sterling lets J. T. keep up with it most. J. T.'s got a scrapbook, and he's got phone numbers and all his information organized. He's into it a little more than Sterling is, because Sterling still has to work and J. T.'s retired.

"Aw, J. T., he just eats it up. He's a little more organized than me. He's got pictures up at his house. When we were at the Grand Ole Opry, they let us get our pictures with some of the players there, and J. T., he got him a picture of him with Roy Acuff. That picture of him and Roy, that was a big thing for J. T. The stars were all real friendly, you know, except, well, some of them were gettin' ready to go on and you couldn't talk to them, but the rest of them, we had our pictures made. I tell you, that was something else. They don't let just everybody do that."

J. T. got to meet Don Knotts. "He said I look a little bit like him," J. T. told me. Sterling had never met Andy Griffith, but he had met a lot of the other cast members—not Ron Howard, but most of the rest of them. "All that's still livin," he said.

In what is today eastern Alabama (about 140 miles southeast of Florence, where J. T. and Sterling would one day win the Andy and Barney look-alike contest) the village of Talladega went over to the Americans. Red Eagle planned to burn the village for treachery. About 120 friendly Creeks took refuge with 17 Americans in a fort built around the house of a half-Creek, half-white son of a Scotsman descended from the first authorized traders who had come into the Indian country. A thousand Red Sticks surrounded Talladega.

A man inside the fort draped himself in a hog skin and on his hands and knees crawled rooting and grunting past the sleeping Red Sticks to alert Jackson. Jackson's army attacked, killed three hundred, lost only fifteen of their own, and broke the siege. (Once again at this point in the tale, I am unjointed by the coincidence of names: not only is Andrew Jackson the name of Sheriff Taylor, but the man who crawled from the Talladega fort dressed as a hog was named Fife!)

When he finished at Talladega (which 150 years later would become the site of the International Motor Sports Hall of Fame), Jackson moved on to the Horseshoe Bend, a switchback on the Tallapoosa River. A thousand Red Stick warriors and three hundred women and children were barricaded on a hundred-acre wooded peninsula. A breastwork of trees and logs eight feet high defended the neck. Jackson sent swimmers to cut loose the canoes and set fire to the huts. His army charged, breached the barricade, and for hours flushed Red Stick warriors from the woods, killing them as they ran. The final count was 557 dead on the ground, with probably 300 more floating dead in the river. Two dozen or so more were found in the woods later, dead from wounds.

The war was over, and the Creeks surrendered 23 million acres, which today makes up three-fifths of Alabama and one-fifth of Georgia.

Jackson's health was wrecked. He had chronic diarrhea and dysentery. For months during the campaign, his arm was still mending from the shootout in Nashville. While he rode against the Red Sticks, pieces of bone worked themselves out of his ruined elbow; Jackson mailed the shards home to his wife as souvenirs.

It was the end of the Creeks, but Jackson was just beginning. He was made major general in command of Louisiana, Tennessee, the Mississippi Territory and what was once the Creek Nation. He marched to New Orleans and became the greatest national hero of his day when he crushed the British forces there. He declared martial law, occupied New Orleans, and, before returning to Tennessee, was honored with a grand ball where, after dinner, he and his wife, Rachel, amused the cosmopolitan Creoles by dancing a country frolic to the jumping tune of "Possum Up de Gum Tree."

The Indian rollback hit a fast pace. The Cherokee were forced to cede land south of the Tennessee River in 1816. The Chickasaws ceded land on the north and south sides of the Tennessee down the west bank of the Tombigbee and all the way west to the Choctaw border in Mississippi. The territory, opened from Tennessee to the gulf, flooded with settlers. Jackson and his friends set up real estate businesses. It was some time during his rampage that Andrew Jackson made yet another contribution to southern culture: he gave the name to "red-eye gravy." He told his whiskey-drinking cook to bring him some ham and gravy "as red as your eyes," and the cook obliged by stirring black coffee into ham grease. In 1819, the Spanish ceded Florida to the United States, and Jackson was named military governor.

By this time, Jackson was taking large doses of mercury and lead to treat his dysentery. He would spend hours draped over a tree branch to help relieve abdominal pains. Two bullets were still lodged in his body; the one in his chest caused frequent coughing spasms, occasional hemorrhages and a continual flow of excessive phlegm.

Jackson was elected president in 1828. His was the first "people's inaugural," and he was mobbed. At the reception, people broke the chains that held them back from the White House. The mob spotted barrels of orange punch and rushed them. Pails of liquor splashed on the floors. Thousands of dollars worth of china and glassware was smashed. Muddy boots stained damask satin-covered chairs as farmers and country folk fought to get a look at the Democrat who had destroyed the British at New Orleans, and who had fought and won against the elitist Washington establishment. Jackson was the first populist outsider to assume the office of president, and the people couldn't get enough.

The White House caretakers feared the mansion would collapse under the weight of so many people. To relieve the pressure, tubs and buckets of liquor were taken out onto the lawn. Spotting the liquor, the crowd bolted, pushing through doors and leaping out windows. It took six days of repair to the White House before Jackson could move in.

The president fought banks, corporations, and other forms of the new growing power of capitalism. Reelected once, Jackson, who cleared the ground for the development of the plantation economy of the South, was even more popular when he went out of office than when he was first elected. He died at his home near Nashville in 1845, but his name was an effective political incantation for decades. Andrew Jackson was a spell to conjure with, and conjure the country did: Jackson, Mississippi; Jacksonville, Florida; the Andrew Jackson Highway, which ran from Chicago to New Orleans; Andrew Jackson Hamilton, who became a governor of Texas; Andrew Jackson Montague, who became a governor of Virginia. Andrew Jackson Borden became Lizzie Borden's dad.

And Andrew Jackson Taylor became the High Sheriff of Mayberry.

\*    \*    \*

Memories of the Creeks remain in the names of the rivers and water-ways along which they lived and travelled: Alabama, Coosa, Tallapoosa, Ocmulgee, Chattahoochee, Ochlocknee, Oconee, Kinchafoonie, Hodchodkee, Alapha, Apalachee, Ohoopee, Altamaha, Muckalee, and the Suwannee, which rises in from the Okefenokee and drains into the gulf. Many others bear names given them by the white settlers and their black Others: the Potato, St. Mary's, Mulberry, Flint, and the Black Warrior, which is actually just a translation of the Muskogean "Tuscaloosa," the name of the great chief of the Alabamas whose power and people were destroyed in the fiercest battle fought by Hernando de Soto and his Spanish army, the first Europeans to explore the South.

It was to the Tired Creek in southwest Georgia that a Baptist preacher came in the early 1800s. The area was sickly, but it reminded him of his home back in North Carolina, so he settled there with his family. Friends and relatives followed him, driving wagons down the Hawthorne Trail. By 1828, they had enough folk to start the Primitive Baptist Church. They received the word of the Lord at Swamp Creek. Those who lived within five miles of the church at Swamp Creek were considered citizens of the community, called, until 1887, the North Carolina Settlement. When they got their first post office and needed an official name, the people chose Calvary, which was the place where Jesus Christ was crucified, and which derives from the Latin meaning skull, or a scalp without hair.

The people of Calvary were Primitive Baptists. Some called them "staunch Baptists"; others called them "hardshell full immersion foot-washing Baptists." They were so fundamentalist they didn't even believe in Sunday School. Those who would be members of the church had to be positive that the Holy Spirit had entered into them and turned them around. Such strict discipline kept membership low, but, even if they weren't born again, the descendents of the earliest members always maintained a respectful loyalty to the church. On up into the middle of the twentieth century, any "hardshell Baptist" who ran for office was guaranteed election.

Each year at the time of Pentecost, all of the "full immersion" folk attended the annual footwashing. Taking place each year on the first Sunday in June, it was a bigger holiday than Christmas (Mayfield 1979). People who had moved off came back to town; everybody wore new clothes and fancy new hats. Only the reborn members of the church could wash the feet of another, or have another wash their own, but all the families and friends and unclean sinners who had not been cleansed in the Blood of the Lamb got together anyway, talking in the church yard and maybe sitting for a while in the church to listen to the marathon of preaching, delivered sometimes by as many as seven evangelists. After the footwashing, everybody took friends and relatives and visitors home for feasts of tomatoes, roasted ears of corn, ice cream and cake. In the years since those days, radio, television, the decline of the railroads and the increase of paved roads have mounted a mighty challenge to the Holy Spirit. The June footwashing is no longer the biggest annual event at Calvary, the Place of Skulls: now it's Mule Day.

Charles Butler has been chairman of Mule Day for the past ten years or so. He runs a farm supply and vegetable brokerage from an office on the side of an old Citizens 77 gas station at the crossroads in Calvary. His warehouse is behind the station. The cracked, weed-sprouted parking lot is scattered with bushel baskets, balls of baling twine, spools of barbed wire, stacks of wooden Pepsi crates. Inside his office, a slingshot carved into the shape of a mule head, the forked prongs representing the ears, hangs from a peg on the wall. Empty green gallon cans of decaf Folgers are stacked on one filing cabinet; on another is a stuffed bobcat. The wall holds a clock made from a cookie box and paper cutout of a laughing mule head. There is a decoupage of old Mule Day newspaper clippings. Also on a wall is the skin of a leopard. When I ask him about it he makes a point of saying, loudly, throwing his voice through a doorway, "My brother-in-law killed that in India. He come up on a sick cat and killed it." He says it loudly because his sister is in the next room, down from Virginia Beach for Mule Day, and she hollers back, "It wasn't sick! He killed it the regular way!"

On another wall in his office magazines hang from a pegboard: *Farm Supply*, *The Grower*, *Produce Business*. They have cover stories such as "Women in the Produce Business," "Tomatoes Making a Comeback," "Fighting the Apple Color Wars," and "Is Your Floral Pricing Strategy Effective?"

"We're down here in a rural area," he says. "I mean *rural* rural. And being in a rural area like this, you know, a lot of Lion's Clubs make money selling light bulbs and brooms. But if you have to travel two, three miles between each house to sell a light bulb, you don't make much profit. So what we did, we got together. We used to grow shade tobacco here. That made a light leaf, and it was used as cigar wrappers, and it required mules the way it was planted and grown and tied up with a string. We'd heard of a Mule Day up in North Carolina, and we didn't know how they did it, but we just got our own ideas about paying honor to the mule, because as you know, the mule was the beast of burden for American agriculture for years and years. We just wanted to start something to raise money for the Lion's Club, and we thought paying honor to the mule was a good way to do it. In a festival-type atmosphere. I guess we hit it at the right time cause it has grown. I think the fact is, we just got lucky. I guess mules is popular."

Since it started in 1973, Mule Day has grown to attract from fifty thousand to a hundred thousand visitors, depending on the weather. The visitors come for the parade of mules and mule-drawn wagons, hearses, carts, carriages, and combines, the packs of riders on various breeds of horses. They come to see the Syrupmakers, the local high school band, march in the parade with eight rows of clarinets and ten rows of trumpets playing a halftime version of "Hey, Baby," and to experience that unique small-town parade pleasure of watching the woodwinds, the brass and the percussion pass down Main Street, of observing their hats fall and catching their eyes and checking the fit of their inherited uniforms and shivering as the sound of each section—brass, woodwind, percussion—stands out with its particular shrill discordance back and forth between buildings with a loud got-to-turn-your-head-and-wince singular din.

They come for the cane syrup that's boiled right there on the grounds, pure and 100 percent cane, because this used to be cane country, and Rodenberry's, the syrup factory, is just over in Cairo, but this cane syrup you can get at Mule Day is made right there by the Lion's Club themselves. (Mule Day is held in November because that's when the cane gets ripe.) The Lion's Club members have their own huge evaporator, finally built after years of just having one old firebox for a demonstration and selling cane syrup made somewhere else. And now the people come to Mule Day to buy the hot syrup and also to stand in the cloud of thick steam coming off the boiling cane juice, and smell its sweetness, and feel the heat from the firebox, which probably more than the sweet steam draws people to the boiling syrup because it can get pretty cold on the first Saturday in November, especially in the early morning. They come to buy sacks of onions and sweet potatoes and bundles of sweetleafed collards off the backs of pick-ups; they come for the pork skins sold by the man who has sold his fried skins at Mule Day ever since its very first year, and who is so famous for them that he's been on David Letterman; they come for the market fair, where more than six hundred vendors of salvage, crafts and art sell ax handles, rusted license plates, jars of buttons, wooden pop guns, hand-forged knives with horn handles, willow chairs; and they come just to come, because down around there there's not much else for them to do. That's what they say.

"Mule Day? It's kind of a celebration," Mr. Butler goes on. "You might call it a gathering. If you take a look over the far western part of the grounds, where the Mule Show is, you'll see we're having a problem with wet dirt, but when that dries out people get together there, have cookouts, camp out, have family reunions, all that. It's kind of a gathering. A little different from a gathering, but like that."

We're sitting in Mr. Butler's office drinking coffee and talking about his fax machine, how it looks like a toy and how it reminds me of the Bavarian Ski Slope and the House of Mirrors, seeming out of place in such a pastoral composition—the machine in the garden, the confession of the mask—and we laugh together about his being in this *rural* rural area wired into the Net, he's got to be so he can make quotes on crops, because that's what he does, being a vegetable broker. We talk about how ironic it is that he's so busy on a day that's supposed to be a celebration of the old, slow days.

The phone rings. "Yello? Hello? Just go to the information booth and they'll give you your number. Yes sir. Thank you, sir."

He turns back toward me. "The locals like it and the Lion's Club likes it, 'cause we generate a good bit of money. We raise money for the blind, for training seeing eye dogs, sight conservation, and we send 'em a good bit a money."

A man comes into Mr. Butler's office, wearing muddy boots and a tired look. "I'm gonna go put up those no parking signs," he says, and Mr. Butler says, "Put two or three more handicap signs up by the fire station. Start up by J. D.'s corner. Up by that culvert up there, and start back on the other side. Make sure the signs 're facing the way the traffic moves."

He goes on, "But generally what people like about Mule Day, and not just the local natives, I think, they like to reminisce. The older people like to reminisce on how it used to be, and they come to point out to their grandkids who want to see what it used to be like."

The phone rings. "Yello? Hey, Joe, what you know? Nope. Don't have nothing yet. Nope. Kinda doubt. Yep."

He says to me, "It's really not a complicated type of entertainment. It's rather simple in a way. It's a outdoor event. It's out in the country. And there's some things going on down there, like the mule show, the syrup, it's what you call like it was back in the old days."

The phone rings. "How much? How much? . . . Those are real nice. The maturity was there I believe. Uh huh . . . New variety I reckon . . . Yeah . . . Ha ha ha . . . Yes suh . . . If I got em. I'll check around. No pole beans? . . . Might have twenty-five or thirty . . . I need 'em at nine . . . Hm mmm . . . Eight bucks . . . Should have a few . . . Alright, sir. When will this truck load? Saturday okay? Tell 'em to come by the office . . . What else? . . . Need any cucumbers?" He hangs up.

"Yep," he says. "Mule Day is what you call like it was back in the old days. What would you call it? Tranquil? That's it. And it seems that people like to stay in touch with a little of that. Those tranquil old days."

I think to myself: tranquil? When was that? No matter how far back I go, I can't find those tranquil old days.

In his essay on the social significance of fighting in the southern backcountry, Elliott Gorn (1985) describes a region that was anything but tranquil. Except for a general agreement that barred the use of weapons, fistfighting in the southern frontier lacked all rules. By 1735, it had become a fashionable and necessary skill for young tidewater Virginia males, along with dancing, fiddling, the handling of small swords, card playing and horse racing. By all accounts frontier fistfighting was a particularly brutal and gruesome practice. In 1746, after four men were mutilated and died during public fighting matches, the North Carolina colonial assembly made it a felony "to cut out the Tongue or pull out the eyes of the King's Liege People." The assembly later was forced to criminalize the biting and cutting off of noses. Virginia legislators also responded to the public habits of violence by discouraging the stomping to death of its citizens. South Carolina made "premeditated mayhem" a capital offense, mayhem being defined as the severing of another's body parts. Fingers and eyes were protected under the premeditated mayhem statute, but noses and ears were not.

In 1774, a New Jersey tutor for a Virginia family wrote in his journal:

> By appointment is to be fought this Day near Mr. Lanes two fist Battles between four young Fellows. The Cause of the battles I have not yet known; I suppose either that they are lovers, and one has in Jest or

reality some way supplanted the other; or has in a merry hour called him a Lubber or a thick-Skull, or a Buckskin, or a Scotsman, or perhaps one has mislaid the other's hat, or knocked a peach out of his Hand, or offered him a dram without wiping the mouth of the Bottle; all these, and ten thousand more quite as trifling and ridiculous are thought and accepted as just Causes of immediate Quarrels, in which every diabolical Strategem for Mastery is allowed and practiced. (Gorn 1985: 19)

Fighters aimed for maximum mauling. Some fighters filed their teeth, the better to bite off appendages. Some tempered their fingernails in fire, sharpened and oiled them, a scoop-shaped thumbnail being especially efficient in gouging out an eyeball. Popping out eyeballs became the knockout punch of backcountry brawling. New Englanders called an empty eyesocket a "Virginia brand."

In one battle, a Kentuckian and a Virginian went at it. The Kentuckian got on top of the Virginian and "snapt off his nose so close to his face that no manner of projection remained." The Virginian then clamped his teeth on the Kentuckian's lower lip and ripped it down over the Kentuckian's chin. Davy Crockett, hero of the Alamo and Tennessee representative to the U. S. House of Representatives from 1827 to 1835, said of one of his fights: "I kept my thumb in his eye, and was just going to give it a twist and bring the peeper out, like taking up a gooseberry in a spoon." Another Kentuckian said of a fight: "So I gathered all the little strength I had, and I socked my thumb in his eye, and with my fingers took a twist on his snot box, and with the other hand, I grabbed him by the back of the head; I then caught his ear in my mouth, gin his head a flirt, and out come his ear by the roots! I then flopped his head over, and caught his other ear in my mouth, and jerked that out in the same way, and it made a hole in his head that I could have rammed my fist through, and I was just goin' to when he hollered: 'Nuff!' "

On another occasion, a passerby saw a beat-up fighter and said, "You have come off badly this time, I doubt?" The fighter smirked and pulled an eyeball from his pocket (Gorn 1985: 19).

*What you call like it was back in the old days. Tranquil? That's it.*

The parade seems to start in silence. At a distance, down the sloping, narrow, two-lane road, the first sign of the parade's approach is the semaphore of silver morning sun glinting off the row of tubas in the high school band. Eventually we can hear the hollow clap of hooves on the asphalt. People close to the sides of the road sit on lawn chairs, bales of hay and blankets; kids are on their knees and families are in rows. I see an old man, thin-wristed and smoking a cigarette, blinking confusedly, wearing a straw hat stapled with brown felt mule ears. Near him his daughter holds a baby in her lap and points up the road, where, when I look again, I see quietly rolling at the head of the caravan the black-and-white patrol car from Mayberry, and, behind it, the high-tossing heads of a mare and a jack mule—the parenting combination that breeds sterile mules—carrying the whipping flags of state and country.

Andy and Barney roll past. I wave. Barney, who is driving, nods his head backward in acknowledgment, then rolls on, once in a while shifting the Galaxie into neutral to gun the engine, and, as they pass, the kids don't really care; it's the parents who lean together and smile in recognition and point and then wave with exaggerated enthusiasm as their friends from Mayberry, the South's favorite TV hometown, lead the parade down the highway, bringing behind them the mule-drawn wagons, mule-drawn carts, a mule-drawn hearse, and packs of riders on horses with silver-studded bridles, and kids on wagons throwing candy onto the asphalt and into the high grass. Then comes a mule-drawn hayrake, Miss Dogwood in a covered wagon, a team of enormous oxen, a small cluster of kilted bagpipers, the Grady County Young Woman of the Year in a red Thunderbird, then the eight rows of clarinets and five rows of trumpets, and behind them a passle of little girls in red Lycra spandex leotards who lift their batons out of sequence and wear little straps that pinch their prepubescent chests into tiny replicas of breasts, their legs high-stepping in dust-brown nylons.

When the parade halts, a mule stops suddenly, a wagon jolts and the riders bounce forward; when they start again the mules' hooves slip vigorously on the road, and when they get traction the wagon jolts forward. One mule suddenly brays, scaring some kids who roll backward onto the blankets into the laps of their mothers. A man laughs and says, "A little starting fluid and I believe that thing'll crank."

I had told Andy and Barney that I would find them after the parade so I could buy one of their autographed publicity photos, so while I wait for the parade to circle up through Calvary and back around again to its final destination, a field of corn stalk stubble, I walk through the Mule Day grounds. I pass the chugging, spitting and popping engines of the Deep South Gas and Steam Engine Club, where a man points to a motor and says it was once used to run a saw at a sawmill, "but that's like cuttin' lumber with a butterknife compared to what they got these days." Indicating another trembling motor that is grinding corn, he says, "When I was a boy, that's how we got all our meal." We watch as two black men wearing thick gloves ram stalks of sugar cane into the dark iron mouth of a grinder run by a slapping belt hooked to the drive shaft of a nearby tractor. The man says, "I wish I had a nickel for every stalk I stuck in one a them things." He motions toward the coughing tractor motor and the crushing iron rollers. "Get your hand caught in there, y'can't say whoa like y'can with a mule."

I move on through the muddy grounds, past the tables of artifacts and relics and salvage and junk, where people pick up iron toys, cap guns, rusted license plates, wooden-handled wrenches, and glass-eyed dolls, showing them to each other and saying, "Momma used to have one like this, I wonder whatever happened to it? If I had all what we used to have, oh, I tell you."

It's true, as Mr. Butler told me, that people come to Mule Day in an effort to recapture what life was like in the "tranquil" old days. But the tranquillity on display here is not authentic; it's refined and imagined, an ideological soporific. It's nostalgia, surely—a bittersweet remembrance of things past—but nothing is as simple as it seems. Nostalgia may give the appearance of being a comforting, wistful state, evoking, for instance, the memory of Aunt Bee serving warm oatmeal on a cold day. But after a while, if you fan away the mist, you begin to remember that the past is laced with anxiety, uncertainty, fear, denial and dread.

The word "nostalgia" was coined in 1688 by Johannes Hofer, a Swiss physician, to describe a condition discovered among Swiss mercenaries who were off fighting in distant European countries (Davis 1979). The lonely, displaced soldiers had a tendency to burst into tears, stop eating, grow numb, surrender, desert. From the Greek *nostos* (to return home) and *algia* (a painful condition), Hofer came up with "nostalgia," meaning a painful yearning to return home. One cause suggested was "the quite continuous vibration of animal spirits through those fibers of the middle brain in which impressed traces of ideas of the Fatherland still cling." Some military doctors suggested that nostalgia was caused by damage to the eardrums and brain cells resulting from the constant clanging of cowbells in the thin Alpine air. But as mass armies formed in the eighteenth and nineteenth centuries, the condition was diagnosed in soldiers from the low countries as well.

By the twentieth century the word had been demilitarized, and nostalgic sentiments became especially evident in America, the land of immigrants, industrialization, displacement, the bulldozer and the chainsaw. Nostalgia means something different from simple homesickness. These days nostalgia is a homesickness displaced from any geographic reality, involving reconstructed versions of the past to evoke a contemplative melancholy that mourns a happiness that is long gone, a remembered serenity that not only replaces the harshness of the actual past but also serves as anodyne for contemporary discontent, a strategy for coping with threats to the continuity of identities. In America we are encouraged to forget the dirt and pain of childhood and think of it instead as a time of innocence. Remembering a revised, obsolete past is the prescribed remedy for those troubling disturbances of the present that keep us awake at night.

Nostalgia has become history without guilt, and, for it to work, remembering and forgetting pull together in harness. Regarding Mule Day, for instance, people might remember that in 1925 four-fifths of the mules in America were in the South, but they forget that it was because, while western and midwestern farmers mechanized, the South's landowners got a better deal working low-wage labor (spending an average of $1.32 a day on the mules, and paying black workers $1.25); they might remember that George Washington and William Faulkner limned praises to the mules, but they try not to recall that between 1940 and 1950 the number of tractors in Georgia increased from nine thousand to sixty thousand, that almost half of all southerners farmed before World War II but by 1980 only 3 or 4 percent did, that from 1940 to 1980 14 million southerners left the countryside for cities and the North, and that the almost half million mules sold by farmers during the 1950s were turned into dog food. People tend to misplace those kinds of memories.

A man in tight blue jeans and snakeskin boots walks up the steps to a flatbed and stands at a chalk line drawn on the planks. Pressing his fingers to his mouth and tilting his head to test the wind, he waits till the moment is right and the crowd is appreciative, then jerks his head forward like a cock crowing and ejects a ropy bolt of tobacco juice from between his lips. The physics of the spit remind me of those of a cast net; the brown juice unrolls and falls apart, and the heftiest of the drops splats twenty-some feet down the length of the truck.

As a man stretches the tape measure, the wind kicks up and the tape flicks, so I hold one end, and the man announces, "Twenty-three feet, six inches." It's not good enough, and for the third or fourth straight year someone named Trim takes home the trophy for the Mule Day tobacco spitting contest with his lob of twenty-five feet, four and a half inches. The other finalists get consolation prizes of cartons of Red Man, and they all walk off with the boxes of chewing tobacco under their arms, their high-heeled horseman's boots pegging wedges in the damp red dirt.

At the mule ring, cotton and sorghum plants are tied to the wire fence, and bales of hay are set around for seats. Nearby at the edge of the field are campers and horse trailers, and the folks who don't want to wait on the lines at the Port-o-lets trail off into the woods. Camp fires and trash piles burn slowly, making thin blue smoke. Around the mule ring women in slacks and earrings and smoking long menthol cigarettes point to the mules and say, "Look at the ears on that one." The farmers in caps and overalls spit and speak slowly to each other in a casual and well-practiced code about the good mules and the purty jacks and the ornry jack mules and the fine red sorrels, and when a fiery horse mule kicks forward at his handler, the overalled men chuckle and spit and offer the skinner their sage advice. "You gotta kick 'em back."

When the plowing contest starts, Number 132, a man wearing a belt that says "Snake" across the back, hitches his mule to the old turning plow. When he flicks the lines the mule bolts and jerks the plow from the ground, dragging the man down a crooked line. The old men laugh and say, "No groceries came from that mule unless he carried 'em from the store."

On a stage decorated with old singletrees, turning plows, cotton plants and milk cans, a group of thirteen-year-old girls with housewife hairdos whip their red-and-black dresses into a froth, their legs brown and flawless, their eyes scanning the audience while they clap and whoop and spin to the tapes of country music with a heavy beat, clogging hard. Their mothers stand near the stage wearing old-style bonnets that cup their faces, making them look like pioneer women on wagons. After the girls, the clogging is done by older women in blue sprays of skirt, moms with weathered faces but still-young lean legs, who grin and kick ankles forward and lift their knees and do the rocking chair and hoist their dresses. Their driving marching rhythm becomes compulsive, the high and sharp tap shoes clattering in concert like the rattle of a snake. Then a single seven-year-old clogs solo to a song with the chorus "I can't stop now, baby / It's too late."

The smell of a stagnant pond comes up and mixes with the wood smoke and meat smoke and smoke from boiling oil. I look at the goods spread out on the tables: stacks of Hank Williams, Jr., hats feathered with synthetic peacock fans, boot knives, Metallica posters, bullwhips, peanut rakes, boxes of fireant killer and beach towels emblazoned with the slogan that nearly everyone at the festival—everyone white, and that was most people—would agree with: "If the South would have won, we'd have had it made."

I'm sitting on the broken porch of the Mule Museum, an old clapboard store moved onto the Mule Day grounds and stuffed full of old farm equipment, laminated family snapshots, canceled checks from defunct banks, corncob dolls, an old stove, and jars of jelly. On a low shelf are school reports on mules, fastened with brass brads, water damaged and gnawed by mice. The Mule Museum is an uncurated cabinet of curiosities, a display of relics and memorabilia governed by only one rule—the items have to be old, to have belonged to a world that is gone.

All day long an endless line of people files through the Mule Museum, the old pictures and rusted mole traps triggering fond remembrances and small smiles. There's more than nostalgia at work here, I decide. I have been to many similar festivals over the previous few years, but it's Mule Day and my encounter with Andy and Barney which kicks my thinking into another gear and gives me the handy trope through which to examine the intangible essence of this cultural impulse.

It is Andy and Barney who have led me to realize that these community festivals are annual institutions erected as mooring for communities that are dissolving, that they are a variety of nativist revitalization movement. Here, at Mule Day in Calvary, I realize that the festivals contain a defining impulse that can be described as a postmodern ghost dance.

The Native American movement that became known specifically as the ghost dance began in the 1880s when a Paiute named Wovoka, who lived in Nevada, visited Heaven and came back with a message from God telling the Indians to dance for five days. He said they had to do this every six weeks. "Do not tell the white people about this. Jesus is now upon the earth. He appears like a cloud. The dead are all alive again. I do not know when they will be here; maybe this fall or in the spring. When the time comes there will be no more sickness and everyone will be young again" (Mooney 1965: 23). He told the people to discard warlike objects and not to fight. He said that if the Indians did all this, the time would come when the earth would be renewed, the game would come back, the whites would be gone. This sounded very good to Native American peoples whose populations were dwindling and whose cultures were disappearing.

What seeing Andy and Barney on Mule Day at the Place of Skulls in south Georgia has helped me understand is that ghost dancing has become an American metaphor for the mournful remembrance of a lost culture. The birth of one South witnessed ghost dancing; the passing of another South sees it again, this time in its signified, postmodern form. After the Civil War, unreconstructed Confederates ghost danced wearing their old gray uniforms like ghost shirts, marching in parades and wishing that things were different. Now, with the times again changing, there is more ghost dancing, and this time the parades are being led by simulacra of the two law enforcement officers from Mayberry, your favorite TV hometown.

Once I have realized this, I know where I have to go to complete my trip through the cracker circuit.

# CHAPTER SEVEN

# AUNT BEE'S DEATH CERTIFICATE

## Mayberry Days at Mount Airy, North Carolina

A tall, whiskered cab driver stands in front of a cinderblock shed. A sign above his head reads "Wally's Service Station—Cold Cokes and Cab Rides." The bill of his cap curls upward in a flip that is the universal symbol for doofus. He twists the cap sideways on his head, stubs out his cigarette, rolls his eyes and slobbers his line for the gathered crowd. "Goober says, Hey!"

The flash from a small camera blinks weakly under a gray, rain-heavy sky that sits over the town like the pillowy lining on the underside of a coffin lid.

Up Main Street from Wally's, a wild-eyed man in a torn vest, dirty cap and unlaced boots drags a sack of rocks up the sidewalk. His shrieking laugh pierces the cool fall air and ricochets off the granite and brick turn-of-the-century storefronts.

"It's me! It's me! It's Ernest T.!"

Cameras click.

A Barney Fife look-alike runs out of Floyd's Barber Shop. He hollers at Ernest T., the backwoods vandal who is notorious for smashing the windows of Mayberry businesses for the sake of love. "Ernest T. Bass, you put down that rock!"

The crowd on Main Street waiting for their pork chop sandwiches at Snappy Lunch goes nuts.

A woman in line grins, says to her friend: This is *soo Mayberry*!

\* \* \*

**Three generations of Barney**

After meeting the Andy and Barney look-alikes at Mule Day and thinking about the web of meaning behind their names and performances, I knew I had to visit Mayberry Days in Mount Airy, North Carolina. Here I would see the purest form of postmodern ghost dancing—the public performance by pop culture simulacra of a simulated golden age. In Mount Airy I would find a town attempting to revive its flagging economy by assuming the identity of an idealized media representation. I would also discover that the negotiation of the dimensions of time and space is a key aspect of the postmodern ghost dance movement.

The birthing of America was greased with the fat of whales and lighted by their burning oils. When the whales began to run out, a Norwegian invented the grenade-launched harpoon, and hunters were able to kill even the fastest whales. Wheels lubricated with fat were good; wheels on rails and lubricated with fat were better; but wheels on rails lubricated with petroleum were the best when it came to lacing up the country according to a new logic of space and time.

When the rail line from Paris to Rouen and Orleans opened in 1843, the German poet Heinrich Heine wrote:

> What changes must now occur, in our way of looking at things, in our notions! Even the elementary concepts of time and space have begun to vacillate. Space is killed by the railways, and we are left with time alone. . . . Now you can travel to Orleans in four and a half hours, and it takes no longer to get to Rouen. Just imagine what will happen when the lines to Belgium and Germany are completed and connected up with their railways! I feel as if the mountains and forest of all countries were advancing on Paris. Even now, I can smell the German linden trees; the North Sea's breakers are rolling against my door. (Shivelbusch 1986: 37)

When the B&O opened a rail line from Baltimore to Charleston, West Virginia, in 1858, journalists, artists and politicians were taken for a ride.

*Harper's Magazine* declared: "The ages of gold, and of silver, of brass, and iron, as described by the poets, are past. The present is the age of steam. . . . The real and the ideal have smoked pipes together. The iron horses and Pegasus have trotted side by side in double harness, puffing in unison, like a well-trained pair. What will be the result of this conjunction Heaven knows" (Eller 1982).

We now know the result. There was a *pulling at the eyeballs* by the passing countryside, a *shaking of the bones* by the metal wheels, and the passengers on trains felt a profound fatigue. Since the early locomotives were, basically, hurtling fireballs, explosive and unstable, and the railroad cars were vibrating, teeth-cracking boxes, people were stunned by their rides. But once the fear of sudden death was calmed by padded seats, travelers got used to the collapsed dimensions of space and time. Cultural adaptation helped fit the people and the machines together, and in the course of it distance became commodified, condensed into a ticket and a panorama. Mountains were crushed by railroads, distances were swallowed, scenery was rendered a blur, and the symbolic permanence and sacredness of the land was voided, with the majesty and grandeur being contained and repackaged for the whimsy of travelers. Tours, trips and visits became industrialized. The landscape—the world out there— became increasingly imaginary. The American landmass had always been imagined and invented by the settlers, whether as a paradise garden or a hellish wilderness, but with the advent of the new industrial technologies, America became local color, framed by a window, a brochure, a novel, a magazine, and, in our current age, by programs where the virtual overwhelms the actual, a country that traffics in mythography and, like the worm Oroborus, endlessly consumes itself.

Like Mayberry being mapped onto Mount Airy, our world is being increasingly remapped by shadow geographies.

Mount Airy, pop. 7,200, is a town of textile mills and granite quarries located in the Blue Ridge foothills of North Carolina. It's also a place where America's television culture has taken one of its quirkiest turns yet: Mount Airy is doing its best to imitate an imitation of itself and become America's official genuine make-believe hometown.

Andy Griffith was born here in 1926, the son of a bandsaw operator at a furniture factory. Andy left town after high school and went on to become, according to a newspaper clipping glued to the wall of the Cinema Theater, "the Mount Airy Boy who made good in the entertainment world." To Mount Airy's good fortune, while writing and shooting the 249 episodes of *The Andy Griffith Show*, from 1960 through 1968, Andy occasionally slipped in the names of people and places in and around Mount Airy. According to the *Mayberry Confidential*, Pilot Mountain (fourteen miles to the south) became Mt. Pilot; Doyle Perdue, a Mount Airy clothier, became Mayberry's Doyle Perkins; and Earlie Gilley's Garage became Earlie Gilley's Service Station. A Miss Rountree appeared on the show, and Mr. and Mrs. Jake Rountree live in Mount Airy; there was a Howie Pruitt in Mayberry and a Howard Pruitt in Mount Airy; Jim Slater in Mayberry was a counterpart to Mount Airy's Jim Slate; Mayberry's Lorraine Beasley had Earlie Gilley's wife's maiden name; and there was a Frank Smith in Mayberry as well as one in Mount Airy. Finally, there's the omphalos of the shadow geography: Snappy Lunch.

It's hard to imagine a smaller thing upon which an alternative universe could be built: Snappy Lunch was mentioned only twice on *The Andy Griffith Show* and never seen. Established in 1923, Snappy Lunch is a regular main street diner, as it's always been, but today it's also the pole star for the pilgrims of The Andy Griffith Show Rerun Watchers Clubs who come to Mount Airy each September for Mayberry Days. The owner of Snappy Lunch, Charles Dowell, has worked there for forty years, and although he can't remember for sure, he's almost positive he would have served Andy at some time when, as a kid, Andy would come in with other kids to buy bologna sandwiches for a nickel, eat slices of pie that were served directly into your hand, and throw their trash on the floor, as was the acceptable custom. These days the must-eat for Andy fans is the $1.85 pork chop sandwich, a piece of breaded boneless pork chop slathered with chili, slaw and sliced tomato on a white bun. During Mayberry Days, Mr. Dowell, small, black-haired and wiry, spends whole days uniformed in white, standing at his windowfront grill frying slabs of pork and passing them down the line where his waitresses sell them in bunches of two or five or fifteen. Above the grill are pictures of Mr. Dowell sitting in a booth with Oprah Winfrey, who shot an episode in Mount Airy after it was named one of the hundred most livable small towns in America. The walls and windows of Snappy Lunch are hung and set with dozens of photos of *The Andy Griffith Show* cast, huge head shots, and slipped into the corners of the picture frames are more recent snapshots of Thelma Lou and Otis and Goober and Howard Sprague, taken when they have come to Mount Airy—their flesh much looser than in that first Age of Mayberry—to stand in Snappy Lunch and pose with fans.

Mr. Dowell once said this about Andy Griffith: "He's the biggest idol I've ever had. If I had the choice of talking to anybody on the face of the earth, it would be Andy Griffith." In 1990, before Mayberry Days, he told the press that he was sure he would finally get the chance to meet Andy. He had had the same dream twice in three weeks: he was at his parents' house, and so was Andy, but every time Charles began to say something, somebody interrupted. "It's so real. I just almost get to him, and I don't. And I want so bad just to say four or five words to him."

The popularity of *The Andy Griffith Show* has been attributed to its success in creating a town with a moral center, an agrarian sense of time, and a believable community of characters. The physical production of the show—the use of a one-camera technique and exterior locations— allowed the producers to effect a convincing portrayal of a geographic place, while the writing succeeded in creating interdependent relation- ships and signifying historical depth.

Andy Griffith's occasional mention of Mount Airy landmarks and people helped *The Andy Griffith Show* conjure up that quirky texture of Mayberry and the magically bizarre idyllic hyperrealism that most critics agree have been unmatched by any television show since. Andy's *giving of himself* bestowed an organic quality on the manufactured Mayberry: the scripts were filtered through Andy's hillbilly homestyle, and the stories were resolved according to a nostalgic, quiescent paternalism in which the order of the home and the town were restored.

Those Mount Airy allusions have had other effects as well. The hypnotic tranquillity of Mayberry—America's favorite small, southern town—has inspired an ever-increasing band of devotees who are flocking by the thousands to Mount Airy, which they call "the real Mayberry," and where they can, in the words of the poem "Mayberry," which is framed in store windows up and down Main Street, "walk the streets that Andy walked."

Mount Airy's attraction, though, is more than simply a few landmarks from our TV heritage; what it offers is a plain, slow-paced ordinariness. That's exactly what the visitors seeking Mayberry want, and in Mount Airy they stroll on Main Street past stores like Hair World, Fabric Menagerie, Fashion Footwear, and the Triple-A Fountain Drug Store, where coffee is 35 cents, hamburgers are $1.10 and the waitress's name really is Lu-Lu. Mount Airy's tourist attractions also have just enough quirk to make the town's ordinariness extraordinary: the town is the site of the "world's largest open-faced granite quarry," and just outside of town is the grave of Eng and Chang Bunker, the original Siamese twins, who married two sisters and raised many offspring before dying in 1874, their body kept in a cellar for years to protect it from grave robbers, their children running looms in the mills. One of the biggest bits of news making its way down the lunch counter at the Triple-A Fountain Drug Store when I made my pilgrimage was that Leonard "Mr. Spock" Nimoy had been in town recently to plan a movie about the twins from Siam. I knew it was big news because they had taped pictures of Nimoy to a shoe store window. Under his portrait was the handwritten caption "A Mayberry Visitor."

Concepts of space and time are socially constructed, which means that people have to agree on their meanings. But space and time are not just matters of opinion: they operate in the world with the full impact of objective fact. Struggles over perceptions of time and space—how fast one would work, where one would live—occurred between Americans and Indians, between capitalists and mountaineers, between self-sufficient farmers and the forces of mechanization, with ultimate hegemony being given to clock time and the cadastral map, which pictures the land as a measurable grid of taxable property. Common lands and seasonal tempos were condemned, and in their place was erected industrial regimentation. Even in the condition of postmodernity, the issues regarding space, while inevitably involving an aesthetic component, are still fundamentally questions of ownership and boundaries, of who tells us where we can and cannot go. Space—whether in dirt, on-line, or in our heads—is almost totally colonized as taxable or fee-serviced property.

Tempo, however, is the antimodernist's last refuge. If the success of any contemporary economy lies in its ability to increase capital accumulation by collapsing distances through the speeding up of time—hurrying—the anodyne is that ancient act of resistance, the slowdown. The Luddites resisted industrial speed-ups by sabotaging machines; the word "sabotage" itself comes from the practice of throwing wooden peasant shoes, *les sabots*, into the teeth of the machines run by resisting French workers. Mine owners in Appalachia disliked hiring mountain farmers, because the farmers showed up when they got there and walked home when they felt they were done. Speed-ups at mills and factories are common reasons for strikes.

While I sit in the basement of The Andy Griffith Playhouse watching back-to-back episodes of the show, I think, Maybe that's why *The Andy Griffith Show* is so popular: a central theme of many episodes is the aberrantly slow pace of Mayberry. In the episode "Man in a Hurry," businessman Malcolm Tucker develops car trouble outside of town on a Sunday and can't get anyone to work on it. The slow pace of Mayberry frustrates him. In "Sermon for Today," a visiting preacher urges Mayberrians to slow down and take it easy. Andy, Barney, Aunt Bee, and friends then wear themselves out preparing for a relaxing band concert. There's an episode in which a Hollywood director wants to film the picture-perfect small town, which results in everybody going nuts and Floyd renaming his barber shop a tonsorial parlor.

With space defeated by cars, the SST, fiber optics, and the Internet, people react by clinging to *place*, and the idea of places. But a sense of place can only develop over time, and it is increasingly difficult for people to remain in one space for enough years for it to deeply become a place. Speed and movement, the acceleration of time and the compression of space, have severed us from wisdom. So, when people look for some kind of identity, be it national, regional, ethnic, sexual, or religious, authenticity no longer matters much. It can't; it's too rare; it costs too much.

As a replacement for real meaningfulness, we cast the world within a cloud and occupy the shadow geographies, remaking our homes inside imagined communities, accepting appliqué in place of depth. There, traditions are invented and reinvented, produced and reproduced; mythologies of the past are reanimated; themes are colonized. These shadow geographies operate through schemes of desire; they are therapeutic and also imperialist, taking over where once was real history; and they are occupied by a type of refugee. Mayberry is a shadow geography in our theme park world. You have to cup your hands around your eyes in order to see. It is a play of light on the land, a flickering in your head that lets you think you see something that really isn't there, like a wish come true.

I knew I had to come to Mayberry Days after meeting the Andy and Barney look-alikes at the Place of Skulls on Mule Day in south Georgia. They had told me about the event and about the pork chop sandwich at Snappy Lunch, and I had been biding my time as the year ran around again to fall so I could make my own pilgrimage to America's favorite hometown, and when I finally got there I discovered the culmination of late-twentieth-century ghost dancing: desire for the past, for a lost world, twisted so far out of shape that the folks were wishing up a time and a place that were already constructs of imaginary times and places when they were originally created in the early 1960s. Mayberry Days has taken the great leap forward: like Swine Time or the Tobacco Festival, Mayberry Days celebrates the way it was in the old days—tranquil— but it's a postmodern nostalgia, celebrating a time and a town that *never existed*.

When I get to Mount Airy in the fall of 1993, it's raining, dark, and overcast. It's eerie; the town feels haunted. It's as though the streets of Mount Airy have been emptied of local residents by some stage manager who has allowed only a few shopkeepers to remain on the set so that too many workers from the local mills won't interfere with the virtuality of Mayberry. Last year, people tell me, the streets were packed with members of The Andy Griffith Show Rerun Watchers Club, but this year the overcast sky and the occasional cool mist of rain have kept down the number of visitors, and I think it's the sparseness of the crowds that adds to the unease I feel. The couples, clusters of four and five, and families of seven and eight are walking the streets that Andy walked, but they seem lonely, deserted, like they're trying to play pretend by themselves, trying to pretend at warmth when they know it's really cold.

Rerun watchers move through Mount Airy's streets like bands of refugees, looking in store windows, following the walking tour of Mayberry, puzzling about where they are supposed to go next—maybe to Holcomb Hardware, where Bill Holcomb will tell you about the young, rambunctious Andy he used to know: "I sat behind Andy in Mrs. Wilson Barber's senior English literature class in 1944. Because of Andy's big frame, I could hide behind him and misbehave without getting caught until he'd doze off and Mrs. Barber could see whatever I was up to. I'll always remember Andy's fine voice when he sang at our junior-senior prom while we danced the night away."

The scene is both poignant and pathetic. It's as though the wandering fans have been sent to repopulate a depopulated community, as though they were assigned to go and be families in the lost American small town, and their job is to perpetuate the myths and offer themselves as weekend repositories for the great and vanquished small-town values. They've been chosen because of their rigorous training: they've all memorized the 249 episodes of *The Andy Griffith Show*. And they readily accept the charge, because pretending to Mayberry is worlds better than their real lives.

As I walk around Mount Airy, I stop to copy down some lines from the poem "Mayberry" propped in the window of a dress shop: "If you like friendly down home folks / and southern hospitality / Then you're just bound to fall in love / With our little town of Mayberry / When you walk the streets that Andy walked / The many sights that you will see / Will leave no doubt as to what inspired him / To make his hometown Mayberry . . ."

Three members of a rerun watchers chapter from Wilmington, North Carolina, walk up. The husband is a printer, his wife hangs wallpaper, and the husband's sister is, she says, just a mom. They say they are proud to be from Wilmington, which is where Andy films *Matlock*.

The wife says, "We meet the first Friday of every month. We decided on that day because we thought it sounded Mayberryish. We play *Andy Griffith Show* bingo, and we always cook something, like buttermilk pie, or sweet tater pone or hoot owl pie. The whole idea is to be homey. We watch the show all the time. We can see it on WTBS, WGN and WXAY. We have 229 of the 249 episodes on tape. We have all the black-and-white ones taped. That's what we watch on the weekends."

She continues, "What do we like about Mount Airy? The spirit of Mayberry is here. You can talk to anybody and they're real nice and friendly. You can talk to people you don't even know and you don't have to worry about anything. You can talk to people in line at Snappy Lunch." She turns to her husband. "Like that man, did you see that man? We just started talking!" She turns back to me. "And a lot of times even in your own hometown you wouldn't talk to people like that. I think that's why we all like to call Mayberry 'Our Home Town.' "

The husband's sister says, "It's like you'd like your family to be. It's the ideal family life. It's not like your own family. Nobody's snide to you. Even when they do get in their spats, they still like each other. And that's the same as when you come to Mount Airy. You can talk to anybody. You can talk to Charles at Snappy Lunch, or Jim Clark [the Presiding Goober of the Rerun Watchers Club], and they all like you. Or at least they pretend to like you."

The wife says, "You can step into any of these stores and it's like stepping back in time. It's like this store where I'm from in West Virginia where I go in there all the time because it's like you can step back right to 1950. They have vanilla cokes, and they still have those cardboards of fingernail clippers on the counter. That's what it's like here."

The husband says, "Sometimes when we go to West Virginia we stop here. We just pass through. When we went to West Virginia two weeks ago, though, we didn't stop because we wanted the feeling to build up. So it depends on how close it is to Mayberry Days if we cut through or not. If it's too close, we'll wait so we don't spoil the feeling."

The wife says, "We've met a lot of the cast members. We met Otis and Don Knotts once. The only thing we haven't done is meet Andy Griffith. He says he don't want to come. I don't know why. But to tell you the truth, it's probably better, because I think that poor man would be mauled."

The husband says, "See, it's not a show type thing. It is, but it's more than that. The spirit of Mayberry is here. It's not the show. It's the spirit. And the thing is, this is real. You can come here any time and it's just like this. There's not some marketing company that's set this up. It's homemade. You can see the stitches in the flag. It's like somebody did this at home one night. That kind of stuff. And, you know, we're worried about it getting out of control. Already you have to make your reservations early."

In one episode, Andy and Barney made a reference to eating Chinese in Mt. Pilot. So every time the Goldens come to Mayberry Days, they eat Chinese over in Pilot Mountain. They've started using black-and-white film when they take pictures of themselves and things. They laugh about how creepy it sometimes seems.

The wife says, "You find yourself saying things, mannerisms, comments, like on the show. Somebody would say something and you would answer them like Barney or Andy, and sometimes it's funny because that stuff just comes out, and you don't even know it. We started out doing it as a joke, you know, he'd answer a question a certain way and I'll know what episode it came from, and he would know, but others wouldn't know. That's another thing about coming here. You can mention a lot of things that most people don't know about, and most people here would know where it came from, so with these people here you always have something to communicate about."

They say the world is so bad these days that if they could get one wish it would be that they could really live inside Mayberry and be there forever. It's as though they would rejoice to find themselves succumbing to a freaky metamorphosis in which they would wake up not as a bug on its back but as a slick-haired deputy steppin' out in the old salt 'n' pepper, snapping, "Nip it! Nip it in the bud."

Later on, I meet a man whose chapter of the rerun watchers club started during the lunch break at the wire factory in Alabama where he works—"We would sit there at lunch and talk dialogue back and forth." I hear about computer bulletin boards where fans exchange lengthy dialogue, with no words of their own. I meet one family who took their Mayberry-mania so far that they've done the next best thing to crawling inside their TV set: they moved to Mount Airy. Cindy, her husband, Steve, and their son, Amos, were living in Phoenix. For twelve years, Steve, who built houses, would shut down the job site and go home to watch *The Andy Griffith Show* in the afternoon. One time, on a trip east, they drove through Mount Airy. "We came through a couple times and we would mention to people we met that we were thinking of moving here," Cindy says. "And everyone would say, 'Well, you just come on. We'd just love to have you.' So we moved! We figured Mayberry is a better place to raise a kid than Phoenix."

It's common for fans to turn off the color when they watch the later, inferior color episodes of *The Andy Griffith Show*. In the same way, the cracker ghost dancers want to bleed the color out of the world itself and wish it back to a never-never land of black-and-white simplicity. Mount Airy is reckoned the Shangri-la of the current form of the ancient pastoral impulse, and the town leaders have spent much time thinking how best to exploit their fortunate situation. They once considered changing the name of their town to Mayberry, or maybe building a Mayberry theme park on the edge of town, but so far nothing's been done about it. If they wait too long, though, this impulse will be spent, the historical moment over, because the desire for the materiality of Mayberry will have evaporated. Andy Griffith himself has already begun the debunking, commenting in his paternal drawl on an anniversary special that Mayberry is fiction and has no connection to his hometown. The true believers, of course, argue among themselves, maintaining that he only said such a thing because he doesn't want legal troubles, or doesn't want too many people coming and spoiling the town. But Andy's betrayal has already begun its corrosive effect, and the spell is unwrapping itself.

I discover that Mount Airy is able to offer the rerun watchers a slow-paced downtown because Main Street there is dried up just like main streets everywhere. The sidewalks are free of jostling, bustling crowds not because Mount Airy has retained the values of the tranquil good old days, but because shopping for life support—groceries, jeans for the kids—has moved out to the highway. The drug stores and markets are

189

closed—the Triple-A Fountain Drug Store, where Lu-Lu works, is just a soda fountain, the shelves of bandages and lineament bare except for cardboard boxes filled with golf balls picked up near the local country club golf course. Up and down the street, between the last holdout clothing stores and shoe repair shops, storefronts are empty, though for the weekend the vacancies are hidden behind photographs of Andy and the cast, taped up on the storefront glass, or pictures of Chang and Eng Bunker, the Siamese twins. Gift shops selling Mayberry souvenirs have taken over from the traditional stores, and in a conversion that seems like the fulfillment of a prophecy, the building made of local stone that once housed the Granite Bank of Mount Airy—a blockhouse temple of financial security—has been turned into the Revelation Christian Bookstore and End Time Ministry. In one window is a poster of a well-muscled Christ, trembling to do a push-up with the might cross of misery and the sins of the world on his back. It said "Lord's Gym." The inspirational slogan read: "Bench Press This."

I know my trek through the cracker circuit has reached its end when I walk into Floyd's City Barber Shop next door to Snappy Lunch. Having finished my pork chop sandwich—huge and delicious—I run into J. T. Garrett and Sterling White (Mule Day's Barney and Andy), and we have a nice moment of reunion. I meet their wives, and they all tell me they are going back for Mule Day again this year. We say we'll see each other at the Place of Skulls in November, and then they tell me I should go next door to the barber shop because "danged if the barber over there don't look just like Floyd."

As it turned out, I was glad I went. I had been noticing throughout Mayberry Days that at all costs the Andy fans avoid theorizing their own facile postmodernity—that is, they avoid becoming fully aware of their simple textuality, their appliqué of ruralism—by fetishizing the actors and the place: Mayberry is real, they argue, because Mount Airy is real; Sheriff Taylor is real because Andy is real; Opie is real because Ron Howard is real; Barney is real because Don Knotts is real. But despite this complex effort to substantiate their preferred virtual reality, inside the City Barber Shop I find a confession of the real terror that underlies all the ghost dancing mythologies.

I walk in and the barber is standing beside a man with two children in his lap who are sitting in the old barber chair having their picture taken. There are maybe two dozen people milling around, waiting for the same thing, waiting to pose for pictures in the barber chair, pictures that later would be tacked and taped and stapled to the wall where there already is a dizzying collage eight feet by twenty of photos of white smiling faces, families come to visit Floyd's here in Andy Griffith's hometown and sit in the barber chair and have their pictures taken with the barber who is not Floyd. Under the mirror along one wall on a marble shelf are bottles of Jerris Hair Tonic, Beau Kreml, and Johnson and Johnson's No More Tears. I am looking at the pictures, curled like drying leaves on the Wall of Fame, waiting my turn for my own picture, when a man in a pink sweater pushes himself up from a wooden chair.

I would find out later that day from Lu-Lu at the Triple-A soda fountain that the man makes a living picking up all those lost golf balls along the border of the local country club, the ones which now line the shelves at the empty drug store. As the man pushes himself up from his chair, I notice that his movements are thrown and ratchety, his fingers forced and splayed, his malady only now expressed as he rises and comes toward me in a lurching gait. He clutches my arm, and I step with him over to his chair. The shop is narrow and crowded and all movements are measured in half steps; one moves best sideways, like a crab or a ninja. With the absolute care of palsied motion he stands me still and lets go of my arm so he can pick up three separate xeroxes from a small table near his seat. The shop is packed and people are pushing past, some just standing, taking turns posing for pictures with the small, wiry barber who is not Floyd.

The man has been speaking to me the whole time, but I have been unable to understand him. His voice comes out from between harshly controlled teeth, and his deeply sighed words are lost in the clatter of the shop. He picks up the xeroxes with stiff unjointed fingers and hands them to me, as he has been handing them to people all morning here at Mayberry Days. When I look at the papers I finally understand what he has been saying.

"Aunt Bee. Aunt Bee. *Aunt Bee.*"

The xeroxes are fifth- or sixth-generation copies, the letters degraded and blurred. The man seems surreptitious as he hands me the papers, as though what he's doing is outlawed, underground, and, in a way, it is. Mayberry Days is a language game, pure textuality, and it has the tenuous existence of a soap bubble. It's premised on a consensual agreement to suspend belief in the harsher logic of material reality in favor of the imagined and the invented, to deny the dirt and worldliness of it all, but what the palsied man in the pink sweater passes me is a note betraying the utopia. It is a confession of the flaw behind hyperreality and the virtual; it is a mirror reflecting the ultimate truth of materiality and mortality and blood and life and death, spoiling the fun of the fantasy weekend. The papers he hands me declare to all who read them that we can wish as hard as we want, can even go so far as to speak lines from our favorite small-town TV utopia or parade behind a carpenter and a gas pump inspector dressed up like our favorite southern law officers, but, no matter how hard we try, it won't work. Our fantasized escapist dreamlands are unreal, tricks of the light. Why the man gives the papers to me, picks me out of the milling crowd, I'll never know. He is a messenger: Hermes with cerebral palsy, guiding me to the underworld.

"*Aunt Bee! Aunt Bee! Aunt Bee!*"

He gives me evidence of the fundamental terror that motivates all faith. I look at the papers. I make out the name on one of the sheets: *Frances Elizabeth Bavier.* I see in bold print: *Congestive Heart Failure. Myocardial Infarction. Coronary Artery Disease. Arthereosclerosis.*

Then the realization of what I am holding in my hand hits me, and I know that my search on the cracker circuit is over. The daydreaming is done; I am looking at the emblem of the ultimate futility of dancing against the forces of time and change: *Aunt Bee's Death Certificate.*

That was it. My trek was finished. I had gone out onto the road and traveled the circuit of weekend civic celebrations and discovered that behind the laughter and rhetoric of economic development that constitute the public face of these festivals, the events are actually the products of a nativistic movement, a response by communities to disintegrating boundaries, structural disruption, commercial transformation. For those whose experience now includes time-space compression and global restructuring, a sense of place is increasingly important. With the small-scale, intimate relations of economic production having been disrupted, certain segments of the southern population are responding by conjuring up images of a lost paradise that never existed, by ghost dancing on the cracker circuit.

# BIBLIOGRAPHY

Abrahams, Roger. 1982. "The Language of Festivals: Celebrating the Economy." In *Celebration: Studies in Festivity and Ritual*. Ed. Victor Turner. Washington, D.C.: Smithsonian Institution Press.

Adair, James. [1775] 1930. *Adair's History of the American Indians*. New York: Promontory Press.

Badger, Anthony. 1980. *Prosperity Road: The New Deal, Tobacco, and North Carolina*. Chapel Hill: University of North Carolina Press.

Bailey, Joseph Cannon. 1945. *Seaman A. Knapp: Schoolmaster of American Agriculture*. New York: Columbia University Press.

Baldwin, Sidney. 1968. *Poverty and Politics: The Rise and Decline of the Farm Security Administration*. Chapel Hill: University of North Carolina Press.

Bartram, William. [1791] 1988. *Travels through North and South Carolina, Georgia, East and West Florida, the Cherokee Country, the Extensive Territories of the Muscogulges, or Creek Confederacy, and the Country of the Choctaws*. New York: Penguin Books.

Berger, Samuel R. 1971. Dollar Harvest: *The Story of the Farm Bureau*. Lexington, Mass.: Heath Lexington Books.

Brunton, Yvonne Miller. 1979. *Grady County, Georgia: Some of Its History, Folk Architecture and Families*. Jackson, Miss.: Quality Printers.

Clayton, Lawrence, et al., eds. 1993. *The De Soto Chronicles: The Expedition of Hernando de Soto to North America in 1539–1543*. Tuscaloosa: University of Alabama Press.

193

Daniel, Pete. 1986. *Standing at the Crossroads: Southern Life Since 1900*. New York: Hill and Wang.

———. 1985. *Breaking the Land: The Transformation of Cotton, Tobacco and Rice Cultures Since 1880*. Urbana: University of Illinois Press.

Davis, Fred. 1979. *Yearning for Yesterday: A Sociology of Nostalgia*. New York: Free Press.

Eller, Ronald. 1982. *Miners, Millhands, and Mountaineers: Industrialization of the Appalachian South, 1880–1930*. Knoxville: University of Tennessee Press.

Falassi, Allessandro, ed. 1987. *Time Out of Time: Essays on the Festival*. Albuquerque: University of New Mexico Press.

Gorn, Elliott J. 1985. " 'Gouge and Bite, Pull Hair and Scratch': The Social Significance of Fighting in the Southern Backcountry." *The American Historical Review* 90, no. 1 (February).

Green, Archie. 1965. "Hillbilly Music: Source and Symbol." *Journal of American Folklore* (July—September): 204–28.

Grose, Elizabeth. 1974. "History of Whigham." Unpublished manuscript.

Hightower, Jim. 1973. *Hard Tomatoes, Hard Times. A Report of the Agribusiness Accountability Project on the Failure of America's Land Grant College Complex*. Cambridge, Mass.: Schenkman Pub. Co.

Hilliard, Sam Bowers. 1972. *Hogmeat and Hoecake: Food Supply in the Old South, 1840–1860*. Carbondale: Southern Illinois University Press.

Hudson, Charles. 1976. *The Southeastern Indians*. Knoxville: University of Tennessee Press.

Irving, Theodore. 1935. *The Conquest of Florida, by Hernando de Soto*. Philadelphia: Carey, Lea and Blanchard.

Jameson, Fredric. 1991. *Postmodernism, or The Cultural Logic of Late Capitalism*. Durham, N. C.: Duke University Press.

Janes, Thomas P. 1877. *A Manual on the Hog*. Circular No. 4 (June 15). Atlanta: Georgia Department of Agriculture.

Kile, Orville Merton. 1921. *The Farm Bureau Movement*. New York: Macmillan Co.

Kirby, Jack Temple. 1987. *Rural Worlds Lost: The American South, 1920–1960*. Baton Rouge: Louisiana State University Press.

Klauber, Laurence Monroe. 1972. *Rattlesnakes: Their Habits, Life Histories, and Influence on Mankind*. Berkeley: Published for the Zoological Society of San Diego by the University of California Press.

# BIBLIOGRAPHY

La Barre, Weston. 1970. *The Ghost Dance: Origins of Religion.* Garden City, N.Y.: Doubleday.

Lears, T. J. J. 1985. "The Concept of Cultural Hegemony: Problems and Possibilities." *American Historical Review* 90 (June 1985): 567–93.

Levine, Lawrence. 1965. *Defender of the Faith: William Jennings Bryan, The Last Decade 1915–1925.* New York: Oxford University Press.

Linton, Ralph. 1943. "Nativistic Movements." *American Anthropologist* 45 (1943): 230–40.

Manning, Frank. 1983. *The Celebration of Society: Perspectives on Contemporary Cultural Performance.* Bowling Green, Ohio: Bowling Green University Popular Press.

Marx, Karl. [1852] 1984. *The Eighteenth Brumaire of Louis Bonaparte.* New York: International Publishers.

Mayfield, Marjorie Maxwell. 1979. "Calvary." In *Grady County, Georgia: Some of Its History, Folk Architecture and Families,* edited by Yvonne Miller Brunton, 53–56. Jackson, Miss.: Quality Printers.

McConnell, Grant. 1953. *The Decline of Agrarian Democracy.* Berkeley: University of California Press.

McLoughlin, William Gerald. 1984. *The Cherokee Ghost Dance: Essays on the Southeastern Indians, 1789–1861.* Macon, Ga.: Mercer.

Mooney, James. [1896] 1965. *The Ghost-Dance Religion and the Sioux Outbreak of 1890.* Chicago: University of Chicago Press.

Neely, Wayne Caldwell. 1935. *The Agricultural Fair.* New York: Columbia University Press.

Otto, John. 1987. "Reconsidering the Southern 'Cracker': The History of an Ethnic, Economic, and Racial Epithet." *Perspectives on the American South* 4: 67–80.

Ownby, Ted. 1990. *Subduing Satan: Religion, Recreation and Manhood in the Rural South, 1865–1920.* Chapel Hill: University of North Carolina Press.

Preston, Howard L. 1991. *Dirt Roads to Dixie: Accessibility and Modernization in the South, 1885–1935.* Knoxville: University of Tennessee Press.

Remini, Robert Vincent. 1988. *The Life of Andrew Jackson.* New York: Harper and Row.

Rosaldo, Renato. 1989. *Culture and Truth: The Remaking of Social Analysis.* Boston: Beacon Press.

Schivelbusch, Wolfgang. 1986. *The Railway Journey: The Industrializa-*

*tion of Time and Space in the 19th Century.* Berkeley: University of California Press.

Scopes, John Thomas, defendant. [1925] 1971. *The World's Most Famous Court Trial, State of Tennessee v. John Thomas Scopes; Complete Stenographic Report of the Court Test of the Tennessee Anti-evolution Act at Dayton, July 10 to 21, 1925, Including Speeches and Arguments of Attorneys.* New York: Da Capo Press.

Scott, Roy Vernon. 1970. *The Reluctant Farmer: The Rise of Agricultural Extension to 1914.* Urbana: University of Illinois Press.

Shapiro, Henry D. 1978. *Appalachia On Our Mind: The Southern Mountains and Mountaineers in the American Consciousness, 1870–1920.* Chapel Hill: University of North Carolina Press.

Smith, Robert Jerome. 1972. "Festivals and Celebrations." In *Folklore and Folklife: An Introduction,* edited by Richard Dorson. Chicago: The University of Chicago Press.

Stallybrass, Peter, and Allon White. 1986. *The Politics and Poetics of Transgression.* Ithaca, N. Y.: Cornell University Press.

Stover, John F. 1975. *History of the Illinois Central Railroad.* New York: Macmillan Publishing Co.

Thornton, Russell. 1986. *We Shall Live Again: The 1870 and 1890 Ghost Dance Movements and Demographic Revitalization.* Cambridge: Cambridge University Press.

———. 1993. "Boundary Dissolution and Revitalization Movements: The Case of the Nineteenth-Century Cherokees." *Ethnohistory* 40, no. 3 (summer): 359–83.

Tilley, Nannie May. 1985. *The R. J. Reynolds Tobacco Company.* Chapel Hill: University of North Carolina Press.

Tindall, George. 1976. *The Ethnic Southerners.* Baton Rouge: Louisiana State University Press.

Tompkins, Jerry R. 1965. *D-Days at Dayton: Reflections on the Scopes Trial.* Baton Rouge: Louisiana State University Press.

Turner, Victor. 1982. *Celebration: Studies in Festivity and Ritual.* Washington, D.C.: Smithsonian Institution Press.

Varner, John Grier, and Jeannette Johnson Varner. 1983. *Dogs of Conquest.* Norman: University of Oklahoma Press.

Waller, Altina L. 1988. *Feud: Hatfields, McCoys, and Social Change in Appalachia, 1860–1900.* Chapel Hill: University of North Carolina Press.

Whisnant, David. 1983. *All That Is Native and Fine: The Politics of*

*Culture in an American Region*. Chapel Hill: University of North Carolina Press.

Williams, Raymond. 1961. *The Long Revolution*. New York: Columbia University Press.

Wood, Peter, Gregory Waselkov, and M. Thomas Hatley, eds. 1989. *Powhatan's Mantle: Indians in the Colonial Southeast*. Lincoln: University of Nebraska Press.

Woodward, C. Vann. 1951. *Origins of the New South, 1877–1913*. Baton Rouge: Louisiana State University Press.

# INDEX

# INDEX

Eco, Umberto, 147

Elizabethtown, 33, 35

Eller, Ronald, 71

Elly May Clampett, author's fixation with, 56

Epperson, Tenn., 84

Evolution, 121–25, 128; law against teaching, 132

Extension Service, 34, 41

Faircloth, Linda, 44

Falassi, Alessandro, xviii-xix

Farm Bureau, 33–42; as "the right wing in overalls," 41–42

Farm Security Administration, 41

Farm-to-market roads, ix

Farmers Day, 35, 38

Farmer's and Farm Women's Day, 34

Festival, etymology of, xviii-xix; as public ritual, xi; as nativistic revitalization movement, xi, 30, 33, 40, 44, 45, 50; polyvalent character of, xv; Rattlesnake Roundup, 3–28; Tobacco Festival, 29–43; and subtext of mourning, 39; Swine Time, 44–55; International Banana Festival, 55–64; analysis of, 59; Hillbilly Days, 65–98; Kudzu Festival, xviii; De Soto Celebration, 99–120; Scopes Trial Play and Festival, 121–43; Mule Day, 145–78; Mayberry Days, 179–92

Fighting, in southern culture, 171

Flint River, 45

Flue-cured tobacco, 31

Foucault, Michel, 18

4-H, 42

French Broad River, 67–68

Fulton, Ky., xix, 55; as "wasplike waist" on the Illinois Central line, 62

Fulton, Robert, 55

Garrett, J. T., 152–54, 158, 163–64, 173

Ghost dance, xi, xii; and Hillbilly Days, 83–84; postmodern version, xv, 154; history of, 83, 89, 161–62, 177; and Civil War veterans, 178

"Gilligan's Island," 18–19

Golden Monkey Restaurant, 138

Goober Festival, 152

*Gopherus polyphemus* (gopher tortoise), 8, 9

Grady County, Ga., 4, 16, 17, 28

Gramsci, Antonio, 18

Grand Ole Opry, 158

"Green Acres," xix, 30, 33, 40, 50

Griffith, Andy, 181–83, 188–90

Gulf of Mexico, 3

Harriman, Averell, 62, 63

Harris, Jim, 70, 80–81

Hatfield and McCoy feud, xix, 72, 85; and "The Andy Griffith Show," 88–89; and Pikeville, 72, 89–98

Hatfield, Devil Anse, xix, 90–98; Italian marble statue of, 98

Hatfield, Ellison, 91

Hatfield, Ephraim, 90

Hatfield, Valentine, 90

Hazard Coalfield, 69

Hegemony, xiv, xvi, 18–20; and "The Andy Griffith Show," 87–89, 126

Heine, Heinrich, 180

Hermeneutics, 145, 148–49

Hermes, 148–49

Highways, and American culture, x; and roads, 69; and music, 79; Robert E. Lee Highway, x; Jefferson Davis Highway, x; Dixie Overland Highway, x; Wilderness Road, 69; Buncombe Turnpike, 69; Daniel Boone Parkway, 69; Kiuka War Trace, 123; Great Wagon Road, 154; Catawba Trading Path, 154

Hillbilly, origin of stereotype, 76, 78–80, 86

Hillbilly Days, xix, 65–98; origin of, 70, 78–80

Hillbillies, Imperial Clan of, 67; initiation rites, 75; origin of, 80–81; trucks, 82–83

*Hillbilly News*, 67

Hindman, Ky., 77

Hindman Settlement School, 77

Historical pageants, 106

History, as form of memory, xv

201

# INDEX